Roosevelt and the Holocaust

Roosevelt and the Holocaust

A Rooseveltian Examines the Policies
and Remembers the Times

Robert L. Beir
with Brian Josepher

Fort Lee, New Jersey

Published by Barricade Books Inc.
185 Bridge Plaza North
Suite 308-A
Fort Lee, NJ 07024

www.barricadebooks.com

A copy of this title's Cataloging-in-Publication Data is available from
the Library of Congress

ISBN 1-56980-311-0

First Printing
Manufactured in the United States of America

To my beloved wife Joan:
"Grow old along with me!
The best is yet to be. . . ."

— *Robert Browning*

"To do justice to a great man,
discriminating criticism is always necessary."

— *Sir Winston Churchill*

◀ ▶

Contents

Foreword

By Ernest Michel

The first time I heard the name Franklin Delano Roosevelt was in 1933 in a movie theater during a newsreel. I was ten years old. Roosevelt had just been elected President of the United States. From my earliest days I was fascinated by history. I remember clipping articles from German newspapers. One of them stated that the American President, Roosevelt, was a descendant of a Jewish family by the name of Rosenfeld, an obviously Jewish name.

I am a Holocaust survivor. I was born and raised in Germany. I was arrested by the Gestapo at age sixteen in September 1939 and spent more than five years in various concentration camps, Auschwitz-Buna, Birkenau, Buchenwald, and finally Berga. Since 1933 the name and image of President Roosevelt played a major role in my life. He was my hope. If the United States and its allies could defeat the Nazis, maybe I had a chance to survive. That became a possibility at Auschwitz, as the Russian army advanced into Poland from the East. On January 18, 1945, Auschwitz was evacuated. Sixty thousand prisoners, I among them, began a death march into Germany. Half did not make it.

On April 11, 1945 the concentration camp Berga was evacuated. Again I joined a death march. That night we slept in an old factory, huddled close together desperately trying to keep warm. The next day, April 12, the Nazi commander announced over the megaphone that "the American warmonger, Roosevelt, is dead" and Germany would now win the war.

Roosevelt dead? It could not be. It was a blow unlike any other I had experienced. That evening 10 prisoners were lined up and shot. Six days later, on April 18, I escaped.

In 1946 I immigrated to the United States under the Harry S. Truman Displaced Persons quota with the support of the United Jewish Appeal and started my new life. I eventually joined the staff at that organization and began a serious study of the history of that period.

What I learned was disturbing. In 1939, nine hundred Jews on board the SS *St. Louis* were turned back from the shores of Miami after having been refused entry into Cuba. The ship with the distraught passengers, as detailed so effectively in this book, returned to Europe. Some thirty percent of the passengers eventually were murdered in the death camps.

Breckinridge Long, the official in charge of the Visa section at the State Department, issued an edict to all American Consular officials to "postpone, postpone, and postpone" the immigration of Jews to the United States despite the fact that the quota was never filled. I was among those he prevented from coming to the United States after, by a miracle, I had obtained an affidavit.

The train tracks to Auschwitz were never bombed. John McCloy's explanation was that the distances were too great and that the punishment in the camps would have been even more severe. More severe than putting Jews into gas chambers? The I. G. Farben factory in Auschwitz-Buna was bombed by Allied planes in the fall of 1944. It happened on a Sunday. I was there.

Throughout the war era, Jews in America overwhelmingly voted for FDR. He was a hero. He was my hero. He was Bob Beir's hero. And yet, when we talk about the Holocaust, the question remains: Where was my hero—a hero to us all—where was Roosevelt?

Much has been written about FDR. Even more has been written about the Holocaust by hundreds of authors, many of them survivors, myself included. The entire tragic period is one of the most reported, analyzed and documented in all of history. And yet Bob Beir has broken new ground. Bob Beir, in this detailed, well-researched, well-documented book, lifts the curtain on FDR's role. The more one reads of this book, the clearer it becomes.

President Roosevelt failed to use his powers, and the huge

resources of the Allied armies, to save European Jews. The President's first and principal objective was to win the war. This he did. Could he at the same time have done more to save Jews? In my opinion, the answer is an unqualified yes.

Does that detract from FDR's greatness? The answer is absolutely not. Franklin Roosevelt is still my hero and he remains a giant in world history. And for good reason. His leadership helped to preserve western civilization.

—Ernest W. Michel

◄ ►

Acknowledgments

I decided, at eighty-five years old, to take on a new challenge: the writing of this book. Writing about the Holocaust, at any age, but especially at eighty-five, is agonizing. Those events took place during my youth. At a time when I was a boy and at play on the Jersey shore, the pogroms in Germany began. At a time when I attended college, Jews in Germany and Austria were scrubbing the sidewalks with toothbrushes, while the SS and the crowds screamed insults. At a time when I went to business school, the massacres intensified. Why couldn't we in America have done more to help those in peril in Europe? That's the question throughout this book. That's the question that I continue to ask myself, relentlessly.

Many times I wanted to quit this writing project. The reasons varied, from health issues to the internal struggle involved in actually doing the writing to the trauma associated with researching this horrific subject. Somehow I persevered and I am amazed now to be writing an acknowledgment section. Certainly, though, I owe a series of people a debt of gratitude.

I relied heavily on three young people for guidance in the writing process, for editing, for support. My son-in-law, Dennis Meade, is a renaissance man. A scholar, a critic, a friend. Dennis never gave up on me; I still find his positive attitude inspiring. Dennis, this book would not exist if not for your efforts and I am forever grateful.

Rhona Silverbush, a professional writer, a Shakespeare scholar, a good friend, saved this project on more than one occasion. I went off base frequently. I took some strange tangents. Rhona brought me back to the story, back to the heart of the matter. Rhona, you are a wonderful counsel and I thank you so much.

Back when this project was in its infancy, I had the good fortune to meet a stimulating lady named Shelley Binder. Shelley has remarkable expertise and knowledge in Holocaust studies, as well as a personal stake. Shelley, your energy, your enthusiasm, your creativity, and your support propelled me to take on this task and to finish it. I thank you.

Another person who encouraged me throughout this project was Dr. Jonathan Koblenzer. He read my manuscript many times; he offered suggestions and insights; but in the darkest days of writing, when I felt the burden of researching the Holocaust and the burden of trying to express my perspective, Dr. Koblenzer urged me forward. Your support and friendship saw me through some rocky times. Thank you.

Many years ago, in fact a quarter of a century has gone by, I started a teaching career at Calhoun High School. That first year I thought I was a failure as a teacher. I learned that teaching is the most demanding of careers. In order to shore up my dwindling sense of confidence, I used to seek solace and advice from one of the most extraordinary educators, and humans, I've ever met. Her name was Kathy McDonough. Her guidance, her patience, her constant encouragement kept me afloat. If not for Kathy, I might never have continued to teach. And without my teaching career, I might not have gone down the same road. Teaching led me to learn more about President Franklin D. Roosevelt, to research the Holocaust, and eventually to write this book.

Several years after I met Kathy, she began to feel lethargic. Kathy was a nun and a woman of great faith and strength. She put off visiting the doctor. As her lethargy grew, I threatened to stop teaching if she didn't get checked out. Eventually she relented. Her cancer by then was too far advanced. However, before she died, Kathy McDonough wrote me the most touching and special letter. I'm brought to tears every time I think about it. In the letter, she wrote that I must continue to teach. In fact, she made me promise that I wouldn't give up. And I didn't. Thank you, Kathy.

There are two more friends whom I would like to mention. Ambassador William vanden Heuvel is the greatest defender of the Roosevelt legacy alive. In fact, I feel sorry for President Roosevelt that he never got to know Bill vanden Heuvel. I doubt the President knew as much of his own life as Bill does. Bill, I have the most profound respect and admiration for you. We may not see eye to eye on some of the history of the Roosevelt era. We may even debate certain aspects. But that's what friends and scholars should do. And afterward they should not allow their friendship to fray. Bill, I will forever be grateful to you. You put me on the Board of the Roosevelt Institute. You started me down this path. But mainly, you've always been there for me and you are a wonderful friend. Thank you.

And then there's Scott Hirsch, who once upon a time was a student of mine. Now he's a colleague. Scott has an unquenchable thirst for knowledge. Scott acted as a sounding board throughout this project. He routinely suggested ideas and books. He loves to play devil's advocate and he does so with talent and tact. Scott, I am blessed by your loyalty, your support and your friendship. Thank you.

I would also like to mention my publishers, Lyle and Carole Stuart at Barricade Books. Thank you both for believing in an unknown author, for trusting in my project, and for taking the risk to see it through to the end.

I had a very insightful and supportive editor. Eileen Brand provided a critical eye, many thought-provoking suggestions, a great deal of knowledge, and a superb diligence. Thank you.

Nearly two decades ago, my wife Joan threw me a 70th birthday party. It was a gala event, with friends and family and even a class of my students. In fact, it was my last year teaching at the Calhoun School. When I got up to make a speech, I thanked everybody. But I forgot to thank the most important person, my wife, who planned the entire celebration. That won't happen here. Joan is my severest critic. She agonized over every passage, every word, written in this book. She edited and re-edited and re-edited. Joan worked so hard that she claimed to have the Holocaust coming out of her ears. I know the feeling. I could never have a better friend, a better colleague, a better confidante, a better partner. Joan is the love of my life.

Robert L. Beir

New York
April, 2006

Timeline of World and Holocaust Events

1919

June 12—Leaders of 32 nations convened the Paris Peace Conference to officially end the First World War. The Treaty of Versailles, signed on June 28, ensured a weak German nation. Germany signed under protest. The United States never ratified the Treaty.

Aug. 11—The Weimar Constitution was signed into German law, creating a federal republic governed by a President and a Parliament. The first article stated that "The power of the nation emanates from the people."

1920

April 1—The German Workers' Party came into existence, based on a 25-point program enunciated by the World War I veteran Adolf Hitler, who was an Austrian by birth. That summer, the Party added the words "National Socialist" to its title, becoming the National Socialist German Workers' Party (Nazi).

1924

May 26—In America, the Johnson-Reed Immigration Act of 1924 further codified a stopgap measure of 1921. The 1924 Act established maximum annual levels of immigration from each country, known as quotas, as well as various qualifications for immigrants. The overall yearly maximum number of immigrants permitted into the United States was set at 153,774.

1925

Autumn—Hitler published *Mein Kampf* (My Struggle), detailing, among his many views, his hatred of the Jews.

1929

October—The U.S. Stock Market crashed, leading to the Great Depression.

1933

January 30—German President Paul von Hindenburg swore in Adolf Hitler as Chancellor of the German Reich.

February 27—The Reichstag, the home of the German Parliament, was set on fire. Emergency powers were granted to Hitler as a result.

March—World famous physicist Albert Einstein renounced his German citizenship.

March—The first concentration camp was established at Dachau, ten miles northwest of Munich in southern Germany. Dachau originally held about 4,800 prisoners, mainly Communists, Social Democrats, and other political opponents of the Nazi Reich. Within five years, the number of prisoners tripled. In 1938, 8,000 Jews were interned following *Kristallnacht* (November 9–10). In 1942, a crematorium was added. In 1944, the camp held over 30,000 prisoners. The number rose to nearly 68,000 by April 1945.

March 4—Supreme Court Chief Justice Charles Evans Hughes swore in Franklin Delano Roosevelt as the 32nd president of the United States.

March 4–June 16—Known as the "The First Hundred Days," Roosevelt used the bully pulpit to introduce his New Deal legislation aimed at alleviating the suffering of the nation. The

First Hundred Days included banking reform, the Civilian Conservation Corps, the Public Works Administration, the Tennessee Valley Authority, and many other programs.

April 1—Nazis staged a boycott of Jewish-owned shops and businesses.

May 10—In a square on Unter den Linden, opposite the University of Berlin, thousands of German students participated in a book-burning. Some twenty thousand volumes were consumed in the flames.

July 14—Nazi Party declared the only political party in Germany.

September 29—Nazis prohibited Jews from owning land.

1934

May—Nazis prohibited Jews from receiving national health insurance and serving in the military.

June 30—During "The Night of the Long Knives," Hitler and his followers purged the leadership of the S.A. (*Sturmabteilung*, Storm Troopers or Brownshirts), including Chief of Staff Ernst Röhm.

August 2—German President Paul von Hindenburg died at age 87.

August 19—In German elections, 90 percent of voters approved Hitler's power seizure. Some four million brave Germans voted against giving Hitler dictatorial powers.

1935

July 15—The first pogrom occurred in Nazi Germany, on Berlin's *Kurfürstendamm*.

August 31—By joint resolution, the United States Congress passed the Neutrality Act of 1935, prohibiting, among its many bans, the export of arms, ammunition, and implements of war to belligerent countries. The Act was limited to two years.

September 15—Nuremberg Laws were decreed, stripping Jews of German citizenship.

October 3—Italian forces, under the orders of their popular dictator Benito Mussolini, invaded Ethiopia.

1936

March 7—Hitler's troops illegally crossed into the Rhineland, the buffer zone between France and Germany. The French, with the largest Army in the world, as decreed by the Treaty of Versailles, refused to respond militarily.

July—Civil War erupted in Spain between General Francisco Franco's Nationals and the Republicans of the government. Three years of bloody battles and changing fortunes for both sides ensued, with Franco claiming victory on April 1, 1939.

August—The world gathered in an outwardly kinder Germany for the Berlin Olympics.

1937

May 1—With the Neutrality Act of 1935 set to expire, the United States Congress resolved to enact further neutrality legislation. The Neutrality Act of 1937 included a concession to President Roosevelt. The compromise, eventually known as Cash-and-Carry, permitted Allied nations to pay cash for American goods at American ports and then transport the goods away in their own ships. The provision was limited to two years.

July—Japan invaded China proper (Japanese invasion of Manchuria occurred in 1931).

July—The concentration camp Buchenwald was established near Weimar. The first 300 prisoners arrived on July 16. By the end of the month there were 1,000 inmates. Two years later, the number reached 8,634. That number climbed to over 37,000 in late 1943, 63,000 in late 1944, and 80,000 in March 1945.

October—At his most prescient, President Roosevelt tried to warn the world, in his Quarantine Speech, of the growing threat to international security. "The peace, the freedom, and the security of ninety percent of the population is being jeopardized by the remaining ten percent who are threatening a breakdown of all international order and law," he announced. The speech caused an uproar. President Roosevelt was accused of trying to circumvent the neutrality laws of America.

December—The Japanese Army launched the massacre of Nanking. In a period of six weeks, according to various estimates, over 300,000 people were brutally murdered. Over 20,000 cases of rape were reported.

1938

March 12—Germany annexed a Nazi-welcoming Austria.

June 4—World-famous therapist Sigmund Freud fled Austria for England.

July 6—In the resort town of Evian-les-Bains on the shores of Lake Geneva delegates of 32 nations gathered to discuss Nazi Germany and the refugee crisis. The Evian Conference, proposed by President Roosevelt, showed world opinion: country after country came forward with a reason for rejecting Jewish immigrants.

July 12—The first fifty inmates arrived at the concentration camp Sachsenhausen, about 20 miles from Berlin. Following *Kristallnacht*, 1,800 Jews were jailed and subsequently murdered. By September 1939, the camp held 8,000 prisoners. In April 1940, the first crematorium was built. In March 1943, a gas chamber was added. In April 1945, as the Soviet army advanced, 33,000 prisoners began a Death March. The Soviet Army found 3,000 survivors in the camp.

July 25—Nazis prohibited Jewish doctors from practicing medicine.

September 27—Nazis prohibited Jews from practicing law.

September 29—Adolf Hitler welcomed delegations from France, Britain, and Italy to Munich. The Munich Agreement permitted the German Army to march into Czechoslovakia. Prime Minister Neville Chamberlain returned to his residence at 10 Downing Street and announced, "I believe it is peace in our time." Simultaneously, Germany invaded Czechoslovakia's Sudetenland without resistance.

October 5—Nazis required all Jewish passports to be stamped with a large red "J."

November 9–10—Thirty thousand Jews were arrested and transported to concentration camps. Ninety-one Jews, according to various estimations, were murdered. The destruction in broken glass came to five million marks, or $1.25 million. And thus the name of the pogrom, *Kristallnacht*, or "The Night of Broken Glass." In America, President Roosevelt responded by extending the tourist visas of nearly fifteen thousand German-Jews here in the States. Simultaneously, he recalled the American Ambassador from Germany. During a press conference, Roosevelt expressed deep outrage and alarm. "I myself could scarcely believe that such things could occur in a twentieth century civilization . . . ," he said.

November 15—Nazis expelled all Jewish pupils from non-Jewish schools.

1939

March 2—Eugenio Pacelli became Pope Pius XII.

May to June—The sailing of the *S.S. St. Louis* exposed the fact that no country wanted to take in Germany's Jews.

August 20—Germany and the Soviet Union signed a non-aggression agreement, known as the Ribbentrop-Molotov Pact (named after the Foreign Ministers). Secretly, the Pact divided up Poland and other parts of Eastern Europe.

September 1—Nazi Germany invaded Poland.

September 3—Great Britain declared war on Germany. France followed a few hours later.

October 11—In a meeting at the White House, the economist Alexander Sachs presented a letter to President Roosevelt. The message, written by Albert Einstein and with the support of other physicists—Leo Szilard, Eugene Wigner, and Edward Teller among them—called on the United States government to explore the military potentials of nuclear energy. In the letter, Einstein warned that the Germans had stopped selling uranium from Czech mines, a clue that the Nazis were trying to build a nuclear weapon. Roosevelt responded, "What you are after is to see that the Nazis don't blow us up." From these beginnings, the Advisory Committee on Uranium was born with a mandate to begin a nuclear weapons program.[1]

November 4—With the Cash-and-Carry provision set to expire, the United States Congress passed legislation prolonging its mandate and permitting European democracies to buy war materials.

November 23—The Nazis required the yellow star to be worn by Jews over age ten.

1940

April 30—Nazis sealed off the Lodz ghetto in Poland, locking 230,000 Jews within.

April to May—After the period known as the "Phony War," the Germans raided Western Europe. Norway and Denmark fell in April. Belgium, Luxembourg, and the Netherlands fell in May.

May 10—Winston Churchill succeeded Neville Chamberlain as Prime Minister of Britain. "I felt as if I were walking with Destiny," he declared, "and that all my past life had been but a preparation for this hour and for this trial."[2]

May 26 to June 4—In a miraculous rescue, a flotilla of ships evacuated 338,000 French and British troops from Dunkirk across the British Channel and over to the safety of Britain.

June 14—A passenger train arrived at a former artillery barracks in a little town named Oswiecim, located some thirty miles southwest of Krakow. The first deportation to Auschwitz carried 728 Polish political prisoners. From such a small beginning grew, in the words of German-Jewish philosopher Hannah Arendt, "quite literally the end of the world." The number of Jews killed at the camp is unknown. Estimates range from as high as 2,500,000— Adolf Eichmann's guess—to a little over a million, according to a contemporary study. Rudolf Höss, the Commandant for most of Auschwitz's existence, agreed with Eichmann's total, but then reduced the number to 1,135.000.

June 22—The French capitulated to the Nazis in the same railway car in which the Germans had surrendered in 1918. "The battle of France is over," Churchill told the House of Commons. "I expect that the Battle of Britain is about to begin."[3]

July 10—The Battle of Britain began. For three months, the German Luftwaffe and the British Royal Air Force (RAF) clashed over the skies of Britain, with London and other cities taking an incredible pounding. In October, the RAF handed the Germans their first defeat. In lauding the RAF, Churchill remarked, "Never in the field of human conflict was so much owed by so many to so few."

September—President Roosevelt traded fifty World War One-era destroyers to Churchill in exchange for the use of Naval bases in British colonies. To American generals, the deal was a disaster, as warships were in scarce supply. To Roosevelt, the deal appeared to aid America's ally while not jeopardizing the President's standing in an isolation-minded Congress. To Churchill, the deal further entangled American and British interests. "I have no doubt," Churchill told the House of Commons, "that Herr Hitler will not like this transfer of destroyers, and I have no doubt that he will pay the United States out, if he ever gets the chance." [4]

September 16—The United States Congress approved the Selective Service Act of 1940, the first peacetime conscription in this nation's history. Passed in an election year, the Act contained numerous compromises. For instance, the Act provided that not more than 900,000 men were to be in training at any one time. Also, service was limited to twelve months. Both stipulations would change in the coming years.

September 27—Japan officially joined the Axis Powers by signing the Tripartite Pact with Germany and Italy.

November—In the general election, President Roosevelt defeated Republican Wendell Willkie and won an unprecedented third term in office.

November 15—Nazis sealed off the Warsaw ghetto, locking 400,000 Jews within.

December 8—In a letter described as "the most carefully drafted and re-drafted message in the entire Churchill-Roosevelt correspondence," Prime Minister Churchill pleaded for American assistance. He noted that Cash-and-Carry would eventually prove "fatal" for both Britain and America because "we may fall by the way in the time needed by the United States to complete her defensive preparations. . . ."[5] In a press conference, Roosevelt announced that "the best immediate defense of the United States is the success of Great Britain in defending itself." This would lead to the policy known as Lend-Lease. Simultaneously, Roosevelt sent his most trusted emissary, Harry Hopkins, to London. Hopkins eased Churchill's mind to a degree. "There he sat," Churchill wrote of Hopkins, "slim, frail, ill, but absolutely glowing with refined comprehension of the Cause [the defeat of Hitler] to the exclusion of all other purposes, loyalties, or aims."[6] Churchill dubbed Harry Hopkins, "Lord Root of the Matter."

1941

March 11—President Roosevelt signed the Lend-Lease Act. The legislation permitted the President to sell or lease materials "to any country whose defense the President deems vital to the defense of the United States." Under the auspices of Lend-Lease, Roosevelt began to aid the Allies. When Germany invaded the Soviet Union on June 22, Roosevelt started arming the Communist nation. In America, the move was extremely unpopular. Roosevelt, who had recognized the Bolshevik government as early as 1933, responded, "Of course we are going to give all the aid we possibly can to Russia." In Roosevelt's worldview, the fascism of Germany was a more dangerous threat to national security than the Communism of Stalin. Responding to an anti-Soviet article in *Liberty*, Roosevelt replied to the editors, "If I were at your desk I would write an editorial condemning the Russian form of dictatorship equally with the German form of dictatorship—but at the same time, I would make it clear that the immediate menace at this time to the security of the United States lies in the threat of Hitler's armies. . . ."[7]

August 9–12—In secret meetings conducted on board warships off the coast of Argentia, Newfoundland, Churchill and

Roosevelt agreed to the Atlantic Charter. The agreement concerned "the final destruction of Nazi tyranny" and promised to support "the right of all peoples to choose the form of government under which they will live."

September 29–30—As part of the continuing massacre, Nazi SS murdered 34,000 Jews at Babi Yar near Kiev.

December 7—The Japanese attacked the United States at Pearl Harbor, Hawaii. Eighteen naval vessels, including eight battleships, were sunk or heavily damaged. Over 180 aircraft were destroyed. Over 2,400 American servicemen perished. Another 1,178 were wounded.

December 8—President Roosevelt addressed a joint session of Congress. "Yesterday, December 7, 1941, a date which will live in infamy," Roosevelt began with a power that nearly sixty-five years later still causes goose bumps, "the United States of America was suddenly and deliberately attacked by naval and air forces of the Empire of Japan. . . ." His conclusion was just as compelling. "I ask that the Congress declare that since the unprovoked and dastardly attack by Japan on Sunday, December 7, 1941, a state of war has existed between the United States and the Japanese Empire." The Congress responded with a near unanimous Declaration of War. There was one single dissenting vote.

December 11—Germany declared war on the United States. Regarding the German-Japanese alliance, Adolf Hitler declared, "Now it is impossible for us to lose the war: we now have an ally who has never been vanquished in three thousand years."[8]

December 22—Winston Churchill arrived in Washington for the Arcadia Conference. For two weeks, the White House functioned as a command post. The leaders and their staffs charged into the business of war. It was here that Roosevelt firmly decided to proceed with the Atlantic First policy, going after Germany before Japan. It was here that Churchill proposed the invasion of North Africa. It was also here that Eleanor Roosevelt became slightly skeptical of the Prime Minister. For Churchill drank a great deal and kept the President up all hours of the night and took naps in the afternoon while Roosevelt focused on the business of the nation. "I like Mr. Churchill, he's loveable & emotional & very human," Eleanor wrote to her daughter Anna, "but I don't want him to write the peace or carry it out."[9]

1942

January—The first United States troops landed in Europe. Between January and March, the number of troops shipped overseas averaged 50,000 per month. In 1944, that number soared to 250,000 per month.

January 20—Leading Nazi bureaucrats convened the Wannsee Conference to coordinate the "Final Solution." Adolf Hitler turned that euphemism into a program. The Nazis meant to exterminate by incineration and other murderous methods every Jew on the planet.

February 19—President Roosevelt signed Executive Order 9066, incarcerating Japanese aliens and American citizens of Japanese descent. In all, some 120,000 Japanese-Americans were forced into squalid concentration camps.

July 19—The Nazis implemented Operation Heydrich (in honor of the slain Reinhard Heydrich), for the extermination of all Polish Jews. Using three extermination camps (Belzec, Sobibor, and the newly opened Treblinka), the deportation of Jews from ghettos began. From late July to early October, approximately 310,000 Jews were moved from the Warsaw ghetto to Treblinka. Before the camps were closed (prisoner uprisings occurred in both Sobibor and Treblinka), the Nazis murdered some 1,400,000 Jews. At Treblinka alone, some 800,000 Jews died.

August—The battle of Stalingrad began. During the next six months, hundreds of thousands of soldiers and civilians died in fierce, guerrilla-style combat. The German retreat from Stalingrad, beginning in February 1943, marked a turning point in the war.

November 8—American soldiers began the invasion of North Africa, known as Operation Torch.

December 17—For the first time, the Allied nations issued a declaration regarding the continuing massacre of Europe's Jews. The

declaration denounced Nazi Germany's "intention to exterminate the Jewish people in Europe," condemned "in the strongest
possible terms this bestial policy of cold-blooded extermination," and announced a "solemn resolution to ensure that those
responsible for these crimes shall not escape retribution."

1943

January 14–24—President Roosevelt and Prime Minister Churchill
met at Casablanca, Morocco. The leaders declared their goal
to be Germany's unconditional surrender.

April 19–29—Representatives from the British and American governments met in Bermuda to discuss the refugee, and specifically Jewish, crisis. The Bermuda Conference dissolved into
secrecy. No recommendations or initiatives were put forth.

April 19 to May 16—The Germans chose the Jewish holiday of
Passover for the destruction of the Warsaw ghetto. The dem-
olition was met by the members of the Jewish resistance, about
one thousand in number. Although the fighters held out for
almost a month, the heavily armed and well-trained Germans
crushed the revolt, capturing 56,000 Jews still in the ghetto,
shooting 7,000, and deporting the rest to concentration camps.

September—After defeating the Germans and Field Marshal Erwin
Rommel in North Africa, Allied forces turned toward Italy.
On September 3, British troops landed on the toe of the Italian
boot, commencing the Italian Campaign. On September 9, the
United States Army, under General Mark Clark, landed along
the Gulf of Salerno. The Germans, holding the high ground,
put up a fierce battle, causing General Clark to begin evacuation preparation. As American lines were fortified, however,
the tide turned and six days later the Americans secured the
beachhead. Salerno, a grinding battle of attrition, became sym-
bolic of the entire Italian Campaign. The Germans did not surrender in Italy until May 2, 1945.

November 28 to December 1—The "Big Three" (Joseph Stalin,
Franklin Roosevelt, and Winston Churchill) met at Teheran,
Iran. Stalin pushed for a second front on the west. Suspicious

of his allies, Stalin worried that Churchill and Roosevelt would sign a peace agreement with Hitler. A second front would alleviate that concern. Ironically, Churchill and Roosevelt were also worried that Stalin might sign a peace treaty with Hitler.

1944

January 22—By Executive Order 9417, President Roosevelt established the War Refugee Board (WRB). The sole duty of the WRB was to save the victims of Nazi oppression, specifically the Jews of Europe. The WRB saved an estimated 250,000 Jews.

March 24—President Roosevelt's war crimes speech began, "In one of the blackest crimes of all history—begun by the Nazis in the day of peace and multiplied by them a hundred times in time of war—the wholesale systematic murder of the Jews of Europe goes on unabated every hour. . . ." At the same time, Adolf Eichmann arrived in Budapest. As he did in Vienna during the *Anschluss* (annexation) and Poland after the invasion, Eichmann quickly put in place the Nazis' Jewish policy: enforcing the wearing of the yellow star, confiscating Jewish property, rounding up the Jews and forcing them into a ghetto. Afterward, as per Nazi policy, he formed a Jewish council to serve as the liaison between the Nazis and the general Jewish population in Hungary.

May 15 to July 7—Eichmann and the Nazis, with the support of Hungarian partisans, deported 437,000 Jews from Budapest to Auschwitz.

June 6—Operation Overlord, code-named D-Day, began with over 160,000 Allied troops and 30,000 vehicles crashing the beaches of Normandy. Allied forces broke through German coastal fortifications, called the Atlantic Wall, and began pushing for Paris.

August 25—The Allies liberated Paris after four years of occupation.

October—At the Kremlin in Moscow, Churchill pushed a sheet of paper across the table to Marshal Stalin. The notes on the paper divided up parts of Eastern and Southeastern Europe between the Soviet Union and the West. According to the notes, the Soviets would be given 90 percent hegemony in Rumania and 75 percent in Bulgaria. Britain would be given 90 percent hegemony in Greece. The Soviets and the West would divide Yugoslavia and Hungary evenly. Stalin, with the check of a pencil, approved the transaction. "Might it not be thought rather cynical if it seemed we had disposed of these issues, so fateful to millions of people, in such an offhand manner?" Churchill said, proposing to burn the paper. "No," Stalin replied, "you keep it."[10]

December 16 to January 28—The Battle of the Bulge essentially marked Germany's last stand. Hitler sent 250,000 troops across an 85-mile stretch in the Ardennes Forest. His troops advanced some fifty miles into Allied territory (creating a "bulge" in Allied lines). The Allies regained the lost territory by the end of January.

1945

January 17—Soviet troops captured Warsaw.

January 27—Soviet troops liberated Auschwitz.

February 4–11—The "Big Three" met at Yalta in the Ukraine. Officially, the Allies agreed to dismember, disarm, and demilitarize Germany. Stalin, under pressure from Roosevelt, agreed to join the United States in its war against Japan. Stalin also agreed to hold democratic elections in all liberated territories. Yalta guaranteed free elections for Poland, Lithuania, Latvia, and Estonia. The guarantee was hollow. "Mr. President," Admiral William Leahy, Roosevelt's Chief of Staff, responded after reading the document, "this is so elastic that the Russians can stretch it all the way from Yalta to Washington without ever technically breaking it." The President answered, "I know, Bill. But it's the best I can do for Poland at this time."[11]

April—The physicist Leo Szilgard met with President Roosevelt. Speaking for Albert Einstein as well as the scientific community, Szilgard expressed the physicists' misgivings: that the bomb would be dropped on civilians. In addition, the physicists worried about the total secrecy surrounding the project. They called for international regulation. Roosevelt, who wanted to wait until the first bomb was tested, did not respond.

April 12—In Warm Springs, Georgia, President Roosevelt died of a cerebral hemorrhage.

April 30—Adolf Hitler committed suicide in his Berlin bunker.

May 7—General Dwight Eisenhower accepted Germany's unconditional surrender at Reims, France.

July 17—Leaders of the Allied nations convened at Potsdam, Germany to officially end the Second World War in Europe. A day before, for the first time, President Harry Truman met Winston Churchill. "He gave me a lot of hooey about how great my country is and how he loved Roosevelt and how he intended to love me etc. etc.," Truman wrote in his diary. "I am sure we can get along if he doesn't try to give me too much soft soap." Twelve days later, Clement Atlee replaced Churchill as Prime Minister and at the conference table. On July 17, Truman met Stalin for the first time. He considered the Marshal just "a little bit of a squirt." The Potsdam Conference did not resolve the key issues of the day. The intractable concerns of Yalta remained: reparations from Germany and the establishment and structure of the Polish government. Truman, however, gave a portent of his presidency. Unlike his predecessor, Truman proved resolute. "I don't want to discuss," he said at the first session, "I want to decide."[12]

August 6—On his way back to the United States from Potsdam, President Truman gave the order to drop the atomic bomb on Hiroshima. Three days later, again under the President's orders in Washington, America dropped an atomic bomb on Nagasaki. Japan formally surrendered on September 2 on board the *USS Missouri.*

November 20—The Nuremberg War Crimes Trial began. Twenty-four of Nazi Germany's highest ranking officers were charged with four indictments, including crimes against humanity. A young Jewish reporter named Ernest Michel, the only Holocaust survivor among the journalists, wrote of the experience, "I pinched myself every morning as I entered the courtroom, to make sure I wasn't dreaming. There sat Julius Streicher, editor of the anti-Semitic hate sheet *Der Stürmer.* . . . There sat Ernst Kaltenbrunner who was among the higher echelon who ran the death camps. He, with Himmler, was responsible for the systematic slaughter of our people in the concentration camps. . . . There sat Von Papen, the patrician, elegant head of the Reichsbank, which became the depository for the billions of dollars worth of Jewish property confiscated by the Nazis. . . . I stared at the lot. I couldn't keep my eyes off them. These were the men who were determined to wipe out the Jews of Europe. . . . Sometimes I wanted to jump from the press gallery to shake them by the shoulders and yell in their faces. 'Why did you do this to us? Why did you kill my friend Walter? Why did you hang Leo, Janek and Nathan? Why? Why?' "[13]

◄ ►

An Introduction: Awakenings

I was born in New York City in April of 1918. Both my parents, though born and raised in America, never quite let go of their German heritage. Many of the German Jews tended to be proud people: confident, intelligent, successful. In the United States, we felt that we were culturally assimilated. American first, Jewish second, just like our German brethren. We never believed that our relatives in Germany could come under attack.

I was eleven when the stock market crashed. I remember the headlines in the newspapers. I remember sitting at the breakfast table with my father, wondering what it all meant. I remember the shocked and serious expression on his face, the gravity. A way of life, suddenly, had been altered. And with the economy plummeting in both Europe and America, anti-Semitism turned more virulent.

I was fourteen when I first experienced anti-Semitism. At Collegiate School, a boy called me a "Dirty Jew." The effects were shattering. I'd been so insulated by my parents, so sheltered. Anti-Semitism was not discussed in our house. Suddenly I became fearful, as the boy put up his fists. Anti-Semitism, as I learned first-hand, instilled a discomfort and a sensitivity to feeling different that remains with me to this day.

Half a world away, Adolf Hitler became Chancellor of Germany. Little by little, step by step, the lurking danger turned into the "Final Solution." In America, we looked the other way. We didn't want to believe and when we couldn't escape the truth of the situation, we didn't know what to do.

I was fifteen when Franklin Roosevelt came to national power. I remember listening intently to his first inaugural on the radio. His eloquent words lifted my spirits. I felt riveted, mesmerized. And so my journey with Roosevelt began.

I was twenty-three when the Japanese bombed Pearl Harbor. I heard the news from a taxi driver on the way from Logan Airport to Cambridge, Massachusetts. I admit I couldn't then identify Pearl Harbor on a map. We Americans typically discover foreign lands as a result of our military involvement. Thus we now know some of the geography of Korea, Vietnam, Afghanistan, and Iraq.

I was twenty-four when I joined the Navy. The enlistment papers asked for preferred place of service. Even though I had no sea experience, I wrote, "Battleship duty. In the Pacific." Not surprisingly, the Navy assigned me to Great Britain.

I was twenty-seven when President Roosevelt died. The news came as a shock. President Roosevelt seemed invincible, immortal even. Suddenly, he was gone. Suddenly, we were dropping atomic bombs on Japan. Suddenly, the war was over.

I was in my mid-fifties when I first started teaching FDR to high school students. Over the next decade, I became a Roosevelt scholar. And the more I learned, the more I came to admire his social programs and his leadership skills, both on the domestic front and in foreign policy. My interest in Roosevelt took on a sense of reverence. I built a private Roosevelt library. I taught the subject of Roosevelt in the schools. I fostered the Roosevelt legacy. I identified myself as a Rooseveltian.

I was in my mid-sixties when David Wyman published *The Abandonment of the Jews*. He leveled some unsettling, damning accusations at Congress, the State Department, and Roosevelt. For me, Wyman's scholarship caused an intellectual and emotional crisis. Could Roosevelt really have abandoned the Jews?

Subsequently, I had the opportunity to question David Wyman following his lecture at Central Synagogue in New York City. "I'm a Rooseveltian," I said, "and I can't believe this. How could Roosevelt have abandoned the Jews?"

"I was a Rooseveltian, too," he replied. "I'm also the son of a Protestant minister—I have no axe to grind—and believe me, I was also surprised. But this is what my research has uncovered."

I faced a heart-wrenching conflict. Could my hero Roosevelt have been indifferent or, at best, passive toward the plight of the Jews? I needed to uncover the facts for myself. I did not know, as I began to study the Holocaust, the conflicts my research would engender. Though I am in no way a survivor of the Holocaust, I began to feel a sense of survivor's guilt. There was a connection. My personal experiences with anti-Semitism in the 1930s and 1940s, a major theme of my memoirs, compelled me to question whether FDR and his administration could have been more proactive in saving Jews during the Holocaust.

I was eighty-five when I started writing this book. What follows is at times a difficult story for me to tell, but a story I feel an overpowering, agonizing need to express. I am writing this story for myself, and my generation, the "Greatest Generation." I am writing this story for my children, and their generation. I am writing this story for my grandchildren, and their generation. I am writing this story, essentially, because I must. Toward the end of our lives, we seek clarity and explanations. These are mine.

My older sister Jeanette, my younger brother
Dickie, and me, 1927.

Chapter 1

◄►

A Blur of Strange Occurrences

I'll never forget the scene after my brother's death. The date was June 7, 1932. Dickie's coffin occupied the space normally reserved for the table in the dining room. The coffin was a splendid object. Beaming white, silk inside. The coffin seemed to rise off the floorboards, to dominate the surroundings. It suggested a towering majesty, like a skyscraper.

I felt suffocated, confused. There was my brother, all of ten years old, a picture of tranquility. I wanted to reach out and shake him. I wanted to jar him from his slumber. Was he asleep? He appeared so.

His illness had seemed so benign at first, a sore throat. A sore throat turned into strep throat. Strep turned into rheumatic fever. The infection attacked his heart. My brother lay in bed for six weeks. Penicillin would have saved his life. Penicillin didn't become a remedy until the early 1940s.

Chairs surrounded the coffin. An overflow crowd gathered, their movement and hushed conversations established a quiet background noise. The noise in the foreground, the noise filling the apartment, belonged to my father, Sidney Beir. He sobbed uncontrollably.

I'd never seen my father cry before. He displayed certain characteristics of our German ancestry: a cerebral intelligence, a dedication to duty, task-oriented, emotionally removed, and often insensitive to the feelings of the family. My father was not a demonstrative man. He never said, "I love you." I never felt his approval. I never saw my father hold my mother's hand, except during the siege of cancer that took her life. Then, he sat by her side. He held her hand for hours. He refused to let go. I found his affection shocking. "Why now?" I thought to myself. "Why not before?"

When my brother's illness took a devastating turn for the worst, my parents put him in quarantine, moving him from our bedroom to their room. Only the family doctor and my parents had visitation rights. Their actions, I suppose, served to protect me. The illness could have been contagious.

I felt shunned. Why didn't my parents explain the gravity of the situation? Why were there so many secrets in my house? "*Das Kinder, das Kinder,*" my parents used to whisper to each other, using the German for not to talk in front of the children. "*Das Kinder, das Kinder*" became a silencer, ending the conversation abruptly, excluding those judged too young to understand. I was always too young to understand.

I felt inferior to my brother. In my mind, my father placed his expectations for the family upon Dickie. In my mind, he set up a strange hierarchy. Dickie was the golden child. Inquisitive, kind, friendly, precocious. In my mind, I held a secondary place. Important but not as essential as my brother. My sister came in last, although she was the oldest. I felt that in my father's eyes the wrong child died. Dickie's death made him unreachable, an icon. How could I compete with such a myth-like status?

In the final days of my brother's illness, my parents sent me up to my aunt's house in White Plains, New York. Her job then, on the ride down to Manhattan and the memorial service, was to reveal my brother's death to me. But how do you do that? What choice words might provide support and concern and sorrow and all the other comforts?

We sat shoulder to shoulder on the train, facing forward. I remember her fumbling. First with a purse, some makeup, her fingernails. The words refused to enter her mouth. I remember the rattle of the train, the jostling, the noise. I remember the scenery zipping by, the beauty and tranquility of the valley. I remember my face in the window reflection. I remember a sense of dread.

"I have something to tell you," she finally managed to say.

"I know," I answered. What a grave moment! My aunt couldn't speak. I couldn't hear. Dickie's death rendered both of us mute.

I don't recall if my parents sent my sister Jeannette away near the end of Dickie's life. I know there was a strain between my sister and my parents. My mother, after my brother's death, turned to me and not to Ginny. Unfortunately, Ginny was not shown the love and acceptance she needed. My parents, I believe, considered Jeannette a difficult child.

Jeannette was five years older. Because of the age difference, we grew up separately. My brother and I were a team, with Jeannette on the other side. There did exist, in the course of our relationship, periods of intimacy. In the immediate aftermath of Dickie's death, for instance, my sister and I became closer. She confided in me, mainly about boys. I remember the many suitors who came to the house. Jeannette was a superb dancer and boys were crazy for her. I remember when one of the suitors asked my father for permission to marry his only daughter. Jeannette and I waited in my room. She was as nervous as could be. My sister had had numerous proposals. My father had declined them, believing the boys were after her money. When my father finally accepted the proposal from a man named Clarence, my sister jumped for joy. I still remember her shouting in the most festive manner. I was thrilled for her. I was thrilled to be an usher at her wedding, and surprised. I didn't think that I'd be included in the wedding party. But there I was, at sixteen years of age, in tails, white gloves, top hat, and cane. I remember prancing around, the proud brother.

The week following my brother's death was a blur of strange occurrences, from the memorial service to my own feelings to my mother's anxieties to the family doctor's peculiar words spoken to me several days after the service. I remember my mother hugging me with a ferocious strength. Her grip was so tight, in fact, that I could feel her blood rushing. Her heartbeat, her pulse, her entire circulatory system seemed an extension of my own. "You're all I have," she whispered into my ear.

Parents don't typically recover from the loss of a child. Franklin and Eleanor Roosevelt already had two children (Anna, born in 1906, and James born in 1907) when they lost an infant son, Franklin Jr., to pneumonia in 1909. A year after that baby's death Eleanor gave birth to Elliott. A few years later she gave birth to another son, Franklin Jr. The last child, John, was born in 1916. In the six-year period following the loss of her baby, Eleanor had given birth to three children. Did her seemingly endless pregnancies assuage the terrible grief? And if so, would that method have served my mother? My Uncle Arthur even suggested that she get pregnant again. For whatever reasons, that didn't happen.

The grieving permanently altered my mother. Yes, she resumed her normal activities. She found solace in the synagogue. She volunteered at the Hamilton House, a settlement for poor immigrants. But that dark cloud of mourning never diminished. I felt like I had to be there for her. So, on Dickie's birthday and the yearly anniversary of his death, I gave her flowers and I went with my parents to the cemetery. These were the actions of a dutiful son. Sometimes I thought I was living for the dead rather than the living.

My reaction to my brother's death was multi-faceted. I experienced a tremendous grief. My brother was my best friend. We attended the same schools, shared many of the same friends, slept in the same bedroom. Always playing practical jokes (on my sister and our nanny), we were very close, in cahoots really.

Simultaneously, I felt important. My brother's death sent a shock wave of attention my way. For the first time, people noticed me. On the street, people would say, "Oh, I'm so sorry about Dickie's death." "Yes," I would answer, "isn't it terrible?" But a part of me didn't feel it was so terrible. A part of me, I think, felt liberated.

That feeling instilled a sense of guilt. I became a bit confused, which was only exacerbated by the family doctor a few days after the memorial service. "You know," he said, "you have to make this up to your mother." These were his exact words and for years they've replayed in my head. What was he trying to say? Did he actually believe that through my behavior I might make up for my brother? Did he actually believe that I might replace my brother?

Did he realize the burden he was placing upon my shoulders? Did he realize the detrimental psychology? I was an impressionable four-teen-year-old. I interpreted his words as: internalize my own needs, make my parents happy, assume a deferential style. I never rebelled. I never clashed. My duty, I believed, was to please my mother.

My father and me, 1951. The portrait of my father was my
surprise gift to him, to commemorate fifty years in business.

Chapter 2

◄ ►

A Decade of
Newsreels

I grew up in an era of newsreels. Besides newspapers and radio, they were the means of disseminating information. We didn't have instant news. We didn't have the bevy, the battering, of cable and its direct access. We learned a little at a time. We went to the movies. Before Judy Garland made her appearance on the screen, or Clark Gable and Vivien Leigh, or Katharine Hepburn and Spencer Tracy, the lights would darken and a newsreel would start. Six or seven short stories lasted a total of five minutes. We learned about current events in this way. We saw world leaders. We glimpsed entertainers, politicians, celebrities. There was a newsreel of Hitler's ascension to power in 1933, and thousands of protesters marching in New York City. There was a newsreel of Mussolini's troops invading Ethiopia in 1935. There was a newsreel of the Spanish Civil War. There was a newsreel of Jesse Owens at the '36 Berlin Games. There was a newsreel of the bombing of Shanghai by the Japanese, and the evacuation of Chinese citizens. There was a newsreel of *Kristallnacht*. In the era before television, there was something special about the footage, something unique. It's no wonder now that in my mind's eye I see newsreels. I see sequences, montages. Here are some of the stories of my life during the 1930s:

The Incident of the Black Eye

The sight of my father crying at my brother's memorial service filled me with fear. Here was an impenetrable man, so strong, so invulnerable. At the memorial, though, he didn't appear so impervious. In fact, he appeared inconsolable. The experience seemed so surreal. My brother was dead. My father appeared broken. How would our lives change? What lay ahead?

In the immediate aftermath of my brother's death, my parents sent me to summer camp. I felt displaced, discarded. I couldn't believe that I'd been sent away. I hated every moment and I yearned to return home. When I did, though, my home had changed. During my absence, my family moved out of the apartment on Broadway. We rented a duplex overlooking Central Park. Clearly, my parents wanted to escape the overriding memories of my brother.

My parents also enrolled me in a prestigious private school named Collegiate. My entire life had changed so suddenly, from attending a Jewish school to leaving my friends behind for the unfamiliarity of a gentile school, from sharing a bedroom with my brother to suddenly having a dead brother, from living in the familiar home overlooking Broadway to peering down on Central Park. I felt like someone had taken a mallet and bonked me on the head, knocking me out cold, and when I awoke the details of my life had been radically altered. I felt dislodged.

I entered a school with a smattering of Jews. At first, the lack of Jews—the people with whom I was most familiar—didn't bother me. My last name wasn't particularly Jewish. My appearance wasn't particularly Jewish. I didn't notice differences. I thought I was just one of the guys. But that changed one day in class when a kid called me a "Dirty Jew." Then he put up his fists.

I was shocked. I was astonished. Still, I had to deal with the threat of violence. "No, not here," I said. I didn't want to get in trouble with the school. "Let's settle it down there." Down there was a gym and settling it meant a boxing match, with gloves and an audience. A large audience, it turned out.

The thought of a boxing match generated in me a sense of fear. The fear of physical harm. The fear of throwing a punch. I'd taken some boxing lessons prior to the incident, but that was different. That was like a game, under supervision. This could become bloody.

The fight wasn't something out of the Joe Louis/Max Schmeling school of boxing. I did manage to scratch my opponent's eye with the laces of my gloves. He showed up the next day with a black eye. I showed up the next day with a sore jaw. A sore jaw can be hidden. A black eye cannot.

For the first time I knew I was different, a member of a hated class. The hurt I suffered at that moment became embedded. I felt stung. No jab could hurt nearly as much.

Sensing those feelings, Wilson Parkhill, the Headmaster of the school as well as my history teacher, called me into his office. He closed the door. He took off his jacket. "Beir," he said, "I have a great idea for you. Why don't you become cheerleader for the school?" I took his meaning to be: let's get back at them, let's make you important.

The interest he showed gave me great comfort. In his office that day, he went through the different cheers. The next morning, during the school's daily assembly, Wilson Parkhill said, "Now, I want to introduce our new cheerleader, Bob Beir." Boy, was I embarrassed. But as I gave the cheers my self-confidence grew. And interestingly enough, I didn't encounter another anti-Semitic incident at that school. In fact, I once again became accepted. Did that have to do with Wilson Parkhill's sensitivity and generosity? Did that have to do with my sticking up for myself?

Anti-Semitism in those days did not generate national headlines. There was the occasional vicious incident—graffiti on a synagogue, an insult hurled, a case of physical abuse—and there was the reaction. Many Jews, in those days, did not force a confrontation. "Keep your nose clean" was my father's philosophy. In other words, don't rock the boat, don't get involved.

Brother, Can You Spare a Dime?

The year 1932 was a fragile time and in the country at large, the turmoil was palpable. The stock market crash of 1929 transformed paper wealth into extreme poverty. Thirteen million Americans lost their jobs in those three years. Unemployment reached a staggering 24 percent of the overall population. As a teenager, I felt scared as I walked to and back from school. Desperation was everywhere. In the men selling apples to try to eke out a living. In the endless begging and that hopeless phrase, "Brother, can you spare a dime?". I felt surrounded by poverty. I felt agitated, as if a darkness clung to our era and would not relent.

The unemployment eroded into homelessness. In New York, for instance, Central Park became a shantytown. Overnight, the flowerbeds and manicured lawns turned into a sea of flimsy dwellings made of anything available, aluminum mainly but also newspaper and cardboard and trash and tree branches. Inhabitants of the shanties tore down low-hanging limbs in hopes of strengthening their structures. Trees in Central Park lost their reachable branches; that was another sign of the Great Depression.

Unofficially, Central Park underwent a renaming: "Hooverville." At a time when thousands of Americans stood in line at soup kitchens, President Hoover's favorite phrases were, "There's a chicken in every pot" and "Prosperity is just around the corner." Meanwhile, the shanties in Hooverville were without foundations. They drifted with the wind. But wasn't that the point? Didn't our society drift with the wind?

In the November election, Franklin Delano Roosevelt won by staggering totals. He gained four hundred and seventy-two electoral votes to Hoover's fifty-nine. He emerged with a 57 percent popular vote to Hoover's 39. Roosevelt's landslide victory was a reflection of the hope he generated. There was confidence in his body language, in his smile, in the rakish way his head angled back to the right when he laughed, in the way he tilted his cigarette holder. There was optimism in his voice, in his words, in his forceful pronunciation. There was strength in those powerful arms that held his crippled body upright.

His inaugural, however, started off as anything but optimistic. March 4, 1933 was an overcast Saturday, the weather a perfect marker of the nation's mood. Yes, a parade snaked down Pennsylvania Avenue and thousands of people cheered the proceedings but a very thick level of anxiety hovered below the surface. "It was very, very solemn," Eleanor Roosevelt said of the first inaugural, "and a little terrifying."[1] The motor ride from the White House to the east side of the Capitol spoke to the somberness and tragedy of the times. President Herbert Hoover and President-elect Franklin Delano Roosevelt exchanged not a word, not even a glance. Their hostility suggested a nation torn apart.

On the inauguration platform, Roosevelt grabbed his oldest son James's arm. In his other hand, he fidgeted with the rim of his silk hat. Inadvertently, he'd picked it up backward. At the rostrum, he raised his right hand and repeated the oath of office. With his left hand, he supported his body with the weight of the lectern. That lectern had been tested earlier for its stability. Roosevelt made a habit of checking the supportability of lecterns.

FDR gazed out at the overflow crowd. If ever there was a time for the impressions of assurance and durability, this was it. With a firm grip on the lectern, he spoke methodically, "I am certain that my fellow Americans expect that on my induction into the Presidency I will address them with a candor and a decision which the present situation in our nation impels. This is preeminently the time to speak the truth, the whole truth, frankly and boldly." And then his voice hummed with a sense of urgency. "This great nation will endure as it has endured, will revive and will prosper." His pledge of "action, and action now" suggested the storm of reform that would become his first one hundred days.

In our apartment, my father and I listened to Roosevelt's voice over the radio. We sat in the living room. Just off the room, a terrace overlooked Central Park. From twenty-one floors above, you gazed out at acres of land. Your eye gravitated to Hooverville. Those shanties imposed an unavoidable chill. The nation required a symbol of regeneration. And who better than Roosevelt, with those ten pounds of metal braces on his legs? My father seemed to recognize the vision of Roosevelt's agenda. He digested each and every word. He was captivated. And I sat there, listening intently to the President while surreptitiously stealing glances at my father. And I was captivated too.

The Searing Effect

Like many high school seniors, I debated my next step after graduation. Attending college was clear. No one in my family had done so. Becoming the first Beir to graduate from college was important to both my parents and to me. The question was: Which college? I'd been thinking Williams or Amherst. Neither of those schools, Collegiate Headmaster Wilson Parkhill advised, would be suitable. I believe he used the word "clique." I believe he meant that both Williams and Amherst accepted only a few Jews. And if I attended, I might find myself facing another anti-Semitic episode, or a series of them.

I applied to Hamilton College, Cornell, and Taft Prep School, the latter in deference to my parents, who thought a year at prep school would better prepare me for college. Taft turned me down. I landed on the Cornell wait-list (which I'm still on today, to my knowledge). Hamilton accepted me. I was all set to go when my mother received a phone call from the Headmaster at Taft Preparatory School. A space had opened up, he said; was I still interested? My parents made the decision for me. I was a young seventeen years old, in their eyes; I needed the seasoning.

Taft offered a superior education. Demanding classes taught by learned men. A rigorous religious curriculum (vespers every night and church on Sundays, regardless of one's religious heritage). Every hour in the student's life accounted for. A dress code. A definite set of socially correct behavior patterns. A curfew not to be contested. The word then was "mores," meaning social customs with almost the force of law. You didn't mess with them. If you did, you paid a steep price. For instance, my first roommate, after sneaking out of the window on successive nights and going into town for some action, was caught and dismissed from school. I'm sure his story was not uncommon.

The school was a reflection of Headmaster Horace Taft, known as "The King." Horace Taft was the antithesis of his brother, William Howard Taft, the 27th president of the United States. Horace Taft was an elegant man: tall and lean, strict but with a gracious smile, rigid but with a soft interior. On the other hand,

President Taft was a jovial, obese man who got stuck in a White House bathtub.

At first I hated the institution. I was homesick and the school's inherent austerity was unsettling. I remember calling my father. I remember begging to come home. He advised me to stick it out for six weeks. During that time, my homesickness mellowed. The school's rigidity became tolerable. I became popular. The King used to invite a handful of boys to his quarters for Sunday night dinner. A great discussion always followed. I was in seventh heaven. Those invites were something to cherish. They also inspired me to study, for the first time in my life. I found that with effort came success.

In those days, Taft permitted one weekend home per student per year. I took mine toward the latter part of the school year. One night I went to a hotel dance, featuring the Benny Goodman orchestra. On my return to Taft a bunch of students were talking about their weekend. I described my evening at the hotel.

"I thought only Jews went there," one boy said. His response took me by surprise. Jews did go there, along with anyone else who wanted to dance and listen to the great Benny Goodman.

"Oh," I replied, "I thought you knew I was Jewish." Taft then had a quota system; I was part of the Jewish 5 percent.

Nobody said a word and the next morning, in the hallways, nobody spoke to me. Not a "hello," a greeting, a remark of friendship. Silence, ostracism, alienation.

That night, I awoke to a gang of boys in my room. I remember my surprise, wondering what in the world was going on. I remember my confusion as I lay on the floor. I'd been dumped out of bed. The boys then scattered, like beads of water dropped on a hot skillet. The incident was never discussed. And I wonder now if the silence that followed wasn't as devastating as the incident itself. In the dumping, I was made to feel tormented, victimized by my friends. In the following silence, I was made to feel shunned by the institution.

Like my Collegiate experience, after the initial anti-Semitic episode, the persecution ended. There was a searing effect, a branding. But then life returned to normal and I became one of the boys again. Still, I never forgot.

A Swastika-Filled Nation

At the end of my year at Taft I again had a difficult decision to make: Which college to attend? Taft was a springboard to Yale and my mother had visions of her son attending one of the two or three greatest universities around. However, as a graduation gift my parents offered me a trip to Europe. That trip conflicted with Yale's admission testing. I couldn't do both.

I drove up to Rhode Island and Brown University with my mother. The admissions officer interviewed me for two hours. He told me not to worry. Sure enough, a month later my acceptance arrived. In those days, a two-hour interview, along with a good scholastic record and the ability to pay (a rarity during the Depression), could get you into an Ivy League school. Not these days.

A month or so before the Berlin Olympics began, my parents and I boarded an ocean liner bound for Cherbourg, France. I was smitten with travel from that sailing forward. The ocean liner experience was a study in charm, elegance, and style. First-class compartments. Tuxedos in the dining room. Strolling along the ship with the roaring Atlantic down below.

The trip took us by automobile through most of Western Europe. In those days, young adults went to Europe *with* their parents. Traveling through Europe wasn't viewed as a form of rebellion but, rather, a form of education. My education included "the Grand Tour." Museums, churches, historical points of interest, anything that might be instructional.

After France, we traveled to England. On the morning of July 16, my parents and I attended the changing of the guard near Buckingham Palace. King Edward VIII made a rare appearance, arriving on horseback to inspect the troops.

Edward must have been in the throes of passion. Five months later, on December 10, 1936, he would abdicate the throne to marry Wallis Simpson. His brother, King George VI, would then grant Edward the title with which we are familiar today: the Duke of Windsor.

As the guard changed, we heard a noise, like a gunshot. Edward's horse reared. A woman standing beside us fainted. Police rushed in from every direction. It was chaotic and confusing. The King was not hurt. In fact, not a single shot was fired.

The next morning, in the newspapers, we read that the would-be assassin, George Andrew McMahon, had come to Buckingham Palace to assassinate the King. The fact that Edward appeared at that moment during the changing of the guard must have been coincidental. Police apparently noticed McMahon as he drew his revolver. In the scuffle that followed, McMahon's revolver hit the pavement (explaining the noise we heard) then slid into the hind leg of the King's horse, nearly throwing Edward to the ground.

McMahon was accused of producing a revolver with intent to alarm his Majesty, a very English charge. Eventually, he was sentenced to twelve months hard labor. And my parents and I had become witnesses to a scary, remarkable moment in history.

After visiting England, my parents and I went back to the continent. At some point, we traveled by plane, my first flight. As part of some necessity in connecting flights, we were routed through Germany. We landed at the Bremen Airport.

What did we know about Nazi Germany then? The newsreels showed Hitler and his many parades. We watched his erect body, his arm thrust upward in the Nazi salute, the legions and legions of goose-stepping soldiers passing under his piercing gaze. The Nuremberg Laws, we knew, took away Jewish citizenship. We didn't know about Dachau, or the sterilization of mental patients, or the Nazis' vast military build-up. We couldn't have known what would follow: *Kristallnacht*, the death camps, the crematoria. We felt, I believe, a growing apprehension.

At the Bremen airport, swastikas were everywhere. As part of the Nuremberg Laws, the swastika had become the official emblem of Nazi Germany. That emblem, up close, was an ominous sight. The future looked dark. I sat in a reception room with my parents, looking at the tarmac. There, I saw a series of airplanes parked in a row, all carrying the swastika insignia. Behind me, around me, on the walls and on kiosks, I saw the swastika insignia. On the clothing of officials, I saw the swastika insignia. I remember the discomfort, the trepidation. Sitting in a swastika-filled air-port, in a swastika-filled nation, I felt an awful foreboding.

A Devilish Vision

During my first semester at Brown University, the fraternity rush-ing season began. The only Jewish fraternity on Brown's campus, Pi Lam, rushed me. At one of the events, I saw my roommate, Tommy Steele. I was caught by surprise: Tommy was Jewish? He had the same reaction toward me. Neither of us looked Jewish. Neither of us had Jewish family names. Later, in our room, we sat on the floor and laughed. "You?" I said. "You?" he replied. Neither of us could quite believe our common Jewish heritage. I'm sure a Brown administrator, with records in front of him, chose the arrangement.

One night there was a knock on our door. Two friends, who usually barged in, asked if they could enter. Slowly, almost timidly, they sat down on one of the beds. Silence followed. Two guys who were normally boisterous were tongue-tied.

"We didn't know you guys were Jewish," they said, eventu-ally. "We were brought up to believe that all Jews had horns and a tail. But you guys are nice."

I've forgotten my reaction. Was I confused or hurt or disgusted? Or did I take it in stride, believing that the best way to deal with anti-Semitism was to let it subside, to wait out the storm? Anti-Semitism, certainly, was ingrained into American culture. The signs were everywhere. There were no Jewish CEOs of Five Hundred Companies or banks in the 1930s, with the exceptions of those entities that were founded by Jews. Jews simply were excluded from top positions. A quota system at universities, particularly for medical and law schools, made it practically impossible for Jews to enter. And if a medical school did accept a person of the Jewish faith, that doctor, after graduation, faced certain obstacles. For instance, Lenox Hill Hospital in Manhattan didn't permit Jews to practice. Today, Lenox Hill brims with Jewish doctors.

In New York, apartments were listed as "exclusive." A euphe-mism for No Jews Allowed. The same could be said for clubs, neighborhoods, resorts. In the late 1930s my family went on holiday at a resort in North Carolina. When my father applied for a room, the desk clerk replied, "I'm sorry, but we are booked."

My father became suspicious. A little while later, he sent my brother-in-law Clarence over to the desk clerk. Clarence resembled the Aryan stereotype: blond hair, blue eyes, and a turned-up nose. Clarence requested a room. Sure enough, the desk clerk found an opening.

Countless Jewish families, I'm certain, could tell a version of this story. On its website, the United States Holocaust Memorial Museum displays a rate card from Barrett's Bald Mountain House in the Adirondacks. A room rate, in the 1930s, went for four dollars per night. A person could rent a room for under 25 dollars per week. Of course, that person couldn't have been a member of the Jewish faith. The rate card read, "Applications from Hebrews not desired." Directly below those words, the card read, "Consumption being classed as a contagious disease, we are compelled to direct persons afflicted with it to sanitary institutions." The inference was clear.

Business Education

It was now 1940. On April 9, Germany invaded Denmark and Norway. On May 10, Germany launched its sweep through Belgium, the Netherlands, and Luxembourg. At the same time, construction began on a concentration camp called Auschwitz. Beginning on May 26, the British and French troops, having been pushed all the way to the sea by the Nazi blitzkrieg, miraculously evacuated three hundred thousand troops from Dunkirk in northern France across the English Channel. Their plight was so desperate that they had no choice but to leave their equipment behind. Also that year, Franklin Roosevelt defeated Republican Wendell Willkie and became America's first third-term president.

The French capitulated to the Germans on June 22, 1940, my graduation day from Brown. The surrender came as quite a shock. The French, after all, had the largest army in the world. The Maginot line, known as the "Great Wall of France," boasted the most modern defense system technology then offered. The French had appeared invincible. The Germans conquered France in six weeks.

The question struck me on graduation day: "Are we going to have to trade diplomas for guns?" Like America itself at the time, I distanced myself from the war. First I went to work for my father in his fabrics business. The calendar turned into the summer of 1941. In England, the Battle of Britain approached its one-year anniversary. The towns of London and Liverpool and Kent still suffered from Luftwaffe punishment. In Warsaw, nearly four hundred thousand Jews had been confined to the ghetto, nearly 40 percent of Warsaw's prewar population interned in 2½ percent of the city's land. In America, legislation to continue the first peacetime draft in the country's history came before Congress. Extending the Selective Service Act passed in the House by one vote.

My father made a suggestion. The First World War was on his mind, as well as the country's. In remembering the horrifying butchery, the gas, the trench warfare, and the piles of bodies, how could he not have had my safety in mind?

"Apply to Harvard Business School," my father suggested. Students then were receiving temporary deferments. Born in 1918, I was the precise age to serve my country. My father speculated that with a temporary deferment I might enter the service on a different military level, as an officer. Perhaps an officer had a better chance of survival.

I phoned up the Headmaster of my old high school. Wilson Parkhill knew someone in Harvard's admissions office. He made a phone call. I entered Harvard that fall (albeit six weeks late, due to bureaucratic red tape). A phone call then could get you into the most prestigious school in the country.

I arrived in Cambridge at the end of September 1941. I moved into the dormitory. My roommate was the son of the CEO of a Fortune Five Hundred company. I immediately buckled down into my studies. I was, after all, six weeks behind.

A few weeks later the Dean called me into his office. "Mr. Beir," he said, "I've found a private room for you." I felt my eyebrows rise in surprise. I felt my head jut back. "I think you'll be happier in your own room," the Dean continued.

My surprise diminished and confusion set in. "I wasn't aware that I was looking for one," I replied.

"Sometimes this happens when students come late to the semester," the Dean responded. "Roommates are usually chosen before the term starts."

My confusion diminished and anger set in. I felt insulted. "Did my roommate ask for this?" I asked.

The Dean replied by repeating an earlier statement, "I think you'll be happier in your own room."

I immediately went to see my roommate. "Did you ask that I move out?" I said.

"Yes," he answered.

"Why?" I asked.

"My parents don't want me rooming with a Jew." I sat there for a moment, dumbfounded. Then I responded, "I feel sorry for you" and I moved out. I couldn't believe that such overt anti-Semitism would occur in graduate school, in such an exemplar of higher learning.

Was I naïve? The evidence suggests so. In 1905, one year after Franklin D. Roosevelt graduated, Harvard President Charles Eliot decided to diversify the applicant pool. He instituted a new policy, emphasizing "merit," as measured by a student's mastery of the traditional curriculum. The College Entrance Examination Boards became the test to determine admission. That decision dramatically increased the number of Jewish students accepted by Harvard. In 1900, 7 percent of entering freshmen were Jews. In 1909, the number of entering Jews increased to 10 percent. In 1915, the number grew to 15 percent and by 1922, entering freshmen of Jewish persuasion reached nearly 22 percent.[2]

Those numbers threw the administration and alumni into an uproar. The President of Harvard during the 1920s, A. Lawrence Lowell, worried that the "Jewish problem" would "ruin the college." He explained in a parallel example: "The summer hotel that is ruined by admitting Jews meets its fate, not because the Jews it admits are of bad character, but because they drive away the Gentiles, and then after the Gentiles have left, they leave also."

In May of 1922 Lowell warned that "the danger [of a large Jewish population at Harvard] would seem to be imminent." His tactic then was to reduce the Jewish demographic. First he proposed a quota, limiting Jews to 15 percent of the student body. Then Lowell tried restricting the number of scholarships given to Jews. Finally Lowell, and his counterparts at Yale and Princeton, changed the admission policy. To the definition of "merit," the Big Three of the Ivy League added the ideal of the "all-around man," including such words as "character," "leadership," and "personality." The application also changed. "Starting in the Fall of 1922," Jerome Karabel wrote in *The Chosen*, "applicants were required to answer questions on 'Race and Color,' 'Religious Preference,' 'Maiden Name of Mother,' 'Birthplace of Father,' and 'What change, if any, has been made since birth in your own name or that of your father? (Explain fully).'"

Further, a classification scheme was instituted. Each Harvard student fell into one of four categories: "J1," "J2," "J3," and "Other." "J1" was assigned "when the evidence pointed conclusively to the fact that the student was Jewish." "J2" was assigned when a "preponderance of evidence" implied that a student was Jewish. "J3" was assigned when "the evidence suggested the possibility that the student might be Jewish." By 1933, as President Lowell's tenure ended, the Jewish population at Harvard had fallen to 15 percent, a fifteen-year low.

Lowell's successor, James Conant, who served as the President of Harvard from 1933 to 1953, held strident anti-Semitic views. For instance, he treated Nazi academics as part of the learned world. He also advised the DuPont Corporation not to hire Max Bergmann, a German Jewish scientist, because he was "very definitely of the Jewish type—very heavy."[3] The *New York Times* described Bergmann as "one of the leading organic chemists in the world."

Anti-Semitism at Harvard, however, didn't end with its top administrator. In 1934, a faculty panel held a mock trial of Adolf Hitler. His anti-Jewish philosophies were ruled "irrelevant." In that same year, a Nazi official and alumnus of Harvard, Ernst Hanfstängl, was invited to the campus for a reunion. Hanfstängl, Hitler's foreign press chief, was a known anti-Semite and yet the

Harvard Crimson (the student newspaper) suggested an honorary award "as a mark of honor appropriate to his high position in the government of a friendly country."

In 1936, Harvard sent a delegation to Heidelberg University to mark that academy's 550th anniversary. By then, Heidelberg had been Nazified. Jewish professors had been expelled. The curriculum reflected Nazi ideology. Also, that university was the site of numerous book-burnings. And yet Harvard sent a delegation to what American newspapers described as a "Brownshirt pageant." This was Harvard, a place of higher learning.

The News That Changed the World

In the late autumn of 1941, the State Department and the Japanese government held a series of negotiations aimed at brokering a peace. These weren't widely known negotiations, of course. Like most Americans, I knew that the Japanese had become a military power. Many of us knew they dominated a wide swath of the Pacific. Their attack in Hawaii, however, stunned America. We simply could not believe the news. Neither could the President. That Sunday, he and Harry Hopkins had just finished a light lunch. Roosevelt had begun work on his stamp collection. The phone rang at 1:47. "Mr. President," Secretary of the Navy Frank Knox said, "it looks as if the Japanese have attacked Pearl Harbor."

"No!" Roosevelt responded. History records that the President needed eighteen minutes to gather himself before taking the next action (placing a call to Cordell Hull at the State Department and sending for General George C. Marshall, who was out horseback riding). And in the days that followed Pearl Harbor the President was not his loquacious self, but rather "businesslike and curt to everybody; appointments were brief, the clock had no mercy, and the President kept time with time."[4]

The general public's response to Pearl Harbor was a desire for revenge. We wanted to attack Japan. An unbridled patriotism consumed America. At Harvard, the dean of the business school called a meeting of the general assembly. He preached patience. His message: "Don't rush into action. Continue to study. Wait out the initial surge. Fight for your country when the time comes. The war will be there. What's the hurry?"

Nevertheless, an exodus occurred. I don't know the exact percentage of students who ignored his advice and went down to the draft board and signed up for service. I would estimate a good 30 percent.

Two months after Pearl Harbor, the Navy came to Harvard Business School looking for officer candidates. I enrolled, feeling both trepidation and patriotism. I didn't want to serve on the front lines; becoming a Naval officer seemed like a safer choice.

The recruitment officer recommended that I finish graduate studies. A few months later I was called down to the First Naval District and interviewed, given a physical, and administered the oath of office. I repeated those immortal words: "I do solemnly swear that I will support and defend the Constitution of the United States against all enemies, foreign and domestic. . . ."

Afterward, I gathered my books and went for the door. The officer asked where I was going. "To take a test," I answered.

He shook his head. "You're in the Navy now!" he said. "You've got four days to get down to NAS Norfolk."

I didn't even know what NAS stood for. I was twenty-four years old.

Continuing Education

At Grand Central, my mother hugged me. What did she feel as she waited for her son to board a train for Naval service and, eventually, the war? She'd already lost one son. What was is it like, for a mother, to contemplate losing the other?

My father couldn't hug me. He couldn't show any emotion. Instead, he put out his hand. He held a watch, a beautiful keepsake. "Good luck," he said, dropping it into my hand. I was startled and overwhelmed.

We shook hands. Tears came to my eyes. That was as close as my father came to reaching out, to expressing anything intimate. It was a very touching moment. I looked away and boarded the train.

Norfolk, Virginia in 1942 stirred with military vigor. The

Atlantic fleet was based there. Service personnel were everywhere. Uniforms dominated the cityscape. There was a deep commitment for the American cause, an overwhelming belief in the war effort. There was in fact no dispute within the nation. No debate. This would be the last war in which such unanimity existed.

I arrived at the Naval Aviation Station (NAS) and immediately reported. I wore civilian clothes. The officer in charge sized me up in a split second. "Why aren't you in uniform?" he hollered. I didn't answer. "Report back here at 0900 tomorrow," he commanded. "In uniform!"

That was my first command, and my first official Naval duty. I bought an Ensign's uniform. Fortunately I didn't buy something more grandiose. Some servicemen came back in uniforms of higher rank. They had to do an embarrassing about-face to the department store (which sold uniforms in those days, particularly in Norfolk, a military town).

The next morning, as I entered the base in uniform to report to the Commander's office, I received a series of salutes. Everywhere I looked, I saw the gesture. Quite suddenly, I felt important. I felt puffed up. "I'm an officer!" I thought to myself.

The Commander asked me a series of questions. If I had any small-boating experience. If I had any fishing experience. I answered no. "What was your major in college?" he asked.

"English literature," I replied.

"Oh, my God," he answered. "What are they sending me now?" And then he pronounced my immediate future in two words. "Code Room."

Norfolk was a drag. I hated the steamy heat. I worked from eight p.m. to eight a.m. I'd come home exhausted. All I wanted to do was sleep but that was impossible in those days before air conditioning. Sometimes I'd drive out to Virginia Beach (as a Naval officer I received a higher ration of petrol, enough to make the trip). On the beach I'd fall asleep. That was the only place somewhat cool.

At the Naval Aviation Station I had no idea what I was doing. I was an Ensign. I didn't know the lay of the land. I didn't know anything about Morse code. I wasn't trained in communications.

I couldn't even identify the flags on the ships. I felt like I was floundering, barely afloat. Slowly, that began to change. I made friends with the old regular Naval personnel, the Chief Petty Officers. I asked lots of questions. Other Ensigns came in and threw their weight around. That wasn't my way. I was a skinny kid. I didn't have much weight to throw around.

In the first few days of my stay in Norfolk, I recognized a fellow from Harvard Business School. I only knew Donald Holms by sight. At Harvard, we hadn't spent any time together. Donald and I decided to room together, sharing a single room in a private home. We quickly became good friends. In the months that followed we double dated. When some of the women began to break dates with me, I became suspicious. "Not again," I thought to myself. Donald confirmed my suspicions. Anti-Semitism seemed so widespread that I couldn't escape it. The question strikes me again today: Was I resigned to it?

As a Naval officer, I was accepted by the Norfolk Yacht Club for a dollar a year. I liked to go there for dinner and dancing and, after almost every shift at NAS, I took my breakfast at the Club. Soon I learned a disturbing fact: the Norfolk Yacht Club, in the 1940s, did not permit Jews. I learned this from Jewish women in town, all of whom refused to frequent the Club with me.

I did not drop out of the Club. "Why should I?" I thought to myself. "Why should I suffer?" But suffer I did, whether I realized it then or not.

To Hell with Habeas Corpus

In February of 1942, President Roosevelt signed the most damning of Executive Orders: number 9066, the internment of the Japanese. The Executive Order also permitted the internment of Germans and Italians living in the United States. According to Attorney General Francis Biddle, Roosevelt differentiated between the two groups. "I don't care so much about the Italians," the President said. "They are a lot of opera singers, but the Germans are different, they may be dangerous."[5] However, six hundred thousand Italian-born legal residents of America became "enemy aliens." Strenuous restrictions were imposed, including curfews, police searches, limitations on travel, a registration and fingerprint requirement, and the confiscation of fishing boats. Ten thousand Italians living in coastal California were forced to move inland. Not only did these people lose their homes but many of them lost their jobs, including a fisherman named DiMaggio, the father of baseball's best player (who, in 1941, set a record by getting hits in fifty-six consecutive games). A leading opera singer, Ezio Pinza, was arrested on suspicion of subversive activities. He spent several weeks in detention before prominent citizens, including Mayor Fiorello La Guardia of New York, came to his defense. In addition, almost two thousand Italians were interned at Fort Missoula in Montana, where many remained for the duration of the war.

As an officer and an American national, I was in favor of the internment, particularly of the Japanese. Consider the climate of the country. The bombing of Pearl Harbor was only a few months earlier. The next Japanese attack on American soil appeared imminent. In fact, while Roosevelt addressed the nation on Washington's birthday, a Japanese submarine surfaced off the coast of Santa Barbara and fired some shells. Although no real damage was done, the assault promoted a culture of fear. In addition, the Japanese unveiled, in essence, the first intercontinental missile: air balloons equipped with bombs and automatic dropping mechanisms. The Japanese launched nine thousand air balloon bombs during the war period, the purpose of which was to cause fear and panic. Two hundred and ninety bombs landed in North America and six people died in Oregon from an attack. Five of them were children who found a balloon and tampered with it.

The scuttlebutt in Norfolk predicted another Pearl Harbor-like attack. The next one in San Diego. A period of caution permeated the country. Roosevelt's Executive Order solidified what the country wanted. Most Americans, I believe, thought the Japanese on the west coast were a threat and as such, aiding their ancestral homeland. How? By using secret broadcasting equipment. By holding out lanterns in the night to identify cities for bombing runs. By giving away our ships' locations. Was it irrational? In hindsight, yes. At that time, though, the country was scared.

Roosevelt, it is interesting to note, began to develop another solution for dealing with the 120,000 Japanese-Americans confined in concentration camps. He advanced the theory of "scattering" the population in a way which would avoid conflict. "He suggested placing two families in every county in the United States, on the ground that such 'distribution' would promote assimilation and resolve the Japanese 'problem.' "[6]

There was no mass public outcry to Roosevelt's Executive Order 9066. No huge demonstration in Washington. Even the liberal newspapers barely objected. Columnist Walter Lippmann, the voice of progressive policies and individual liberties during the New Deal days, supported the internment, calling the Pacific Coast a "combat zone."[7]

"Because there had been no clarion call of protest," James MacGregor Burns wrote in his seminal work, *Roosevelt: The Soldier of Freedom*, "the President was never faced with a compelling set of alternatives and arguments." Even in Roosevelt's Cabinet, opposition was tempered. Henry Morgenthau and Harold Ickes, typically the voices of liberalism, didn't oppose the order. The most vociferous opposition came from Attorney General Francis Biddle, who argued that such an order ran contrary to civil liberties. Roosevelt replied that when you're at war, you listen to the generals. Biddle, without allies in the Cabinet, acquiesced.

One other voice of opposition should be noted. At a White House dinner, Eleanor Roosevelt asked the President to assist the one million enemy aliens (the Japanese, Germans, and Italians combined) who, the First Lady argued, were the targets of discrimination and persecution. Winston Churchill, present at the dinner, suggested following the British example: setting up loyalty hearings. "We separated the goats from the sheep," Churchill said, "interned the goats and used the sheep." Eleanor Roosevelt continued her crusade. She opposed mass evacuation. She lobbied against the severity of the measure. In her newspaper column she profiled one Japanese-American. "This should remind us," she wrote, "that among the group are really good and loyal Americans and we must build up their loyalty and not tear it down." When she further pressed the issue with the President, however, he cut her off.[8]

In retrospect, the internment of 120,000 Japanese-Americans (and the others) was one of the gravest travesties of civil rights. The Japanese-Americans were innocent. There is no way today to justify what happened then. No way to excuse the racial intolerance. No way to defend the horrendous conditions within the camps. No way to rationalize the undermining of the Constitution. In retrospect, the internment was one of Roosevelt's biggest mistakes. In those years, though, we didn't question the policy.

Are there parallels today, concerning the Patriot Act and the internment of Arab-Americans? Sadly, there seem to be. And it's too easy to blame terrorism, to call the incarceration of an ethnic group a casualty of war. It's an egregious error. In 1942, Westbrook Pegler, an anti-Roosevelt columnist who later became a staunch McCarthyite, wrote that every Japanese in California should be under guard "and to hell with habeas corpus until the danger is over."[9] Actually, something similar was the policy in Lincoln's day. Is that the policy now?

My first year in the Navy, 1942.

Chapter 3

◄ ►

Impressions of
War-Torn Britain

T he newsreels of the 1940s offered a much different flavor than the newsreels of the previous decade. There was a different urgency to the 1940s. There was a sense of desperation at first, then the urge for revenge after Pearl Harbor, and then a challenge to end worldwide tyranny. There prevailed an unfettered belief in the righteousness of our actions. The newsreels reflected these attitudes. There was a newsreel of Pearl Harbor. There were newsreels of American soldiers in training and in battle. There were newsreels of nurses (perhaps used as propaganda to recruit women to the war effort). There was a newsreel of B-17 bombers ruling the skies over Europe. There was a newsreel of Iwo Jima, and a newsreel of V-E Day, and a newsreel of the Yalta Conference. There was a newsreel of President Roosevelt addressing Congress directly after Yalta, when he sat during the speech, the only time in his presidential career in which he did so. Here are some of the stories of my life during the 1940s:

London

In January of 1943, I received orders to report to COMNAVEU (Commander, U.S. Naval Forces in Europe). The trip to London, England, which these days would be a straightforward flight, became a five-day adventure. My orders stipulated that I report to Idlewild Airport (JFK after the name change) in civilian clothes, carrying a State Department diplomatic passport. I did not know the reasons for these directives. I boarded that plane not knowing my future. The question "What lies ahead?" occupied my mind.

The seaplane carried some major VIPs, including Junius P. Morgan and W. Averell Harriman, who would soon become the Ambassador to the Soviet Union and, eventually, the Governor of New York and presidential aspirant. First Lady Eleanor Roosevelt may also have been on that plane, although that could be a figment of my memory. Mrs. Katherine Chapin Biddle, the Attorney General's wife and an avid Red Cross volunteer, may also have been on that plane. Memory, I've learned during this writing process, can be a tricky source of reliability.

The plane flew to Bermuda, where we stayed overnight to refuel. Then to Fornes Airport in Northern Ireland. Then to Foynes Airport. We slept in the fishing village of Adaire. The next day we took off for England, flying low over the Irish Sea to avoid German fighter planes. At some point along the way, the pilot observed the German Luftwaffe. The pilot made a quick return to Ireland, landing in Limerick. Again, we stayed overnight. The next day, we took off again. This time we reached our destination: Poole, England. From there, the non-VIPs boarded a train for the long trip to London.

I arrived in England with a cold, like most of the other passengers on that trip. In those days, the heating systems weren't very well developed. The cabin was freezing cold. We all wore blankets to keep warm. There was another way to keep warm: Irish whiskey. My first introduction to that famous drink.

We arrived in London in the middle of the night. Of course, the whole city was blacked out. I had no idea where to stay. Fortunately, the Red Cross met the train. Some of us were taken to a facility and put up overnight.

My apprehension was growing. I didn't know, for instance, why we all wore civilian clothes until much later. The answer was that travel to a neutral country (in this case, Northern Ireland) dictated it.

The next morning I reported to COMNAVEU headquarters, located at Grosvenor Square. The officer in charge pored over a stack of papers. He couldn't find my orders. Finally, they turned up and revealed that I wasn't supposed to report for another two weeks. Typical Navy snafu.

The Navy, like the other military branches, had a vocabulary all its own. Snafu stood for Situation Normal All Fucked Up. "Bloody" was a word we used relentlessly, at least in Britain. "Scuttlebutt" was another. Also in the Navy, we cursed a lot.

Since I had no assignments for two weeks, all I had to do was report at 0900 and then the rest of my day was free. I toured the city. Nearly a year and a half had passed since the Battle of Britain and yet German bomber planes still flew overhead nightly. The extensive damage to London was hard to believe: buildings leveled, neighborhoods destroyed, rubble everywhere. To quote a German communiqué from the time, "One great cloud of smoke stretches from the middle of London to the mouth of the Thames."[1] To quote from my letter home dated January 29, 1943, "Most appalling sight—takes your breath away—is incredible—gruesome—depressing—bitter to take." And yet the British fighting spirit remained, the deep commitment to serve and persevere.

The surroundings I saw echoed Winston Churchill's most stirring words, given in the House of Commons on June 4, 1940. ". . . We shall go on to the end. We shall fight in France, we shall fight on the seas and oceans, we shall fight with growing confidence and growing strength in the air, we shall defend our island, . . . we shall fight on the beaches, we shall fight on the landing grounds, we shall fight in the fields and in the streets, we shall fight in the hills; we shall never surrender. . . ."

That deep commitment to serve and persevere kept King George VI and Queen Elizabeth in London, instead of fleeing to Canada as they'd been advised. Officially, the King and Queen remained in Buckingham Palace, although they often escaped to Windsor Castle to avoid bombing raids. During one raid, a lone German bomber attacked Buckingham Palace, nearly killing the Royals. The bomb exploded in a Palace courtyard, not far from the residential wing.

The King and Queen, throughout the war, went on morale-boosting tours, visiting bomb sites and munitions factories. Their popularity among the British was unrivaled. On one tour, Queen Elizabeth and her younger daughter Margaret stopped at a little store, where a couple of Navy officers, buddies of mine, were shopping. In a letter home, dated Wednesday, April 21, 1943, I wrote:

> *There were only the two boys, the Queen, the Princess, and a body guard in the shop at the time, and the boys didn't even notice the Royal family until one of them spotted the crowd outside the store. They then were aware of the freak luck chance had played upon them and decided to remain within the shop, "hoping but never for a moment believing," to get a word with the Queen. After remaining there for about 25 minutes or so (and very obviously, as they expressed it) the Queen walked over and started conversing with them for several minutes. They were so excited they could barely answer. According to one of the boys, the Queen was charming and quickly put them at ease. . . . They fell in love with her.*

I fell in love with the British. So stoic. So determined. Londoners slept in bomb shelters during the night. The next day, they went to work. Not a complaint uttered. I found their resolve inspiring.

Once I reported for active duty, I was assigned to the Code Room then located in the basement of Selfridge's Department Store. For the next three months, I was among a handful of officers cleared to decode top secret messages from President Roosevelt to the "Former Naval Person," as Prime Minister Winston Churchill liked to be called. Both the President and the Prime Minister were Navy men. Both rose to high ranks. Roosevelt became Undersecretary of the Navy under President Woodrow Wilson. Churchill became First Lord of the Admiralty during the First World War. Both men chose to correspond through the Navy, rather than the State Department. Although top secret, the messages themselves were much generalized. Today, I search my memories for specific information. I can't remember a directive.

After deciphering the messages, I remember, the decoder strapped on a .45 caliber pistol and delivered the communication to 10 Downing Street. But this too may be a part of my imagination.

I was issued a .45. That I remember specifically. I never learned to fire the pistol. The term then for recruits after three months of basic training was "90-Day Wonder." I never had a single day of basic training. The following episode proves my inexperience. In the latter part of my tour of duty, the Secretary of the Navy, Frank Knox, arrived for an inspection of the port. As one of the senior officers, my duty was to put the men at attention and ensure the full military routine. Without a day of training, and feeling inadequate, I turned my duties over to the Chief Warrant Officer. After the Secretary had passed through, we all broke up in laughter because I wasn't even trained to handle a basic inspection.

The code work had an ebb and flow to it. Always we felt a tremendous responsibility, an importance for the work. Sometimes we were extremely busy, decoding an avalanche of messages. Other times there was nothing to do but wait. During those hours, I wrote letters home. My mother, much to my surprise, kept my correspondence. Years later, when my wife discovered the letters, I felt like I had unearthed a lost world, a treasure trove.

What was life like for the American serviceman in London? My letters tended to reflect a certain ease, even amusement. There were reasons for this tone. On a subconscious level, perhaps, I wanted to protect my mother, to shield her as the family doctor had suggested in the immediate aftermath of my brother's death. On a military level, all letters from servicemen were under the stern rebuke of the censor. We couldn't write about our duties or our location. We had to be very careful. As such, I chose to focus on the more relaxed side. For instance, in one letter home, dated Friday, April 2, 1943, I recorded a grand evening. Even as I reread this letter, I am amazed that the British continued to live the remnants of a jovial era. I wrote:

> *Around six o'clock after I had had my usual afternoon tea, I went to a very exclusive party which for some reason or other I was invited to. It was a farewell party for the Lady*

so-and-so, who had worked at the Red Cross and was resigning to conquer new fields in the way of different war work. As usual I was the first to arrive (forty-five minutes after I had been told to come), and found myself before a palatial mansion (a left-over from the good old days). As I entered, one butler took my coat, another my hat, and another asked me for my name and rank, and then I was very, very ceremoniously ushered into a huge, paneled room overlooking a beautiful garden, and suddenly heard my name shouted out—Ensign Beir. Needless to say I was slightly embarrassed to express it mildly to find an almost empty room. I was then introduced to Sir and Lady Ha-Ha, and a Mr. Somebody (he was one of the hosts who just never did get around to being knighted). . . . It wasn't long until I heard a few more Lords and Ladies names shouted into the room, and then Mr. and Mrs. Biddle made their entrance [the Attorney General and his wife, I assume. Or could it have been Anthony Biddle, the U.S. Ambassador to many of Europe's governments-in-exile, and his wife?] The RAF, English Army (two Colonels), the American Army, a Major and a Colonel, and the U.S. Navy, another Ensign, were all represented. I had the time of my life, I assure you. One could never have an empty glass, so I drank prewar scotch as long as they insisted (and they never did stop insisting). I vaguely remember a very tall, rather good-looking girl talking to me, or maybe I was talking to her. Anyway I think I asked her out after the party. How it all happened to this day I'm not altogether certain, but I faintly recall leaving, after many thank-yous, being ushered into a waiting taxi and the next thing I knew we were at the Chesterfield Club for dinner, a party of about 12. Apparently the reservations had been made, and I was expected to join though I knew nothing about it. I ate very, very little dinner but managed to sober up enough to dance my way through dinner with that same girl I must have invited out. Of course I didn't have the slightest idea of her name, and she kept calling me Beir with the most awful inflection. Once again someone took me by the arm and I found myself in another taxi headed for the Red Cross. We arrived there just in time for the last dance, had some waffles and lots and lots of coffee. Someone then came through with a suggestion that we go to the Embassy Club to top the evening off. Still again, I was led to another taxi and whisked over to the Embassy. One of the girls was a member so we barged into the club. . . . Again we danced, this time to a good band, and I found that one of the girls in the party was a beautiful dancer, so the next two hours passed by rapidly. It was five o'clock before I got to bed, and I think I have a date with one of the girls for tomorrow night. I slept all this morning, had some lunch, and went back to bed till dinner, and here I am on watch. . . . You may think I have exaggerated this story, but honestly it seemed just like I described it. Everything was unexpected and I was just led from one place to another. It was all good fun. . . . At least I hope to convince you in this letter that I am not continuously suffering, though I must confess most of us do get homesick, and miss the states very much. . . .

Of course, there was an underlying fear. These were not playboy days. These were the days of heavy anxiety. These were the days of not knowing what the next day would bring. I touched on that theme in a letter dated Thursday, April 8, 1943. I wrote, "We have had some activity here on and off, but generally and comparatively speaking, things have remained calm, though of course no one knows what's in store, now that Spring is here. The consensus seems to be that we may have some fun soon. 'Jerry' has been unusually quiet for a couple of weeks."

That consensus proved correct. In a letter home, dated Wednesday, April 21, I wrote, "No doubt you have been reading in the U.S. papers of some and rather frequent, though light, activity in these parts. 'Jerry' has paid us more visits lately, but on a very, very small scale and of very short duration."

On one such occasion, I heard the siren wailing and I suppose my curiosity and my stupidity were equally strong. I did not run for the shelters. Instead, I stuck my head out the window of my hotel room. The hotel was situated beside St. James's Park. In those days, St. James's accommodated a multitude of anti-aircraft guns. Hundreds of them at that moment were going off. You couldn't tell the difference between the bombs in the sky and the anti-aircraft fire. It was all a rain of light.

Suddenly, I experienced a surge of fear. There I was, exposed. Instinctively, I ran from the window. But my room was a typical hotel room, not exactly a bomb shelter cavern. I ducked under the bed.

Later, I laughed at my behavior. How could I have been so stupid? Fortunately, the bombs dropped elsewhere.

I went through lonely days. Like most American servicemen, I yearned to return home. Add to that longing, the important though repetitive work, the terrible food (I wrote to my parents that "I was turning into a brussel sprout"), and of course the gloomy weather, and a bit of melancholy became a rather predictable result.

One day, after work, I went to a neighborhood restaurant. I sat alone at a table. The rest of the details I documented in a letter home to my parents:

> *A few moments later, a rather distinguished fairly elderly English gentleman asked me if I objected to his joining me, to which I replied, "Of course not." We struck up a conversation and he divulged that his son was stationed in New York City as an English Naval Officer of my rank. Naturally, I told him New York was my home, and the conversation "glowed" from there on. He asked me if I liked London, if I had done much sight-seeing. I informed him that I liked all of England very much. . . . He then asked me if I had ever been to a Trade Guild Luncheon and I said no. He took my name and address and I his card. I soon forgot the incident, when yesterday in the mail I received a note from him with an enclosed invitation, quote: "The Master Wardens and Court Assistants of the*

*Worshipful Company of Gardeners request the honour of
the Company of Ensign Robert L. Beir U.S.N.R. at
Luncheon at the Inholders' Hall, College St. Dowgate Hill
E.C.4 on Thursday the 29th of April, 1943 at 1 for 1:15
p.m." Unquote. I understand these luncheons are steeped
in the tradition and history of old England having survived
throughout the ages, and though being somewhat anachro-
nistic today, are held occasionally to revive and keep alive
an old tradition. Wigs and gowns used to be worn, and I
don't believe they have been discarded yet. . . . I am not
on watch Thursday, the 29th and am accepting the invitation with much anticipation. . . .*

And what an experience it was. I detailed the experience in a
letter dated Thursday, April 29th, 10:30 p.m. And here again as
I reread this letter, I am amazed that the pomp and circumstance
continued during the war. I wrote:

*Remember I wrote you about being invited to a Gardeners'
Guild luncheon by this English gentleman I had met in a
restaurant? Well, the luncheon took place today and I
arrived there 10 minutes late to find that they were waiting lunch for me, the last of over 200 men to arrive but it
was in an old section of the City of London (near Guild
Hall and St. Paul) and I had difficulty finding the place.*

*Mr. Gardner, the gentleman who had invited me, ush-
ered me into a paneled (mahogany) room with magnifi-
cent low hanging chandeliers and portraits. The Inholders'
Hall is one of the few halls where Guild Luncheons are
held that was not bombed out in the blitz. The stained windows were shattered and replaced by plain glass, and the
entire block had been wiped out, but the hall stubbornly
remained, almost defiantly outlined amongst inconceivable
wreckage and ruins as the one symbol of all England. Its
very existence, almost stoic in nature, surrounded by deeds
of havoc, and a witness to the rape of London, in itself
was sufficient evidence of Hitler's failure. That building*

*seemingly echoed the voice of the English people in refus-
ing to admit defeat was possible. This description may
sound dramatic, but after visiting that section of London
which seemed to be Hitler's most frequent target, and seeing block after block reduced to ashes and stones—blocks
where Johnson and his circle met, blocks that supported
Guild Hall in which the Lord Mayor of London presided
for so many centuries, blocks steeped in the history, legend,
and folklore of England, then one fully realizes the irrepara-
ble damage committed, and the full significance of that one
remaining Hall silhouetted against empty background.*

*The luncheon itself reflected the building in which it was
held. For the members stubbornly refused a war to interfere
with tradition, and carried out the entire function apparently oblivious to the limitations war imposed upon them.*

*True, it was not a banquet in the former sense of the
word, but neither was it stark simplicity or mere frugality
as one of the members expressed, when apologizing for the
meal to the guests. We had soup, duck, vegetables, dessert
(or a trifle called here), cheese, and three wines with cigars
and cordials. The affair was held in the best and most typical British manner. Toasts were drunk to all the illustrious guests including, "the sole representative of the United
States of the United States Naval Reserve, Ensign R.L.
Beir." Mr. Ernest Brown, Minister of Health, was the guest
of honor, and spoke magnificently. All the speeches were
excellent and anyone who claims the English don't have a
sense of humor will have a difficult time convincing me.
The Guild has a Master elected each year who presides and
two Wardens, an upper and lower Warden, each presiding
over a table. My host was a "past Master" who was the
only member of the Guild to serve two terms in the history of the organization (since 1500 and something). He
refused to run this year. I guess he's a combination of Mr.
Coolidge, "I do not choose to run" and Mr. FDR for
breaking tradition! There were many lords present, many
of whom I met later and found most affable. The Master*

of ceremonies (he had another official title, but can't recall it) spoke very well. He mentioned the distinguished guests present and after Mr. Brown's name, he said, "And last but not least, it gives me special pleasure to welcome a friend from America who is here today in the uniform of an Ensign in the USNR, Ensign R.L. Beir to whom I propose a toast." Where upon they all stood while I turned all colors and they shouted, "here, here (pronounced heah, heah)." I never was so petrified in my life for I didn't know whether I was supposed to acknowledge the toast as all the others had done or not. However, my embarrassment was short lived, for the Master of ceremonies quickly continued as soon as the members were seated, and I once again felt at ease and enjoyed the remaining speeches. I felt like "King for a moment" and never again expect to have a toast drunk to me by so illustrious a gathering.

Gourock

Eventually I became restless in the Code Room. I yearned for active duty. I applied for sea duty. In June of 1943, I received new orders. Not exactly sea duty. I became a Port Officer in Gourock, Scotland.

Located on the Clyde River, Gourock was one of four major U.S. port offices in the British Isles. Unlike the other offices, however, the port at Gourock was deep enough to accommodate the *Queen Mary* and the *Queen Elizabeth*. These ships carried close to fifteen thousand American soldiers per trip across the Atlantic. During the course of the war, the *Queens* carried over a million and a half troops. They traversed half a million miles. They did so without an escort despite the lurking Nazi submarines. At top speed, the *Lizzy* and the *Mary* made thirty-four knots. They could out-run and out-maneuver enemy ships. According to the Nazi rumor mill, Hitler offered a quarter of a million dollars to any U-boat captain who sank a *Queen*. According to the German press, a U-boat torpedo hit the *Lizzy* on November 11, 1942. If that occurred, the torpedo rendered little damage.

My duties were numerous. I was one of the few officers cleared for confidential messages. I embarked and disembarked various high-ranking Naval emissaries and dignitaries, including Prime Minister Winston Churchill (who, when he traveled on the *Queen Mary*, went under the name "Colonel Warden"). I was responsible for checking the health of the armed guard personnel serving on board the ships. I remember trying to climb the Jacob's Ladders. The launch brought you within arm's reach. I remember the choppy waters, the ropes swinging this way and that, the tumult and turbulence. I remember holding on for dear life. A leg could have been smashed during those moments, or far worse.

I also served as a liaison to the Royal Navy. Convoy ships arrived all the time from America, as part of Roosevelt's Lend-Lease policy. Congress had passed the Lend-Lease Act on March 11, 1941. The legislation permitted the President to "sell, transfer title to, exchange, lease, lend or otherwise dispose of, to any such government any defense articles." Thanks to Lend-Lease, the Allied nations hung on during the darkest days of the war and American war production escalated.

Convoy ships had to refuel and resupply in Gourock. During these stopovers, the skippers received their sealed orders at what we called "Convoy Conferences." We knew where they were bound: Murmansk, Russia. That journey passed through some of the most hazardous waters on earth.

The convoy ships were predominantly underarmed Liberty Ships, the work horses of World War Two. As part of Roosevelt's "bridge of ships" from America to Europe, over two thousand Liberty Ships were built during the war. They transported everything from grain to ammunition to trucks and troops across the Atlantic.

Escorted by Destroyers (DDs), the Liberty Ships moved at a snail's pace, perhaps 8 to 10 knots. If they were lucky, they carried 3-inch guns and 50-caliber machine guns. They had practically no armor and were readily attacked by German submarine wolfpacks and the Luftwaffe. These were the early days of the war and the casualties were unbelievably high. In fact, less than a third of the convoy ships reached their destination.

On occasion, after an attack, survivors would be picked out of the sea, returned to Gourock, and interviewed. Their tales were harrowing: experiencing the panic of a ship capsized, floating in the frigid water, their buddies dead, the Germans in the vicinity. Very chilling stories. Incredible tales of survival.

Back at the port, these tales reached the armed guard sailors, frightening those who had to man the guns on upcoming missions. Some of these men used their shore leave to go to Glasgow and frequent the local prostitution houses. When the initial signs of venereal disease surfaced, these sailors went to pharmacist mates at the hospital at Rosneath. I had to accompany them. "Drop your pants," the pharmacist mates would order. If the infection had set in, the sailors received a shot of a new drug called penicillin and they had their names removed from convoy duty. I didn't exactly begrudge them. The risks of venereal disease couldn't compare to the risks of convoying to Soviet Russia.

Gourock was not the most exciting place on the planet. In a letter home, dated Saturday, May 8, 1943, I wrote, "Gourock is a very small town and as I understand it, the principal occupation is drinking, poker, etc. . . . I must say I chose a most depressing day to arrive. It is like winter here, driving rain, cold dampness, and high winds. (And I arrived at the end of spring!) . . . The surrounding countryside is beautiful, and I have walked quite a bit of it. However, there are no other recreations, no dancing, one small dirty movie house. I've gone from one extreme to the other, London and all its many diversions, Gourock with none, from 'city slicker' to 'country hick' overnight."

When I first arrived in Gourock, I stayed at a small hotel. The place was a dive, a cesspool for rodents and vermin. One night I heard a huge BOOM! coming from the other room. I rushed over. "God damn," the officer inside said, "I missed the son of a gun."

He'd shot at a rat with a .45. The bullet tore a hole in the wall. The gun was literally smoking. Although I cracked up at the scene, I loathed the hotel. Fortunately, in a few weeks, I found suitable accommodations. Some rooms opened up in a private house, for thirteen dollars a week. In a letter home, dated Monday, May 31, 1943, I wrote:

> *I finally moved yesterday into a pretty good set-up. A large bedroom, sitting room, bath and shower (the first one I've seen since I've been overseas). . . . The landlady is an old maid of about 50. She seems very nice and the place is immaculate which is amazing! Clean sheets, linen, towels, etc., though very little heat or hot water. . . . It is not too convenient a location, for it's a 25, 30 minute walk or 10 minutes on bus, but busses don't run after 10 o'clock at night. However, I think I shall be satisfied. At least I won't be chasing rats all night, and cleaning bath tubs before taking a bath.*

It was a good deal. I was even allotted a Jeep, which made my commute easy. My landlady, Dorothy Harding, turned into my European mother. Her home became my second home. We became great friends; she even corresponded with my parents back in the States, easing their minds a little. "You no doubt will be surprised to hear from me," she wrote to my parents, in the autumn of 1943, probably the first time she'd written them. "I thought it might be a comfort to you if you heard from someone that your son looks very well indeed and seems happy." She then, in her nearly illegible handwriting, touched on the transitions of her own life. "What changes this house has seen since the outbreak of war. But mother was alive then and everything happened in a perfectly sane and civilized manner. We had our big Blitz three weeks after her death and since then I've had evacuees with their children, Army, Air Force and now I seem to be running a home for sharp Americans." In the end, she wrote the same lines she would in subsequent letters. "Please don't worry too much. B.B. is in fine form." Dorothy Harding was the only person who ever called me B.B.

Occasionally a room opened up in Dorothy's home. Typically, she found an officer or Red Cross member to rent the space. At one point, a room became available and I recommended an acquaintance, who happened to be a Major in the Army. Dorothy agreed to take him in and he was thrilled.

A few nights later at the port office, a bunch of guys gathered around for a rap session. The Major started talking about the Jews. The discussion turned nasty. I interrupted. "I want in on the conversation," I said. "I'm one of those Jews you're talking about." Silence followed. You could have heard a pin drop.

"You are?" the Major finally said. There was surprise in his voice. "But you're a nice guy," he said. The universal response, apparently. The next day, the Major changed his mind. He did not rent the room. Was it a coincidence?

What did servicemen in Great Britain know about the Holocaust during this time? The answer, simply, was nothing. We did not have access to the *New York Times*. If I read the London *Times*, I don't recall. Certainly, I didn't read about any Jewish massacres. We read *Stars and Stripes*. We worried about our future. We hated the Germans because they were our enemy on the battlefield. Meanwhile, the Nazis were trying to keep the Holocaust as secret as possible. In the late summer of 1943, the Nazis were in full Final Solution mode. In August, the Nazis deported 1,260 Jewish children from the Bialystok ghetto to the concentration camp Theresienstadt. All of the children would later die at Auschwitz. On September 18, 2,000 Minsk Jews were deported to the concentration camp Sobibor. On October 9, in commemoration of the Jewish Day of Atonement, 1,000 Auschwitz prisoners, judged too sick to work, were sent to the gas chambers.[2]

In Great Britain, we knew nothing of this.

During my two-year stay in Scotland, I received orders to report to other port offices. For instance, I spent a summer in one of the most isolated places on earth, Loch Ewe, at the northern tip of Scotland. I also opened a port office in Oban, Scotland. I was the only American officer. The N.O.I.C., Naval Officer in Charge, was a British Captain. In peacetime, Oban was a beautiful resort. In fact, during my stay, I rented a room in a luxurious hotel. During the war, Oban became another working port. Why the Navy needed a port there, I had no idea.

I awoke one morning to find, shortly after opening the office, approximately thirty Liberty Ships in the bay. A few days later, a platoon of African-American soldiers arrived. I then received our orders. All the gear from the ships had to be removed. My specific orders were to board the ships and make certain nothing of value remained. I didn't know why these orders were given, but I followed them.

Some weeks later, toward the end of May 1944, I awoke to find the ships all gone, sailed out of the harbor. My mysterious assignment apparently was complete, but I kept my office until I received orders from London to return to Gourock. There, I learned of the Normandy invasion. Those same Liberty Ships (known as Gooseberries) had been sunk off the coast to form artificial harbors called Mulberry harbors.

The Allies knew that the Germans were dug in around the ports of Western Europe. Seizing such a defended port was judged too treacherous by the commanders in charge. The Allies therefore created these artificial harbors in the immediate aftermath of the Normandy invasion. Within twelve days of D-Day, two Mulberry harbors were operational. They supported the Allied armies for ten months. At the Mulberry harbor off Gold Beach, an estimated two and a half million men passed through. So did a half-million vehicles and four million tons of supplies. To this day, steel girders from the Lobnitz Pierheads (giant tables, seven Lobnitzes side by side, created a fourteen-hundred-foot-long pier) are still visible off the coast of Normandy.

It dawned on me suddenly. By stripping those Liberty Ships, my men and I had played a small role in the Normandy invasion. That invasion, and all the men who gave their lives, paved the way for the defeat of Germany. The casualties there, and the brutality of the fight, still stagger my mind.

A few weeks later I received orders from London to report to Normandy to help with landing soldiers on the beaches. Immediately my superior officer in Gourock spoke to the London office. He said he could not afford to lose me, that I was the executive officer, second-in-command, and the only experienced officer at that time. When he got my orders canceled, I lucked out.

Two of my fellow officers from Gourock died during their service in Normandy. The Germans had sabotaged the area, laying mines and such. Those officers stepped on one.

Overfed, Oversexed, and Over Here

Many American servicemen were spoiled. These were the "Ugly Americans." I wrote about the arrogance in one of my letters home:

> *A Yank and a Brit were seated at a bar in a pub, both gentlemen feeling no pain, when the Yank turned around and said, "Well, I guess the war will be over soon, now that we're here." No answer. A few minutes later, the Yank once again (he was now well on his way to another world) said, "Don't worry, we'll fight your war for you" and sneered savagely. Finally, and very calmly, the Brit turned around, cast a disdainful look at the Yank, and said, "You speak bloody good English for a Russian." That's my sentiment too.*

Great Britain was populated with an abundance of available women. British men were on the continent fighting the war; American men took advantage. The saying then went like this: "The British were underfed, undersexed, and under Eisenhower. The Americans were overfed, oversexed, and over here."

I had many dates, many flings. I fell in love once. At one of the Convoy Conferences in Gourock, I met a young Wren officer named Lavender Keyes. She was a relative of Lord Keyes, the first Director of Combined Operations until his forced retirement in 1941. I fell for Lavender quickly. She was kind, caring, and so lovely to listen to. We frolicked. We had a wonderful sense of companionship. She was highly educated, classy, with a typical British sense of humor which I adored. We became inseparable.

At some point in our relationship, Lavender and I began to talk about our future. I was nearing the end of my tour of duty and, once I received orders to report to New York, we expected to spend only a short time apart. I thought I'd get settled in the

States. She intended to finish her military stay. Then we planned on her coming to the States, to be my bride.

But I didn't send for her. At first, I missed her terribly. We corresponded regularly. But once I returned home, I settled into my former life, with friends and family, and as time went by our correspondence dwindled. How do you explain it? Did the doubts creep in, as I became more integrated into life in the States? Was she a part of that life—the war, Britain—and not a part of my life here? Was the feeling mutual? It must have been; the correspondence soon halted altogether. I guess I wasn't ready for marriage then.

Many American servicemen in Great Britain did marry. I don't know how many weddings I attended. All you needed, according to the code at the time, was your commanding officer's permission. I gave my permission to marry to many men under my command. I remember one incident specifically. An enlisted man came to me in a quandary. His British girlfriend was pregnant and she demanded a wedding. As I remember, he didn't want to marry her and he didn't know how to handle it. I suggested that he take his girlfriend over to Rosneath Hospital for a pregnancy test. Sure enough, the test eased his mind. She was not pregnant. Like many others, she just wanted to become an American citizen. The enlisted man was very relieved when I withheld permission.

My father had worried about this very issue. "Son," he wrote, "I know you well enough to know that you wouldn't do anything stupid like getting married abroad." No, Dad, I wouldn't. Although I nearly brought her back to the States.

Washington, D.C.

The final major battle on the Western Front, the Battle of the Bulge, began on December 16, 1944. For all U.S. personnel stationed in Europe, leaves were canceled. There may have been no more bloody, vicious, determined battle in the entire war. The Germans knew this was their last stand. For a month in the Ardennes, they threw everything they had at our soldiers. Nearly 80,000 Americans were killed, injured, or captured. On January 28, 1945, the battle ended with an American victory. The Germans retreated into Germany. About a month later, the American Army crossed the Rhine.

At the same time, I received orders to return to the States. After three years in Great Britain, I was ready to go home, ready to return to things familiar. My military experience did not include combat, for which I now confess relief. Why I requested, and fervently wanted, sea duty, I have no idea. The hunger of youth, I suppose. My military experiences were full of many hours in a decoding room. My military experiences were full of the important work of a Naval attaché. My military experiences were full of the frigid days of British winters, drinking Scotch to keep warm, waiting for letters from home. My military experiences were also full of people: both military personnel and civilians. The times were intense and I formed many friendships.

At the end of my stay, my friends threw a going-away party in my honor. I was flattered and touched. I remember the party's sentimentality. Yes, I was happy to be going home. Yes, after three years away I was eager to make the return voyage. But I also felt like I was losing something. A part of myself. The part that grew up during the war. The part that matured. I had shouldered some big responsibilities. I'd learned how to take care of myself. I was twenty-four when I boarded the plane in civilian clothes at Idlewild Airport. I was twenty-seven upon my return. My early adulthood was spent in Europe. When I left Great Britain, I left that part of me behind.

I sailed home on the *Queen Mary*. Having boarded the ship so many times in Gourock, I knew all the officers. I was able to wangle a private stateroom normally reserved for flag officers. I returned to the States in unbelievable luxury and comfort, unlike my journey to Europe three years earlier. Upon sailing into the New York harbor, I did not, for instance, arrive with a cold.

I had four days to report to New York. I was apprehensive. I didn't want to be sent out to the Pacific. So instead of waiting in New York, I flew down to the capital immediately and met with a Naval personnel officer whom I knew. Explaining that I had served over three years abroad, I requested duty in New York or nearby. The personnel officer thought he had just the right position for me in Washington. Captain Eliot, who was a relative—a grandson, I believe—of Charles Eliot, the famed President of Harvard, was looking for someone with just my experiences abroad. I went to see the Captain. He studied my record and offered me a position. However, he said he probably wouldn't need me for another three months. So I flew back to New York and moved back in with my parents.

This was now April of 1945. On the 12th, I remember listening to the radio while taking a Naval correspondence course. Suddenly a funeral dirge came over the air waves. I was half-listening. Then an announcement. The President was dead. I was shocked, as was the whole country. FDR was a fixture in our lives: a man of great stature, a beacon of power. At a time of so much uncertainty, he seemed to be the one constant, the one reliable. For thirteen years, he dominated. He was the definitive Commander-in-Chief.

For me, he was even more than a Commander-in-Chief. He was even more than a skilled politician. He represented something paternal. He offered a sense of protection. This made him, like Abraham Lincoln, a great war leader.

One thought perplexed the country, and perhaps the world, in the immediate aftermath of FDR's death. What would happen now? The battle leading to Berlin was raging. The Japanese promised to defend their island at any cost. These were not such certain days.

In the Oval Office, Harry Truman was sworn in as the new President. A few days later, he addressed Congress. A huge audience tuned in on the radio. What would this man say, we wondered? How could he replace Roosevelt? Truman began to speak and then came an interruption. "Just a minute, Harry," said the Speaker of the House, Sam Rayburn, using the familiar first name rather than the reverential "Mr. President," "let me introduce you."[3] This caused even more apprehension in the country. Was Truman up to the task?

A few days later I received orders to report immediately to Washington and Captain Eliot. On my twenty-seventh birthday, my mother and I drove down to the capital. When I reported to Captain Eliot, I said, "I thought you didn't need me for three months."

"Things have changed," he responded, "they're going faster than I expected and I need you now."

Washington, D.C., then was the center of the world. During Roosevelt's era, the city grabbed the imperial spotlight. There was so much activity, so much life. It seemed like important decisions were being made every day. The maelstrom swept me up. I felt challenged and excited.

Finding housing in Washington, however, was not an easy task. The city simply couldn't accommodate the huge influx of personnel. Desperately, I looked around for some place to live. I found a bedroom in the basement of a rundown house. The place was dismal. I stayed there for a couple of months before lucking out. I read an ad placed by an elderly couple. Their apartment was available for a year, while they vacationed in Florida. In the interview, they grilled me. I felt like I was up for a Cabinet position. Finally they decided the apartment would be safe in my hands. I sublet it. Relieved, I settled in.

My service in Washington was hectic, demanding, interesting, and quite important. I found myself thrust in with Generals, Admirals, Ambassadors. I worked in the U.S. Naval Transportation Department. In a temporary building. One of many.

In the beginning, I served as a liaison officer with the other departments of the government, mainly State, the Pentagon, and the War Shipping Administration. By then, I was full Lieutenant. I couldn't believe how much responsibility was thrust upon my shoulders. The experience was challenging indeed.

On May 7, 1945, Nazi Germany surrendered. May 8 became V-E Day and there was great rejoicing in the land. In July, President Truman sailed to Germany, where the leaders of the Allied nations were gathered at Potsdam. During the meeting, Truman's Secretary of War, Henry Stimson, received a coded message from General Leslie Groves in Washington. "Doctor has just returned most enthusiastic and confident that the little boy is as husky as his big brother," the message went. "The light in his eyes discernible from here to Highhold and I could have heard his screams from here to my farm."[4]

What did the decoding officer think at the Army Message Center? Did he believe that the Secretary of War, age seventy-eight in 1945, was a new father? Secretary Stimson explained the message to President Truman. "The little boy" signified the atomic bomb. Its healthful huskiness meant that the test in Alamogordo, New Mexico, had been successfully completed. The sound carried fifty miles. The flash of light could be seen for two hundred and fifty miles, the distance in fact from Washington to Highhold, Stimson's estate on Long Island.

At Potsdam, Truman told Churchill of the test. Then he went to the Soviet leader. "I casually mentioned to Stalin that we had a new weapon of unusual destructive force," Truman reported later. "All he said was that he was glad to hear it and hoped we would make 'good use of it against the Japanese.'"[5]

Truman did not identify the weapon itself. He didn't have to. Stalin had a spy in New Mexico, the German-born, British citizen and physicist Klaus Fuchs. Stalin already knew every detail.

On his way back to the United States, Truman gave the order to drop the bomb on Hiroshima. Still, the Japanese did not surrender. Four days later, from Washington, Truman ordered the bomb to be dropped on Nagasaki. The Japanese surrendered immediately.

Today, decades later, we debate the humanity of Truman's decision. We watch footage of those bombs exploding and we shudder at the effect. We imagine, perhaps, the incredible toll. In Hiroshima alone, the bomb killed eighty thousand persons, injured tens of thousands more, and wiped out 60 percent of the city. The death toll for both bombs combined has been estimated at between 110,000 to 200,000 Japanese civilians.

More than sixty years ago, we celebrated. When Japan surrendered on August 15 (though formally, the surrender didn't take place until September 2 on board the *USS Missouri*), America sighed a national breath of relief. The invasion of Japan, America realized, would have been the most difficult invasion ever attempted. Consider the perspective of a soldier. Paul Fussell, a 21-year-old Second

Lieutenant, had spent the year 1944 fighting his way through Europe. At the time of Hiroshima, he was among those soldiers scheduled for the invasion (known in military circles as Operation Olympic). Upon hearing the news of the bomb, Lieutenant Fussell reacted, "We learned to our astonishment that we would not be obliged in a few months to rush up the beaches near Tokyo assault-firing while being machine-gunned, mortared, and shelled, and for all the practiced phlegm of our tough facades we broke down and cried with relief and joy. We were going to live."[6]

My task, following the Japanese surrender, was to reroute hundreds of thousands of troops on their way to the Pacific theater back to the United States. Rerouting these men, including men like Lieutenant Paul Fussell, became the highlight of my Naval career. There was nothing less than a sense of exhilaration in the work. Those poor men, who had fought a brutal war in Europe, would have had to do the same in Japan. As we rerouted soldiers, we felt more than relief, more than satisfaction. We felt jubilation. We worked day and night, finding ports in America. We were over-joyed to serve. This was a definitive moment in America.

Just recently, Charles Sweeney (the pilot who dropped the bomb on Nagasaki) died. His obituary told the story of his return to Japan, alongside Paul Tibbets (the pilot who dropped the bomb on Hiroshima), many years later. Both men expressed great sorrow for the devastation and the lives lost. But when asked if they felt regret, both men said. "No, dropping the bombs ended the war."

The Japanese, Truman and his Administration knew, would have fought for their nation with a stubborn ferocity, as they had in the islands. In addition, the Japanese had broken the American code. The Japanese knew about Operation Olympic, scheduled for November 1945. They knew that the American military intended to land in southern Kyushu. The U.S. strategy called for the attacker to outnumber the defender by at least three to one. The American military, estimating that the Japanese would have three divisions on Kyushu, planned on attacking with nine divisions. In addition, the American military anticipated that the Japanese would possess 2,500 to 3,000 planes. American air strength, the military leadership estimated, would be four times greater.[7]

But in mid-July, American intelligence identified a huge military buildup on Kyushu. Japanese ground forces totaled ten divisions. Japanese aircraft amounted to 6,000 to 10,000 planes. According to an American intelligence officer, the Japanese defenses threatened to "grow to the point where we attack on a ratio of one (1) to one (1) which is not the recipe for victory."

Had Truman not made his fateful decision and if the United States had gone into Japan using manpower, how many soldiers would have died? The War Department estimated between five hundred thousand and a million American soldiers. How many civilians? How long would the invasion have taken? Would the American people have had the stomach for another year or more of war? In addition, there were shocking consequences for the populations under Japanese authority. According to estimates, between 250,000 to 400,000 Asian prisoners of war, most of them civilians, were dying each month the war persisted. Perhaps these considerations compelled Harry Truman to order the dropping of the bomb. Perhaps Harry Truman wanted to send a message to Joseph Stalin. Did Truman fear that Stalin would take advantage of a prolonged American war in Japan to further his territorial expansion in Europe? Or worse yet, did Truman fear that Stalin would join an American invasion of Japan, become entrenched, and then apply Soviet domination to Japan as he had to Eastern Europe? Truman made his decision. If he had regrets, they didn't show. Truman claimed that he went to bed every night with a clear conscience.

When we finished rerouting the troops, my job ended and I expected that I would go home. Then my Admiral, Admiral Callaghan, invited me to his house. That was unique; Admirals didn't invite Lieutenants to their homes. But this was an unusual Admiral with an unusual family history. Admiral Callaghan's brother, Rear Admiral Daniel Callaghan, commanded the flagship, the *San Francisco*, during the Naval portion of the battle at Guadalcanal. On November 13, 1942, Rear Admiral Callaghan was shot and killed on the bridge of his ship by the Japanese. Posthumously, he received the Congressional Medal of Honor for "his courageous initiative, inspiring leadership, and judicious foresight in a crisis of grave responsibility."

After dinner, before Admiral Callaghan began his pitch, he sat me down on a sofa, squeezed in between two other Admirals. I was almost blinded by all the gold on their uniforms. I had served the Navy well, his speech went, would I consider joining the Navy as a career? I was flattered. I was, I admit, amazed by the persuasion. I had no sea experience. I was a Jew among gentiles. Why did they want me?

At the end of the evening I thanked them but declined the offer. I wanted out. I felt it was time to go home. The Admiral was not deterred. A few days later he came to me and offered a spot promotion to Lieutenant Commander if I signed for another six months. "Admiral," I replied, "I will stay as long as you need me. Six months, a year, longer if need be. But I don't want to commit myself to a specific time."

The Admiral recommended me to the personnel department for the spot promotion. But because I wouldn't sign for six months, personnel turned down the upgrade. So I resigned my commission. I have since regretted that I didn't accept the spot promotion. If nothing else, it would have given me time to clear my head and consider my options. Perhaps, during those six months, I would have found a suitable position and a direction in my life. But in Washington I felt like I was in a vise. I felt like I couldn't move. I felt like the obstacles were too enormous to overcome.

One obstacle included my housing. The elderly couple from whom I rented were returning from Florida. I took that as sort of a sign; I didn't look for housing. I didn't move into a hotel, which would have been adequate short-term housing. I did not accept a personnel position within the State Department (I had applied for a diplomatic position due to my experience as a liaison officer). State was known as an anti-Semitic institution (the degree of which was not known then). The question dawned on me: How high could a Jew rise?

I moved back to New York. I moved into my parents' apartment. Then I floundered. For three months I went rousting at night and slept until noon. I felt empty and lost. I had never fought on the front lines, never fired a gun at an enemy, and yet I wasn't ready to return to civilian life. For three years I had shouldered tremendous responsibility and commanded hundreds of men. I was part of something much larger than daily concerns, part of something with a heroic goal. The letdown was tremendous. And once at home, questions went through my mind: What had the Navy prepared me for? What were my talents? Where did I belong? And most important, where could I find a position as stimulating and important as my Naval career?

I didn't find the answers. Did I give myself enough time? My father suggested that I return to Harvard Business School on the GI Bill of Rights. I couldn't, however, conceive of going back to the classroom, not after the intensity and urgency of my military experiences.

Three months passed. When my brother-in-law had a heart attack, my father asked me to help out, temporarily, in the family business. My temporary stint in Arthur Beir and Company (ABC) Fabrics turned into a fifteen-year career, regrettably. In retrospect, I think I took the easy way out. I must admit that bothers me to this day.

Chapter 4

◀ ▶

The Kind of Man Roosevelt Hired

My uncle, Arthur Beir, had a big personality: gregarious, accommodating, and kind. He was a natural salesman. In the early 1900s, he held a job as a salesman in a fabric house, which required many hours on the road, taking fabric orders and sending them back to the home office for shipping. That fabric house, however, was crooked and only half-fulfilled the orders. Furthermore, unordered goods would be added to the shipments. My uncle discovered his company's practices when he returned to the stores in subsequent visits; the merchandise managers complained to him. My uncle knew his reputation was at stake.

One day he confronted the head of the firm. "I need your guarantee that the orders will be shipped as I write them," he said. "I can't go back out there without it."

"I will run this business as I choose," the head of the company said. "If you don't like it, you can leave." In the middle of the afternoon my uncle phoned my father. My father held a position in the financial department of a firm. My uncle knew that my father was a natural manager and merchandiser, and he was sure they'd make a great team. Mr. Inside, Mr. Outside.

"Sidney," my Uncle Arthur said, "I'm going into business for myself. I have some money. I think we can borrow the rest. Will you join me? Yes or no?"

"I don't know," my father replied. "Can we talk about this later?"

"No, I need to know now. Yes or no?"

"Well," my father said, "what will you pay me?"

"Twenty-five dollars a week."

"I'm making that now," my father replied.

"Yes or no, Sidney?" my uncle said. The answer was yes. ABC Fabrics would be born and a synergistic partnership would be built with my uncle running the sales side and my father administering the financial and merchandising end. ABC Fabrics would become a highly successful enterprise.

My father had witnessed the business demise of his own father. My grandfather ran a dry goods business in the town of Lockport, New York. It failed, crushing my grandfather in the process. That failure left a deep impression upon my father. That failure became the impetus for his striving to succeed. He swore to himself that failure would never happen to him.

ABC Fabrics started with linings for coats and other products. The firm quickly expanded. ABC generated, among our many lines, one famed product: the ABC percale, a kind of cotton fabric (80 square). ABC sold percales in the millions. We became known as the Tiffany's of our field.

I grew up idolizing my father. He was a mastermind. He created a thriving business during the boom years of the twenties and as the times changed, he found ways to adapt. For instance, the Stock Market crash of 1929 transformed America overnight. My father, though, kept ABC prosperous. During the Depression, few people had the money to buy dresses from department stores. So many Americans returned to making their own clothes, buying fabric and stitching to patterns they chose from Butterick and McCall's and Simplicity Pattern catalogs. ABC sold the fabric. In this way, the firm weathered the storm.

When the Stock Market crashed, my father lost a great deal of money in the market on paper. Fortunately, though, he had never bought on margin and he never sold any of his distressed stocks (most of which eventually recovered, even if it did take many, many years). Friends of his were not so fortunate. They lost everything. Paper millionaires one day, living the high life, went broke the next. Some friends, desperate to provide for their families, committed suicide to collect the life insurance, which was legal in those days. My father extended financial assistance to several friends. I remember my father's best friend losing his entire fortune. Before the Depression, he'd had a thriving business, a beautiful apartment. He'd invested heavily on margin in the market. Suddenly he had nothing. My father kept him afloat financially. This was an admirable part of my father's personality. He was very loyal, very dependable. His peers admired him immensely. There was an aura about Sidney Beir. He was prescient. He was a visionary. He was remarkably similar to the leader of the era: Franklin Delano Roosevelt.

Both men were aloof, charming, indomitable. Both men were devious, controlling, powerful. Both men loved the potency of their positions. My father built ABC Fabrics into a thriving business. His office became his sanctuary. Roosevelt loved the Presidency so much that he held on to it even when he was gravely ill.

Both men healed quickly from tragedy. After the emotional shock of my brother's death, my father returned to his unemotional ways. If he suffered, he didn't talk about it. If his business suffered, only he knew it. In the late summer of 1921, Roosevelt became deathly ill. He ran a high temperature with severe pains in his legs and back. The first physician believed that Roosevelt had a bad cold. A second physician diagnosed Roosevelt's illness as a blood clot in the lower spinal cord. Within a day, Roosevelt couldn't walk. The paralysis took over his bladder. A third doctor diagnosed the polio, with infantile paralysis. Within a few weeks, Roosevelt's paralysis had spread to his arms and back. In a New York hospital, one month into his illness, Franklin Roosevelt didn't even have the ability to lift his head.

Externally, Roosevelt exhibited courage and cheer. Below the surface, he suffered from a deep clinical depression. He questioned whether God had abandoned him. He grew irritated over what he perceived as a lack of medical treatment. He employed "the psychological defense of denial" and "was highly unrealistic about his future physical condition."[1] For instance, for nearly a decade, Roosevelt thought he would walk again.

The depression didn't last. At the 1924 Democratic Convention, Roosevelt negotiated the fifteen feet to the podium on two crutches. The twenty thousand Democrats in Madison Square Garden fell silent, momentarily. When Roosevelt quoted Wordsworth and nominated Alfred E. Smith as "the 'Happy Warrior' of the political battlefield," the Convention exploded. The electricity echoing throughout the arena paved the way for FDR's move to the national stage.

Like Roosevelt, my father was secretive. Like my father, Roosevelt was elusive. Roosevelt used speech in place of his feet. He freed himself with words. When officials would visit the Oval Office, Roosevelt would smile and go into storytelling mode. A half hour would pass and at the end of the meeting the visitor would leave with his agenda barely discussed. "Whenever I visited Roosevelt on official business," Congressman Emanuel Celler wrote, "I found a man adroit, voluble, assured, and smiling. I was never quite sure he was interested in the purpose of my visit; we spent so little time on it. Mostly he talked. He talked with seeming frankness, and when I left, I found that he had committed himself to no point of view. At the end of each visit I realized that I had been hypnotized."[2]

Both Roosevelt and my father were imposing. I wonder if the Roosevelt children were overwhelmed by their father. I wonder if the Roosevelt house was a difficult place for growing up. In my youth, I felt intimidated by my father. I felt I could never measure up. He was too indomitable for me to be myself. I never wanted to risk his disapproval. For example, I remember an unnerving phone call I had to make while I was still in school. A college roommate and I went to a party while at home in New York City, my first stag party. The event was stylish—the men in tuxedos—and quite risqué, with strippers and plenty of alcohol. After the party, we went to a dance hall. We were, I admit, looking for action. We were twenty-one and horny. We tried to pick up two women, both employees of the hall. Later that night, I remember, we sat on a bench, chatting with the women, asking when they got off work. Suddenly, I looked up and saw blood rushing down my roommate's face and staining his tuxedo. And before I could react, a belt buckle hit me square in the face. The attack came from two Marines, who must have been dating these women. The owners of the hall hailed a taxi and ordered the driver to rush us over to Roosevelt Hospital. After receiving seven stitches in my scalp, and then enduring the setting of my broken nose without anesthesia, I had to deal with my real pain: phoning my father, asking him to pick us up. I don't know if I've ever felt so ashamed. Blood on my tux, two black eyes, a concussion, my head all stitched up, and I had to face the disapproval of my father. I was humiliated. Somehow I made the phone call and my father drove down to the hospital. I feared that I would get another lecture from him. Surprisingly, he didn't say a word. But my anxiety was immeasurable. (A side story: the next day, our respective mothers concocted a story that we had been in a taxi accident. Neither wanted to admit that her son was in a fight over dancè hall girls.)

My father loved me. Saying it, expressing it, demonstrating it, wasn't a part of his nature. My father was stern with me. He presented a hard façade. He was the youngest of ten children, in fact the seventh son of a seventh son, but he quickly became a caretaker for his immediate and extended family. He protected us. He provided financial security. He deserves an immense amount of credit: his keen investing saw us through the worst economic disaster in this country's history. At the same time, my father was insensitive to my feelings. Instead of support, he lectured me. Instead of encouragement, he put me down. He made me feel impotent. He crippled my self-esteem. Conversely, I craved for his approval. Growing up in his house was not easy.

My father was a man of great pride. On his deathbed, for instance, my father had a barber give him a shave and a haircut. He wanted to die with dignity. The next day, he did.

Roosevelt was imbued with the same kind of pride. He gave orders not to photograph the wheelchair. Most photographs show the President from the waist up. The nation never knew the extent of his vulnerabilities; it was such a well kept secret. The same can be said for the international community. "During the 1930s," John Gunther wrote, while living in Europe, "I repeatedly met men in important positions of state who had no idea that the President was disabled."

Roosevelt was never alone, except when he slept. He once told John Winant, the American Ambassador to London during the Second World War, that his "utter lack of privacy" was the "hardest single thing" he had to bear. Rarely did Roosevelt let his guard down and reveal the helplessness of his position. On one such occasion, he concluded a late meeting with Labor Secretary Frances Perkins (the first female Cabinet member in the history of the United States). He rang for his valet but no one answered. "Please find Prettyman [his valet]," Roosevelt confided to the Secretary of Labor. "I am helpless without him."[3]

There were differences between FDR and my father, of course. Roosevelt liked to laugh. He liked to chitchat. One of his favorite amusements was summoning J. Edgar Hoover to the Oval Office and getting the lowdown on Washington gossip. He wanted to know who in Congress was sleeping with whom. Hoover's information typically provoked a deep cackle from the President. This was his form of relaxation.

My father was not a gossip. His sense of humor had an edge. Sometimes clever. Sometimes cute. Sometimes hurtful and prickly. Usually sharp.

President Roosevelt was a terrible investor. There are stories of FDR plunking down five thousand dollars on a wide array of failing stocks. He was impulsive and reckless and he liked to speculate. My father maintained a very focused and profitable portfolio. He was cautious.

Roosevelt was the eternal optimist. My father was a realist. Roosevelt was a politician. My father was a businessman. Roosevelt was a storyteller. My father was didactic. Roosevelt smoked cigarettes. My father smoked cigars. Roosevelt mixed martinis. My father was a Scotch man.

My father was the kind of man Roosevelt hired. Roosevelt's Administration brimmed with smart, cerebral, highly functional, assimilated Jews. My father, a great administrator, would have made a superb chief of staff.

My father had no problem saying no. President Roosevelt could not say no to anyone. For instance, he let several politicians believe that each would be the vice presidential candidate in Roosevelt's final election. The list of possibilities included: Vice President Henry Wallace, the ardent New Dealer; House Speaker Sam Rayburn of Texas; Illinois Senator Scott Lucas; Senate Majority Leader Alben Barkley of Kentucky; and Senator Harry Truman of Missouri. In addition, the President supported Supreme Court Justice and Roosevelt favorite William Douglas and the seeming front-runner, James Byrnes. Roosevelt encouraged them all. "Roosevelt never pursued a more Byzantine course," historian James MacGregor Burns, then a member of the White House staff, later wrote in *Roosevelt: The Soldier of Freedom.*

The nomination, of course, went to the man who least wanted it: Harry Truman. In fact, Truman had a speech in his pocket nominating Byrnes. The story goes that during the Democratic Convention Truman and Bob Hannegan, the Democratic National Committee Chairman, met in a hotel room. Hannegan picked up the phone to hear Roosevelt's voice. "Whenever Roosevelt used the telephone," Truman later said, "he always talked in such a strong voice that it was necessary for the listener to hold the receiver away from his ear to avoid being deafened, so I found it possible to hear both ends of the conversation."[4]

What Truman overheard was Roosevelt's reaction when told of Truman's reservations. "Tell the Senator that if he wants to break up the Democratic Party by staying out, he can," the President roared. "But he knows as well as I what that might mean at this dangerous time in the world."[5]

"Jesus Christ!" Truman exclaimed. "But why the hell didn't he tell me in the first place?"

Good question. Roosevelt played one against the other to consolidate and maintain power. His tactics for the choice of Vice President "incited charges that he had been a treacherous, aged tyrant lopping off the heads of those who might dare challenge him."[6]

My father used similar tactics. He routinely pumped his salesmen and executives for information. Then he'd cross-check. Nobody took advantage of him. Nobody ever became too powerful, including me. In the early 1950s, my father went to the executives of ABC Fabrics and offered a choice: a pension fund or a 50 percent share of the profits after taxes. Of course, the executives chose the profit plan. Unfortunately my father never consulted me, although I was the vice president of the company at the time. When I learned about it from one of the executives, I was deeply hurt. And furious. I couldn't understand how my father, a gifted and keen businessman, could make such a compromising decision. I knew my father's plan would create an economic wedge issue. When the business was doing well, the executives would be financially rewarded. When the business went through a down period, the executives would complain. With my father's plan there was no way to keep in check the good during the good times and the bad during the bad times. My father's agreement with the executives effectively created a payment plan of extremes.

As happened, the next year the Korean War broke out. ABC enjoyed the largest profits in our history. Merchandise was so scarce that you could sell it at any price. Meanwhile, we had a huge inventory. We sold out our entire warehouse.

The executives, who prior to the plan were making a reasonable salary, plus incentives, made huge bonuses. The year following the Korean War was a difficult one. Profits fell significantly. The executives questioned the drop in bonuses. A rebellion nearly occurred. They were incredulous. They turned to me. What could I do? I was placed in an awkward position. As the vice president of the company and the would-be successor, I felt like the first mate on a mutinous ship, squeezed between an elusive captain and an enraged crew.

I realized then that the executives could not be appeased. At the same time, the unions were clamoring for better pay and fewer hours. A divide went up. We were becoming a very unhappy organization.

During the same period, the fabrics business underwent a sweeping transformation. Discount stores became large buyers of fabric. J.C. Penney and Sears, in particular, offered huge orders, three million dollars and up. But making such deals threatened our regular customers. And once you consented to sell to the discount stores, it wouldn't take them long to demand lower prices. ABC Fabrics would have been at their mercy. I felt like I had a rope around my neck. I knew I had to sell the business in order to preserve our assets.

When I suggested this to my father, he struck an unyielding chord. "We're only losing a little money," he replied. "You have a job, a salary, recognition." And then he blew his top, "What would you do if you didn't have the business? You'd become a bum." Eventually he relented, "You won't find a buyer. Who would want to buy this business?" In an almost challenging voice, he added, "But go ahead and try."

Incredibly, I found a buyer. Protracted negotiations ensued. They were complex and arduous. At the point when everything seemed to be going smoothly, the union made demands for a larger severance pay. That nearly devastated the negotiation process. "I'm not giving them anything!" I told my friend and attorney, Jimmy Mathias. I was angry and adamant. Jimmy Mathias presented a very simple and effective argument. "It's better to swallow your pride than be forced to liquidate the business," he said. I took his advice to heart.

When I approached my father with the done deal, he screamed at me for an hour. He couldn't believe that I'd given in to the union. He couldn't believe that I hadn't gone to him for advice. Then he broke down. His business defined him. ABC Fabrics was his identity. When we sold in 1960, he was eighty years old. He must have been asking himself a very difficult question: What now? I was asking myself the same question.

In retrospect, I felt bad for my father. At the same time, I was thrilled to free myself from a sinking ship. This was the first time I had defied my father and succeeded. In standing up to him, my hero, I wonder if I made it easier to question my other hero, Franklin Roosevelt, years later.

Chapter 5

◄►

"What Have
I Got to Lose?"

The 1960s for me began in such an uncertain way. Professionally, after selling ABC Fabrics, I formed an investment company with my father and my cousin. We used a familiar name: Arthur Beir and Company. When we sold the business, we sold the trademark but kept control of the name.

Personally, I was coming off a very difficult health crisis. Sometime in the late 1950s, I began to feel sharp pains in one of my testicles. I couldn't tolerate the slightest pressure there and although I didn't think anything was seriously wrong, I decided to consult the family doctor. The family doctor recommended a urologist. The urologist recommended testicular surgery. I sought a second opinion. That urologist concurred with the first. I sought a third opinion. What was I looking for? An alternative to surgery. Something to curb my fear.

The third urologist not only confirmed the first two diagnoses but suggested I might have testicular cancer. The thought had not even entered my mind. Cancer? That to me was an older person's disease. I wasn't quite forty years old. I was a healthy man, or so I thought. Suddenly, my life was in jeopardy.

I had the surgery. While recovering in a hospital bed, I asked the family doctor if I had cancer. He denied it. I so wanted to believe his words. I did not question their veracity. But shortly before I left the hospital, the family doctor suggested that I take radiation treatment. Naturally, my mind jumped to the first conclusion. "Then I have cancer," I said.

"I didn't say that," the doctor replied. "It's just a precaution."

Just a precaution? Since when is testicular surgery just a precaution? Since when is radiation treatment just a precaution? I was frustrated and scared. I couldn't get any answers. The word "cancer" was not mentioned during the 1950s. Not by the radiologist. Not by the urologist. Not by the family doctor. It took a heated argument with my wife for the word to be said. That's how society dealt with cancer back then: a secret, a whisper, an accidental slip of the tongue.

I began six weeks of radiation treatment. Six terrible weeks. I lost my appetite. I lost weight. I lost my energy. I was exhausted, enervated, depleted. In those dark ages of cancer treatment, radiation was so primitive. I was also anxious. To be honest, I feared impotency. Fortunately, that did not materialize.

Meanwhile, my marriage of nearly ten years was falling apart. The differences were irreconcilable. What do I remember about my first marriage? Shouting, hostility, antagonism, a long and ugly divorce proceeding, a deep hurt. On the very positive side, my son Chip was born in 1953.

All of these issues—cancer, the selling of the family business, my divorce—triggered a serious bout of depression. I felt weighed down, burdened, taxed. One day my sister Jeannette suggested that I try talking to a therapist. "I don't need therapy!" I scoffed. "Don't be ridiculous!" But as I wrestled with the overwhelming issues of my life, I realized that therapy might not be such a bad option. Therapy, in fact, would prove exceedingly useful.

I scoffed at my sister's suggestion for a specific reason. I didn't believe in it. Therapy then came with a stigma: if you needed help, you weren't a real man. I bought into that attitude. Fortunately, Jeannette's persuasion rescued me from my machismo.

My sister died at the age of sixty-one, after an excruciating period with her own cancer. Originally, she was diagnosed with breast cancer. She had surgery. A few years later, she came down with colon cancer. Again, she had surgery. Then the doctors found cancer in her lungs. Yet again, she endured surgery. Finally, the doctors found cancer in her brain. She did not have surgery. Witnessing her illness was the most dreadful experience imaginable. Jeannette suffered intense pain. I reacted in a brotherly fashion; I tried to reach out to her, to discuss our childhood, to discuss our relationship, to discuss cancer.

Jeanette's second husband formed a protective barrier around her. He became her gatekeeper. He never left her side. He rarely gave anyone a moment of privacy with her. At the same time, he never addressed her condition. His response always was, "She's getting better."

One day Ginny said to me, "Bobby, you're the lucky one, not I." What did she mean by that? Was she alluding to my relationship with our parents? Was she thinking that I had survived cancer? Did she know that she was going to die?

Jeannette succumbed to cancer in 1974 and in her death, I felt horribly empty. There was a great deal of unfinished business between us. Unfinished words. Unfinished thoughts. An unfinished history. We never had the chance to reminisce and reconnect. We never had the chance to say goodbye. It's strange to bury your siblings without any sort of closure.

A few months after the divorce, I started to date again. I certainly wasn't in a hurry to remarry. Commitment was the furthest thing from my mind. I simply wanted female companionship.

New York then (and this may be true today, from what I've heard) contained numerous single women. Some of them divorced. Some of them career-minded. Like other single men my age, I found myself in demand. Everyone wanted to fix me up. I don't know how many women I dated during this period. Many.

Several months later, a friend called me. "Are you involved?" he asked.

"What do you mean involved?" I responded.

"Are you seriously dating a woman?"

"Somewhat," I replied, sounding cautious and defensive, having gone on many blind dates that didn't turn out.

He told me that he knew a woman recently divorced. "If I were single," he said, "she would be the first woman I'd ask out."

Upon such a strong recommendation, I took her number. A few days later, I called. We chatted amicably. We set up a date.

Joan was living in New Rochelle at the time and I invited her to my apartment at the Hampshire House in New York City. I'll never forget the scene. The year was 1962. She walked in like the old Ajax ad, a whirling white tornado. She had been married some sixteen years. This was a new, and clearly stressful, experience for her. I suggested dinner at the Oak Room in the Plaza. Ironically, our courtship included very few dinners at fancy restaurants. This turned into a running joke. On dates with other women, I went to the opera, to the theatre, to plush restaurants. With Joan, there was just so much to talk about. There wasn't time for those other entertainments. Typically, our dates consisted of conversation and late-night trips to the Mayflower for pancakes.

At the Oak Room, our discussion veered to Fidel Castro. The subject of Castro, in fact, incited a heated but challenging dinner conversation. Joan thought that Castro was a liberator. She was not alone. There were many Americans at that time who supported the Castro Revolution. "Thank God Castro kicked out that crook and dictator Batista," she said. I knew right then that I was dealing with a true blue liberal.

No one can doubt that Fulgencio Batista was a crook. Havana under Batista was the most wide-open and lurid city in the world. Gambling was everywhere. So were "circuses," places to view sexual intercourse. The drug trade, I'm sure, was quite rampant.

Havana also was a fabrics haven. ABC Fabrics had routinely sold off seconds and closeouts. As a result, we maintained a representative there. A crook, it turned out. On my first visit to Havana to unload merchandise, I found that he was skimming off the profits. Apparently, he was taking a cue from Batista.

"Joan," I said, "do you know that Cuba just opted for a Communist?"

"He's not a Communist," Joan responded. "He's a Revolutionary."

"He most certainly is not," I replied. The conversation petered out from there.

After dinner, I walked Joan to her car. My mother believed in etiquette, which included seeing a woman to her front door. The front door in New Rochelle, though, was too far away. I put Joan in her car, closed the door, and cautioned her to drive safely. That was our first date. I didn't think there would be a second.

Three weeks later, I reversed course. Why did I dial her phone number? Joan was outspoken, intelligent, and beautiful, all of which appealed to me. Obviously, I was attracted. Joan did not expect to hear my voice on the line. She did not hang up, however. "You know," I said, "we may not have gotten off to the best start, but I'd like to try again. What do you think?"

"I'm game if you are," she replied. And so we tried again. In July of 2004, we celebrated our fortieth anniversary. I guess it worked out.

About a decade later, Joan made a suggestion that altered the direction of my life. We lay in bed one night. Joan was studying for her master's degree in social work at Columbia University. I was reading a biography of Franklin Delano Roosevelt. "Did you know that Franklin Roosevelt was the first president to fly in an airplane?" I quizzed her. She did not respond. "Did you know that Roosevelt was the first sitting President to attend his party's convention?" I said. Again, she did not respond. "Did you know President Roosevelt's greatest fear was fire?" I said. This time Joan did respond. "You know so much about Roosevelt," she said, "why don't you teach a course on him?"

I found her suggestion simply astonishing. "I'm a businessman," I replied. "I'm not a historian." I had spent my adult life up to this point in two businesses, fabrics and investments. Yes, my knowledge of Roosevelt was growing. However, I wouldn't have called myself a scholar.

My wife shrugged her shoulders and returned to her studies. I returned to my reading. I thought the idea would die. It didn't. For weeks, it swirled around in my mind, a force all its own. That led to a meeting with the Headmaster of the Calhoun School in Manhattan.

My connection to Calhoun began with Lisa, Joan's younger daughter. Through her years in the school, I realized its potential.

The school, however, was hurting. There were major financial questions. There were building issues. When I went on the Board in 1970, I knew none of the school's difficulties. Two years later, the Board voted out the existing President and elected me as his replacement, all without my advance knowledge. For the next four years, I served as the Board's President. And gradually the school began a transformation, from an all-girls school to a co-ed school, from a traditional, rigid curriculum to a progressive, open one. Calhoun developed a new philosophy; we wanted the students to learn how to learn and to foster independent thinking. And as the years passed, the school began to receive recognition. Enrollment increased. Our economics became sounder. Calhoun turned into a leader in the field of progressive education.

Shortly after Joan's suggestion in bed, I went to the Headmaster, Gene Ruth, with a proposal to teach a mini-course on Roosevelt. I had no idea what he would say. His response took me by surprise. "What have I got to lose?" he said.

Chapter 6

◄►

A Journey
with Roosevelt

The first few classes were difficult. I entered the classroom with a feeling of apprehension and insecurity and I found myself floundering. I felt inadequate in front of the students; I felt like I couldn't connect to them. I thought about quitting. I might have had I not received tremendous encouragement and support from Kathy McDonough, an extraordinary educator and person. The question strikes me now: Had I quit, where would I be today? Would I have gone down the same road? Would I have become a Roosevelt scholar, a Holocaust researcher? Would I have written this book? Life takes many surprising turns. Teaching became a source of great inspiration and motivation.

Teaching Roosevelt then had a sense of hero worship to it. The major writers on the man and his Presidency, from John Gunther to James MacGregor Burns to Arthur Schlesinger, Jr. put Roosevelt on a pedestal. I certainly agreed. Roosevelt's Presidency saved the capitalist system at a time when America could have turned to Communism. He turned fear into hope. He gave Americans someone to believe in. And when America entered the Second World War, he shone as the most brilliant Commander-in-Chief in this nation's history.

A student, however, raised a provocative question. "What about the *St. Louis*?" she asked in class. I nodded in a meaningful, contemplative way. Later, I raced home. In my library, I stared at titles. Names jumped out at me. A wall of Churchill. Eisenhower and the Normandy invasion. The concentration camps. In that particular section of my library, I found *The Voyage of the Damned*. In truth, I didn't know the story of the *St. Louis*. Or perhaps I'd forgotten. The *St. Louis*, in June of 1939, was headline news in the *New York Times*.

In the spring of 1939, the *SS St. Louis* set out from Hamburg, Germany for Cuba. Nine hundred and thirty-seven Jews were on board. They'd paid the fares, paid the Cubans for landing permits, even paid the Nazis an additional 230 *Reichsmarks* (ninety-two dollars) for the return trip, just in case some special circumstances surfaced and the ship had to re-cross the ocean.

The *St. Louis* took two weeks to cross the Atlantic. After anchoring in the Havana harbor, the passengers prepared for disembarkation. Tragically, only a few were allowed to go ashore. One can only imagine the dismay of those forced to remain on board. The Cuban President ordered the ship to move out of his nation's waters, or face the consequences from the Cuban Navy. The *St. Louis* sailed slowly up the coast of North America. Close to U.S. waters, the Passengers' Committee sent telegrams to the State Department and the Oval Office, pleading for assistance.

The pleas fell on deaf ears. The *St. Louis* re-crossed the Atlantic. Along the way, the American Jewish Joint Distribution Committee negotiated with four Western European countries. As a result, none of the passengers went back to Nazi Germany. That was a short reprieve. Three months later Nazi Germany invaded Poland. In the spring of 1940 the construction of Auschwitz began. Thirty percent of the *St. Louis*'s passengers perished in concentration camps.

Once I learned about the *St. Louis*, a sickening feeling rose from the pit of my stomach. For the first time I began to question our government's policies. I began to question Roosevelt. Why didn't the President act? Why didn't he grant temporary visas? Why didn't he sign an executive order? Why didn't he do everything in his power to land those passengers? Was he afraid to challenge and further alienate an anti-immigrant, isolationist, and anti-Semitic Congress? His overriding priority in 1939 was the arming of Great Britain and the Allies. Wasn't it possible that he could have accomplished both tasks?

In 1984, shortly after David S. Wyman's *The Abandonment of the Jews* hit the bookshelves, two members of the Roosevelt Institute paid me a visit. One was Schuyler Chapin, an impresario of New York's cultural scene and a dedicated Rooseveltian. The other was Franklin Delano Roosevelt, Jr., the fourth child of Franklin and Eleanor Roosevelt. They'd heard about my interest in Roosevelt and asked if I was interested in joining the Franklin and Eleanor Roosevelt Institute's Board of Directors.

Initially I thought: What a great idea! What better place for a Rooseveltian like myself than on the Board primarily responsible for his legacy. But a flicker of reservation crossed my mind. To Franklin and Schuyler, I mentioned *The Abandonment of the Jews.* "That couldn't be true," Franklin responded, "because my mother would never have let that happen."

"Let me think about it," I told the Roosevelt Board members.

A week later, I received a phone call from Ambassador William vanden Heuvel and an invitation for lunch. Then the President of the Roosevelt Board and its strongest advocate, Bill convinced me to join the Board before dessert.

Yet, a nagging presence remained: my hero, Franklin Roosevelt, had seemed indifferent to the Jews of the Holocaust. At first, I tried to submerge my feelings, to work tirelessly and incessantly for Roosevelt's legacy. But that nagging presence persisted. I was saddled with my own anti-Semitic experiences. I couldn't let either my history or the history of the Holocaust alone. I felt compelled to delve further.

In July of 1942, President Roosevelt sent a statement to a rally at Madison Square Garden, sponsored by American Jewish groups. "Citizens, regardless of religious allegiance, will share in the sorrow of our Jewish fellow-citizens over the savagery of the Nazis against their helpless victims," the statement read. These words marked Roosevelt's first public response to Hitler's crimes against the Jews. They would be followed by a policy: the best way to save the Jews of Europe was to win the war. In other words: retribution, not rescue. This policy would jump from the White House to the State Department to Congress to the media to the public at large, including Jewish organizations. This policy would essentially strand those Jews imprisoned in Hitler's Europe and, in future years, lead to the belief that Roosevelt and America abandoned the Jews. What follows in the ensuing chapters is a history, tracing the arc of this policy, and America's response, to the Holocaust. A personal warning: it is a disturbing story.

Chapter 7

◀▶

"The Best Jew
Is a Dead Jew"

In January of 1933, five weeks before Franklin Roosevelt's first inaugural, by chance on the President's birthday, the new Chancellor of Germany, Adolf Hitler, watched a torchlight parade of some twenty-five thousand Nazi soldiers pass by the Chancellery. The parade took hours. "Hitler looked strangely tense, like a coiled spring. His eyes welled with tears of excitement," Robert Payne wrote in *The Life and Death of Adolf Hitler*. "Once he whispered, 'No power on earth will ever get me out of here alive.'"

Shortly thereafter, Hitler consented to an interview with an American. James G. McDonald, acting as the League of Nations' High Commissioner for Refugees, broached the subject of Germany's Jews. Hitler declared that he was not making war on the Jews, but rather Communists and Socialists. McDonald, however, discovered a different opinion from Ernst Hanfstängl, the head of the Foreign Press Bureau in Berlin (and the very same man who was honored in 1934 at Harvard). Hanfstängl, a friend of McDonald's from their college days together at Harvard, related a conversation he'd had with Chancellor Hitler. Hanfstängl, who "spoke poetically" of the Nazis to McDonald, reported that Hitler "beat his fists and exclaimed, 'Now we shall show them that we are not afraid of international Jewry. The Jews must be crushed.'"[1] The plan then in the works had the Nazis assigning members of the SA (*Sturmabteilung*, otherwise known as Brownshirts or Storm

Troopers) to each Jew. That plan proved too costly in terms of man-hours. Dachau, the newly constructed concentration camp, proved much more efficient.

In his younger days Hanfstängl, a gregarious personality, had befriended men who would become world leaders. For instance, he'd made friends with Franklin Roosevelt. The two sometimes dined together around the year 1909 at the Harvard Club in New York City. Roosevelt then was a state senator.

In the summer of 1932, Hanfstängl had met with Winston Churchill, then a member of the British Parliament. Churchill was touring Germany in his research for his *Life of Marlborough*. In 1705, John Churchill, the first Duke of Marlborough, and ancestor of Winston Churchill, marched his army from the Netherlands to the Danube, winding through the Rhine Valley. Churchill, in 1932, followed the same path. "I naturally asked questions about the Hitler movement," he wrote in *The Gathering Storm*,[2] "and found it the prime topic in every German mind. I sensed a Hitler atmosphere." In Munich, Churchill met with Ernst Hanfstängl. "As he seemed to be a lively and talkative fellow," Churchill wrote, "speaking excellent English, I asked him to dine. He gave a most interesting account of Hitler's activities and outlook. He spoke as one under the spell. He had probably been told to get in touch with me. He was evidently most anxious to please." In the course of the conversation, Hanfstängl suggested a meeting between Churchill and Hitler. "Nothing would be easier to arrange," Hanfstängl declared.

"I had no national prejudices against Hitler at this time," Churchill wrote. "I knew little of his doctrine or record and nothing of his character. I admire men who stand up for their country in defeat, even though I am on the other side. He had a perfect right to be a patriotic German if he chose." However, during the discussion, the subject of the Jews arose. "Why is your chief so violent about the Jews?" Churchill asked.

Hanfstängl, Churchill wrote, "must have repeated this to Hitler, because about noon the next day he came round with a serious air and said that the appointment he had made with me to meet Hitler could not take place."

"Hitler produced a thousand excuses," Hanfstängl recalled, "as he always did when he was afraid of meeting someone." And so a meeting between Churchill and Hitler never took place.

Unlike Churchill, Franklin Roosevelt did know something of Hitler's character. In 1933, he read the English translation of *Mein Kampf* and noted that the English version had been severely watered down, suppressing Hitler's fiercest anti-Semitic viewpoints. President Roosevelt commented, "This translation is so expurgated as to give a wholly false view of what Hitler is and says—the German original would make a different story."[3]

Former Senator Alan Cranston, a reporter for the International News Service in the 1930s, translated and published an unabridged version of *Mein Kampf*. His edition sold over 500,000 copies before the American publisher sued him for copyright violation.[4]

As for sales of *Mein Kampf*, the book sold 9,473 copies in 1925, according to royalty statements seized by the Allies in 1945. The following years saw a downward turn. In the early 1930s, however, as the Nazi Party began to expand in both members and power, sales jumped. The book sold 54,086 copies in 1930. In 1932, sales soared to 90,351 copies. In 1933, *Mein Kampf* sold one million copies. Only the Bible sold more copies during the Nazi era. By 1940, six million copies of *Mein Kampf* had been sold in Germany alone.[5]

If there was anyone on the world stage who foresaw the danger of Adolf Hitler, it was Franklin Roosevelt. From the earliest date, Roosevelt realized the acute danger of Nazi Germany. "The situation is alarming," Roosevelt remarked, referring to the treatment of Jews in Germany. "Hitler is a madman and his counselors, some of whom I personally know, are even madder than he is."[6] So it was no surprise, in the spring of 1933, when McDonald returned from Nazi Germany and went to the White House that Roosevelt "seemed deeply concerned [about the treatment of Jews] and said he wanted to find a way to send a warning message to the German people over the head of Hitler."

Roosevelt, however, had his hands full with his domestic agenda and his legislative plan known as the New Deal. The subject of German Jewry barely made his radar screen. Roosevelt held eighty-two press conferences throughout 1933. The persecution of the Jews surfaced once. A reporter asked, "Have any organizations asked you to act in any way in connection with the reported persecution of the Jews over in Germany by the Hitler government?" Roosevelt responded, "I think a good many of these have come in. They were all sent over to the State Department." This would become Roosevelt's standard response. The State Department would become the institution mainly responsible for immigration and, once the war began, rescue of the Jews. Paradoxically, the State Department's reputation included deep-seated anti-Semitism.

Meanwhile, Hitler began to consolidate his position by ridding the country of his enemies. As would become part of his routine, Hitler caused a conflagration and used the event to go on a violent spree. On the evening of February 27, 1933, Hitler dined with Propaganda Minister Joseph Goebbels and his family. "Suddenly," Goebbels wrote in his diary, "a telephone call from Dr. Hanfstängl: 'The Reichstag is on fire!' I am sure he is telling a tall tale and decline even to mention it to the Führer."[7]

Hanfstängl's "tall tale" proved accurate. Flames from the Reichstag filled the sky. The Nazis immediately proclaimed the fire a Communist crime. And indeed, on the surface, a Dutch Communist named Marinus van der Lubbe claimed responsibility. According to his confession, he entered the building and started a series of fires in the great hall. Van der Lubbe, however, only had his shirt for kindling. Considerable quantities of chemicals and gasoline were needed to ignite such a blaze, according to expert testimony (given at the Reichstag fire trial before the Supreme Court in Leipzig in the fall of 1933). Without the necessary incendiaries, how was Van der Lubbe able to produce the blaze? Van der Lubbe simply was a dupe.

An underground passage, a heating system, connected the Reichstag to Herman Goering's palace. Karl Ernst, the leader of the S.A. in Berlin, along with a few of his colleagues, maneuvered through the passageway. In the Reichstag, they started the fire. Afterward, they returned the way they came.

The Nazis used the Reichstag fire in a variety of ways. A

"Communist Conspiracy" was alleged. "The burning of the Reichstag was to be the signal for a bloody insurrection and civil war," the Nazified Prussian government stated. "It has been ascertained that today was to have seen throughout Germany terrorist acts against individual persons, against private property, and against the life and limb of the peaceful population. . . ." This statement provoked a landslide of fear among the general populace. Germany, according to Nazi rhetoric, was on the verge of a Bolshevik Revolution.

That threat influenced President Hindenburg. With his support, Hitler instituted the Decree of the Reich President for the Protection of the People and the State, suspending those sections of the Constitution that guaranteed individual and civil liberties. The Nazis described the decree as a "defensive measure against Communist acts of violence endangering the state."

At the same time, the Nazi terror began. Throughout Germany, Storm Troopers arrested "enemies" in mass. Beatings and torture became commonplace. The Communist press was suppressed. Social Democratic newspapers were suspended. The meetings of the democratic parties were either banned or broken up. Over four thousand Communist leaders were arrested, as well as many leftist leaders, including members of the Reichstag (who, according to the law, were immune from arrest).

One month after the Reichstag fire, Hitler introduced the Enabling Act, or in Nazi parlance, the "Law for Removing the Distress of People and Reich." The law, if sanctioned by a two-thirds majority in the Reichstag, would remove from Parliament the powers of legislation, including the control of the budget, the ability to make treaties with foreign states, and the amending of the Constitution. Those powers would be transferred to the Reich Cabinet for a period of four years. In addition, the powers of the President would remain "undisturbed." "The government," Hitler promised, "will take use of these powers only insofar as they are essential for carrying out vitally necessary measures."[8]

When the vote came before the Reichstag, the Center Party, representing the political movement of the Roman Catholic Church, voted for the bill. Ironically, the Center Party chose this position despite the Nazis' opposition and violence toward

Catholics. In all, 441 members of the Reichstag voted for the bill and 84 (all members of the Social Democrats) voted against it. The Enabling Act, in essence, ended the days of parliamentary rule.

Hitler's wooing of the Center Party and its parent organization, the Vatican, went far beyond the Enabling Act. In July 1933, Franz von Papen, the Vice-Chancellor of Germany, and Eugenio Pacelli, the Vatican Secretary of State (and future Pope Pius XII), signed the Reich Concordat. Not only did the agreement dissolve the Center Party; not only did the agreement reverse the German Bishops' denunciation of National Socialism; not only did the agreement block the Bishops and their followers from protesting the Nazi movement, but the Concordat gave Hitler power over twenty-three million German Catholics. Hitler, according to Cabinet minutes, "expressed the opinion that one should only consider it a great achievement. The Concordat gave Germany an opportunity and created an area of trust that was particularly significant in the developing struggle against international Jewry." Or in the words of papal scholar John Cornwell, "the perception of papal endorsement of Nazism, in Germany and abroad, helped seal the fate of Europe."[9]

Simultaneously, the Nazis began to issue anti-Jewish laws. In the spring of 1933, Jews were forbidden from holding public office, civil service positions, and most of the professions including journalism, education, farming, and the arts. On April 1, Hitler proclaimed a national boycott of Jewish shops. Meanwhile, Propaganda Minister Goebbels began the cultural divide, purging Jewish organizations and others assumed to be politically or artistically suspect. The German Student Association, with the blessing of Goebbels, proclaimed a nationwide "Action against the Un-German Spirit" to climax in a literary purge, otherwise known as a book-burning.

The Student Association, in an evocation of Martin Luther, published twelve theses. These declarations had a threefold effect: attacking Jewish intellectualism; announcing a pure German language and literature; and demanding that the universities develop German nationalism.

On May 10, 1933, students in various chapters of the Association burned twenty-five thousand volumes of "Un-German" books. Works by Franz Kafka, Lion Feuchtwanger, Heinrich Mann, and many others went up in flames. As did the books of another famous figure, Sigmund Freud. "What progress we are making," Freud responded sardonically from his home in Vienna. "In the Middle Ages they would have burned me. Now they are content with burning my books." Five years later, the Gestapo would make Freud nearly eat his words.

What did we know in America? Were we aware of the early brutality imposed by the Hitler regime? Did we read about the Reichstag fire and realize that this might endanger our German brethren? Were we in an uproar over the boycott of Jewish shops or the book-burning bonfires?

In America there was a sense of puzzlement. The mainstream press portrayed events in Germany in a confused manner. On the one hand, the *Chicago Tribune* reported that the entire Jewish population in Germany was living "under the shadow of a campaign of murder which may be initiated within a few hours and cannot at the moment be postponed more than a few days." On the other hand, both the *Chicago Tribune* and the *New York Times* called the Nazis' plans for massacre of the Jews "wild rumors." Skepticism pervaded. For instance, the columnist Dorothy Thompson traveled to Germany and wrote to her husband, writer Sinclair Lewis, that the Jewish situation was "really as bad as the most sensational papers report. . . . It's an outbreak of sadistic and pathological hatred."[10] Thompson, the first American correspondent expelled from Nazi Germany, developed a huge following. *Time* Magazine called her the second most popular woman in America, behind the First Lady. At the same time, another popular columnist, Walter Lippman, advised his readership not to judge Germany on the basis of Nazi radicals. He argued that people possessed a "dual nature." He wrote, "To deny that Germany can speak as a civilized power because uncivilized things are being said and done in Germany is in itself a deep form of intolerance."

My memories of Walter Lippman are very strong. I read his column regularly. Actually, I *reread* his column regularly. Lippman was very difficult to understand. He was arrogant. He was pedantic. He was the Henry Kissinger of his era. His column took an effort to digest. He also worked for a conservative newspaper, the *Herald Tribune*, although he was a true blue liberal.

Walter Lippman joined segments of the mainstream press and accused the Jews of acting as provocateurs. In rationalizing the violence in Germany, he wrote, "Who that has studied history and cares for the truth would judge the French people by what went on during their terror? Or the British people by what happened in Ireland? Or the Catholic church by the Catholic church of the Spanish Inquisition? Or Protestantism by the Ku Klux Klan or the Jews by their parvenus?" Here was a Jewish American, and the most influential columnist of his era, not only excusing Nazi brutality but introducing an undercurrent of anti-Semitism. Although Lippman never identified himself as a Jew (as many leading Jews did not), his philosophical self-hatred made it easier for other publications to take an anti-Semitic viewpoint. The *Christian Science Monitor* wrote that Jewish "commercial clannishness . . . gets them into trouble." The *Monitor* recommended that Jews "within Germany and without might give some attention to the problem." *The Christian Century*, the most prominent Protestant journal in America, wrote, "May we ask if Hitler's attitude may be somewhat governed by the fact that too many Jews, at least in Germany, are radical, too many are communists? May that have any bearing on the situation? There must be some reason other than race or creed—just what is that reason?" In America, a poll published in April 1938 found that 60 percent agreed that the persecution of European Jews was either entirely or partly the fault of Jews.

The fault of Jews; this is the sentiment echoing throughout the ages. Jews killed Christ. Jews murdered children and used their blood to bake Passover matzah. According to *The Protocols of the Elders of Zion*, international Jewry will bring down the state. Or as Hitler told Hanfstängl, "The Jews must be crushed." This is the message so pervasive and destructive.

In Germany, the Nazis' consolidation of power continued. According to Nazi propaganda, Adolf Hitler placed a loaded gun on the table. Across the way, Ernst Röhm, the chief of the S.A., refused to take his own life. Hitler pushed the gun closer to Röhm's hand. Again, Röhm declined. Shortly before bullets from members of Hitler's bodyguard filled Röhm's big body, he cried out in loyalty, "*Mein Führer, mein Führer.*"

The date was June 30, 1934. At that point in time, there were two and a half million Storm Troopers. Enrollment in the regular army, limited by the Treaty of Versailles, reached one hundred thousand men. This discrepancy in manpower had given Röhm an authority surpassed only by Hitler. Consequently the perception arose within the House of Hitler that Röhm was a dangerous threat.

According to Nazi propaganda, Hitler and a few associates stormed a Munich hotel where Röhm and the S.A. were meeting. The hotel was strenuously fortified with guards loyal to Röhm. Armed only with a bullwhip, Hitler rushed upstairs and found Röhm in bed with a young boy. (Within Nazi circles, Röhm was infamous for his flamboyant homosexuality.) Hitler arrested the S.A. chief on the spot. Hitler, according to the propaganda, wanted to "deprive" Röhm of his position. However, he sensed a mutiny. "In these circumstances I could make but one decision," he later reported to the Reichstag. "Only a ruthless and bloody intervention might still perhaps stifle the spread of the revolt."[11]

Two weeks passed before Hitler announced the putsch. He called "The Night of the Long Knives" an accomplishment of self-interest. "I alone was able to solve this problem. No one else!" he told his chief architect, Albert Speer.[12] "The Night of the Long Knives" took place in the daytime.

According to Nazi propaganda, German forces executed sixty-one of Röhm's men during the purge. According to more accurate sources, the Nazis executed at least a thousand people, including the two highest ranking officials in the German Army, General (and former Weimar Chancellor) Kurt von Schleicher and General Kurt von Bredow. Hitler explained his actions to the nation: "In this hour I was responsible for the fate of the German people, and thereby I became the supreme judge of the German people. . . . Everyone must know for all future time that if he raises his hand to strike the State, then certain death is his lot."

From President von Hindenburg, the beloved patriarch of the country, Hitler received a telegram, thanking the Chancellor for his "gallant personal intervention . . . that stopped treason in the bud . . . and rescued the German people from a great danger."[13]

That "great danger" laid the foundation for Nazi terror. The stretch from budding dictatorship to genocide began here, with the eradication of Hitler's supposed allies. It began here, by shocking the German people into obedience. It began here, with the terror becoming law.

A year later, a new set of laws defined German citizenship. The Nuremberg Laws included three key provisions:

1. The Law for the Protection of German Blood and German Honor prohibited marriages between Jews and Germans and also forbade German females under forty-five years of age from working in Jewish households.
2. The Reich Citizenship Law stripped Jews of German citizenship.
3. An addendum gave the Führer and Chancellor of the Reich (as Hitler called himself in the immediate aftermath of President von Hindenburg's death) the power to release anyone from the provisions of the administrative decree.

In the United States, condemnation was swift. Many news publications called the Nuremberg Laws a throwback to more intolerant times. *Newsweek* Magazine, for instance, remarked that the Nuremberg Laws "relegated Jews to the Dark Ages."[14]

On a political level, Governor Herbert Lehman of New York, a prominent Jewish leader and Roosevelt ally, cabled the President. Lehman proposed doubling the number of German Jews admitted to the United States from twenty-five thousand a year to fifty thousand. Roosevelt responded sympathetically; he advised Consular officials to offer "the most considerate attention and the most generous and favorable treatment possible under the laws of the country."[15]

Roosevelt's pronouncement did little to facilitate immigration. According to the quota, in the years before 1938, 25,957 immigrants from Germany could legally enter America. In 1935, 5,532 German immigrants were accepted. In 1936, the number improved to 6,642 German immigrants. In 1937, the number improved to 11,536 German immigrants. That number, of course, didn't fulfill half the legal limit.

The reasons for these low numbers varied. These were the days of severe American anti-immigration. In Congress, the lawmakers were extremely restrictionist-minded. They included Senator Robert Reynolds of North Carolina, Representative William Elmer of Missouri, Representative Leonard Allen of Louisiana, and Representative Edward Rees of Kansas. Together, they formed a potent voting block. But more significantly, they represented the will of the American populace. A poll taken in 1938, for instance, revealed that 67 percent of Americans wanted refugees kept out of the country altogether.[16]

These were the days of great American isolationism. The memories of the First World War turned America inward, seemingly safe within our borders. The "war to end all wars" deeply impacted the American psyche. There was no stomach for sending soldiers abroad. There was no stomach for another savage battlefield. There was no stomach for more atrocity stories. In 1915, the French press produced a photograph of a baby whose hands, according to the story, had been cut off by German soldiers as the child clung to his mother's skirt. The American press gave great coverage to the "Belgian Baby Without Hands." After the war, investigators failed to find any such children. Clearly, the "Belgian Baby Without Hands" was war propaganda. But that story, among other factors, caused the isolation of America. The mood across the nation was clear: Let Europe fight its own wars.

That overriding sentiment compelled the Congress to pass, and the President to sign, the first Neutrality Act, proclaiming a mandatory arms embargo and making it illegal for the United States to "export arms, ammunition, or implements of war to any port of belligerent states."

These were the days of Father Charles Coughlin, the magnetic man in the clerical collar, who attracted an estimated forty million people to his radio sermons. He became "one of the nation's most notorious extremists: an outspoken anti-Semite, a rabid anti-communist, a strident isolationist, and, increasingly, a cautious admirer of Benito Mussolini and Adolf Hitler."[17]

These were the days when Charles Lindbergh and his wife, Anne Morrow, responded with awe to Hitler. Anne Morrow called her trip to Berlin in 1936, in which the Lindberghs attended the opening ceremonies of the Olympics as guests of the Reich, "ten perfectly thrilling days." "Hitler," she wrote, "I am beginning to feel is a very great man, like an inspired religious leader—and as such rather fanatical—but not scheming, not selfish, not greedy for power, but a mystic, a visionary. . . ."[18] During the same trip, Charles Lindbergh lunched ceremoniously with Reichsmarshal Herman Goering, one of the architects of "The Night of the Long Knives." He stood for photographs with Goering. At the same time, Lindbergh inspected the Luftwaffe, Germany's new force in the sky. He toured the factories. He piloted some of the aircraft. "There is certainly a great ability [in Nazi Germany]," he declared, "and I am inclined to think more intelligent leadership than is generally recognized. A person would have to be blind not to recognize that they have already built up tremendous strength."[19] In his reports to the governments of the Western democracies, Lindbergh wrote that the Germans had considerable air superiority and were capable of wiping out the great cities of Europe. His reports, in fact, would play a significant part in inducing Neville Chamberlain of Great Britain and Edouard Daladier of France to capitulate at Munich.

Lindbergh influenced another isolationist: Joseph Kennedy, Ambassador to Great Britain. Kennedy was convinced that a war with Germany would destroy American capitalism. He continually sought a personal meeting with Hitler, without State Department approval, hoping to facilitate a peace between the United States and Germany. Kennedy was also a notorious anti-Semite. "Individual Jews are all right, Harvey," Kennedy told one of his trusted aides, Harvey Klemmer, "but as a race they stink. They spoil everything they touch." Years later, Klemmer reported that Kennedy generally referred to Jews as "kikes or sheenies."[20]

These were the days of American Jews acting behind the scenes. My aunt brought over a whole family living in Nazi Germany. My father brought over a cousin, Franz, who arrived with a sense of entitlement. He continually pointed to the "Fatherland" and its greatness. Of course, he was referring to an earlier time. A time of Jewish integration. A time of serving the nation, when one hundred thousand German Jews volunteered to fight for their homeland during the First World War. A time of the Weimar Republic and a more open society. Clearly, Franz wasn't referring to Hitler's Reich. But this way of thinking helped to explain why many German Jews remained in Germany during the 1930s. They loved their country. They believed the era of Hitler would pass. They believed in perseverance.

Here in America, there were many Jewish families who tried to bring over friends and relatives. Arthur Sulzberger, the owner and publisher of the *New York Times*, was one such example. Beginning in the mid-1930s, Sulzberger and his wife Iphigene began to receive a steady stream of requests from German Jews asking for an affidavit guaranteeing financial support (a mandatory part of the immigration application). The stream of requests turned into a flood. "Arthur and I couldn't see our way clear to vouching for complete strangers," Iphigene Sulzberger wrote in her memoirs. "We rationalized our reluctance by saying that the situation wasn't as bad as people said, and we put the letters aside. Ever since then, I have wished we had taken the chance. I wish I had signed for them all—I wish to God I had."[21] Working behind the scenes, as Sulzberger spurned attracting attention as a Jew, the Sulzbergers signed many affidavits. When those relatives reached America, the Sulzbergers were generous with financial support. But I am haunted by a question, the same question that apparently affected Iphigene Sulzberger. During the 1930s, when support could have been given, did American Jews do enough for the Jews suffering in Germany? Were these outreaches—bringing over a relative, for instance—sufficient? And did our assimilation, our relative comfort, get in the way of a more effective response?

A corollary question arises: What would my response have been?

Had I been an adult, a man with the means and heart to help, would I have found a successful approach to aid my German brethren? Or would my attentions have been local, trying to make a living during the Great Depression, making sure to support my family, reading about the horrible events in Germany but seeing them at a distance, somewhat separate from my life here in America?

I am haunted by these questions. I am haunted by the history. I am haunted by Storm Troopers shouting, "The best Jew is a dead Jew." In Berlin in the summer of 1935 two hundred Brownshirts raided theaters and restaurants on the *Kurfürstendamm*, the center of the city's cosmopolitan culture. Anyone with a Jewish appearance was subject to attack. An American journalist witnessed this first pogrom in Nazi Germany. His name was Varian Fry and during that summer, he traveled throughout Germany, writing for the journal *The Living Age*. On the *Kurfürstendamm*, Fry "saw with my own eyes young Nazi toughs gather and smash up Jewish-owned cafés." Fry "watched with horror as they dragged Jewish patrons from their seats, drove hysterical, crying women down the street, knocked over an elderly man and kicked him in the face."[22]

This scene never left the psyche of Varian Fry. In the summer of 1940, he would travel to France and, through extraordinary measures, rescue thousands of Jews in dire circumstance. He knew the specifics of Hitler's form of terror. He'd personally heard the Brownshirts shouting that horrible slogan, "The best Jew is a dead Jew."

I am also haunted by another history. There was an American named Thomas Watson. He was a capitalist, driven by new markets and larger profits. Watson was a "conqueror." And "like any conqueror, he would vanquish all in his way, and then demand the spoils."[23]

In 1914, at the age of forty, Thomas Watson joined a company called CTR (Computing-Tabulating-Recording Company). He became head of the organization a year later. In 1922, he renamed the company. International Business Machines, or IBM, came into existence. The IBM credo suggested the character of its leader: "IBM is more than a business—it is a great worldwide institution that is going on forever."

In 1932, Watson supported Roosevelt for President. He became one of the campaign's leading donors. That gave him access to Roosevelt after the election. In fact, Roosevelt and Watson developed a friendship, corresponding regularly. Roosevelt, according to historian Edwin Black in *IBM and the Holocaust*, "came to rely on Watson for advice. White House staffers would occasionally ask for Watson's schedule in case the President needed to contact him quickly. Watson visited Hyde Park for tea several times and even stayed overnight at the White House. Eventually, Roosevelt offered to appoint Watson Secretary of Commerce or Ambassador to England. But Watson declined to leave IBM."

In 1933, Hitler became Chancellor and began to consolidate power. Simultaneously his government became "statistics-friendly," wrote the chairman of the German Statistical Society. In fact, Hitler's government became statistics-obsessed. "Very important problems are being tackled currently, problems of an ideological nature," wrote another member of the German Statistical Society. "One of those problems is race politics, and this problem must be viewed in a statistical light."

The Nazi government needed to know who was Jewish and where that person lived. From a logistics perspective, the Holocaust began here, with statistics. In fact, the Holocaust began with a machine.

In the days before computers, the Hollerith machine relied on punch card technology. Any trait could be identified on a card: gender, occupation, religion, etc. The card could then be fed into a reader. The information could be quickly processed. The Hollerith machine "could render the portrait of an entire population—or could pick out any group within that population."

The Hollerith machine was invented by Herman Hollerith around 1884. Hollerith used the technology to form a company, which would later become IBM. Hollerith's company began as a census tabulating company. Its first overseas census involved Russia and Czar Nicholas II.

The IBM Hollerith machines were not sold to the Nazis; they were leased. That meant regular maintenance and upgrades. That meant training. That also meant custom design. "IBM machines were useless in crates," Edwin Black wrote. "Tabulators and punch cards were not delivered ready to use like typewriters, adding machines, or even machine guns. Each Hollerith system had to be custom-designed by Dehomag [IBM's German subsidiary] engineers. Systems to inventory spare aircraft parts for the Luftwaffe, track railroad schedules for Reichsbahn, and register Jews within the population for the Reich Statistical Office were designed by Dehomag engineers to be completely different from each other."

The IBM punch cards had to be custom designed, too. For instance, consider the cards for prisoners. There were "columns and punched holes detailing nationality, date of birth, marital status, number of children, reason for incarceration, physical characteristics, and work skills. Sixteen coded categories of prisoners were listed . . . : hole 3 signified homosexual, hole 9 for anti-social, hole 12 for Gypsy. Hole 8 designated a Jew.

"Column 34 was labeled 'Reason for Departure.' Code 2 simply meant transferred to another camp for continuing labor. Natural death was coded 3. Execution was coded 4. Suicide coded 5. The ominous code 6 designated 'special handling,' the term commonly understood as extermination, either in a gas chamber, by hanging, or by gunshot."

As for the systematic killing of Jews, IBM maintained a policy: Don't ask, don't tell. Apparently Thomas Watson, as the leader of IBM and its ethical center, faced no moral dilemma. In turn, he aided the German economy as it prepared for war. He disregarded the international boycott of German goods and services. From New York, he ignored Germany's anti-Semitic brutality throughout the 1930s and he looked away during the genocide of the 1940s. Thomas Watson viewed Adolf Hitler as a vital trading partner, second only to U.S. markets. Nazi Germany "offered Watson the opportunity to cater to government control, supervision, surveillance, and regimentation on a plane never before known in human history. The fact that Hitler planned to extend his Reich to other nations only magnified the prospective profits. In business terms, that was account growth. The technology was almost exclusively IBM's to purvey because the firm controlled about 90 percent of the world market in punch cards and sorters."

IBM leased more than 2,000 machines to the Nazis for use in Germany and thousands more to the Nazis and their accomplices throughout occupied Europe. In addition, IBM sold perhaps 1.5 billion punch cards to the Nazis annually. How did the Nazis pay for this expensive technology? One way was through Jewish bullion, literally by extracting the gold from the mouths of Jews.

For Thomas Watson, Nazi Germany also offered other riches. In the summer of 1937, Watson traveled to Berlin and met separately with, among others, Joseph Goebbels, Herman Goering, and Adolf Hitler. The specifics of Watson's conversation with Hitler remain unknown, but Watson condensed the exchange for the *New York Times*. "There will be no war," Watson reported. "No country wants war, no country can afford it."

One evening, in the Wannsee section of the city, at Friedrich Wilhelm III's eighteenth-century castle, the Nazis threw the most elaborate party reported during the entire Nazi era. Three thousand guests attended at a cost of four million *Reichsmarks*. Watson and the other guests were greeted by "hundreds of charming Berlin schoolgirls daintily outfitted in white blouses over white silk breeches and white leather slippers. Each girl waved a white fairy's wand and angelically bowed." The guests then drank at "a bar of seemingly endless length, manned by eighty bartenders pouring and mixing any cocktail. . . ." A dinner "remembered as gigantic" followed. "Thousands of chefs, waiters, and their kitchen helpers whisked dome after dome of gourmet specialties back and forth across the lawns. . . . Enchanting Prussian porcelain figurines were bestowed upon the wives. Ballerinas and singers from a nearby artist's colony performed an enchanted display of dance and song beneath a prodigious rotunda, which later became an immense dance floor."

The party was all in celebration of Thomas Watson. Hjalmar Schacht, then the president of the Reichsbank, presented Watson with a medal of honor specifically created for the IBM leader. The Merit Cross of the German Eagle with Star recognized "foreign nationals who made themselves deserving of the German Reich." The medal ranked second in prestige, behind Hitler's German Grand Cross.

In addition to Watson, there were other famous Americans who received medals of honor from Nazi Germany. James Mooney, General Motors' chief executive for overseas operations, received the Order of the German Eagle with Star, June 9, 1938. Henry Ford received the Grand Cross on his seventy-fifth birthday, July 30, 1938. Charles Lindbergh received the Order of the German Eagle with Star, October 19, 1938.

How much profit did IBM generate during the years of Nazi Reich alliance? There are no definitive totals. At the end of the war, however, IBM's German subsidiary was valued at more than 56 million *Reichsmarks* ($230 million today) with a gross profit of 7.5 million *Reichsmarks* ($30 million). This at a time when the rest of Germany was essentially bankrupt.

These numbers are chilling. Here are some more. Thomas Watson became the highest paid executive in America. He received a 5 percent bonus on all IBM profits worldwide and he was dubbed "the thousand-dollar-per-day man." In 1935, Watson's salary totaled $364,432, a veritable fortune for those days. He made nearly as much as the salaries of the Chairmen of Chrysler and General Motors combined. And yet he never had to answer for his alliance with Nazi Germany. He walked away a multimillionaire.

Chapter 8

◄ ►

The Avery Brundage Effect

In 1931, two years before Hitler became Chancellor, the International Olympic Committee awarded the 1936 Summer Games to Berlin. About a year before the games began, Hitler's Germany came under the microscope and a debate raged: Should an international event of the magnitude of the Olympics be staged in a land of unbridled persecution? Europe responded by calling for a counter-Olympics, known as the "People's Olympics." Barcelona was picked as the site. The outbreak of the Spanish Civil War, however, ended the possibility of an alternative event in Spain.

In the United States, the question of participation became a controversial topic. An editorial in the *Washington Post* called for a boycott "to let the Germans see what the outside world thinks of their present rules."[1] Those rules, in the view of Judge Jeremiah Mahoney, the President of the Amateur Athletic Union, went against the Olympic principle forbidding discrimination based on race and religion. Participation, in his view, would mean an endorsement of Hitler's Reich.

Former Governor Al Smith of New York lent his support to the boycott. So did Governor James Curley of Massachusetts. So did Mayor Fiorello La Guardia of New York. A Gallup Poll taken in 1935 showed that 43 percent of the entire population favored a boycott. Within Jewish organizations, there were some, like the Jewish Labor Committee and the American Jewish Congress (founded by Rabbi Stephen Wise), who took a public pro-boycott stance. And there were others, like the American Jewish Committee and B'nai B'rith, who stayed in the background, fearing an anti-Semitic backlash both in the United States and Germany.

In Congress, Brooklyn Representative Emanuel Celler encouraged the boycott. He said, "The Jew who is jeered on the streets simply because he is a Jew cannot be cheered in the arena because he is a champion."[2]

Two Jewish-American athletes took Celler's words to heart. Milton Green and Norman Cahners, both members of the Harvard track team who had qualified for the national Olympic trials, boycotted that event.

On the other side of the debate stood Avery Brundage, the President of the American Olympic Committee (A.O.C.). The boycott, Brundage knew, was meant to undermine the Nazi movement. However, Brundage believed that sports and politics should be strictly separate. Should the American athlete be made "a martyr to a cause not his own"? Brundage asked. He answered his own question: "The A.O.C. must not be involved in political, racial, religious, or sociological controversies."[3] Brundage's criteria were clear: he asked that Nazi Germany accept Olympic rules and allow German Jews to try out for the German team.

With that in mind, Brundage traveled to Nazi Germany in September 1935. For two weeks, he toured the Reich, meeting with high-ranking German officials. "I was given positive assurance in writing by Tschammer [and] Osten, Germany's official Olympic representative, that there will be no discrimination against Jews," Brundage announced to the American press. "You can't ask more than that and I think the guarantee will be fulfilled."

Somehow, during Brundage's tour of Germany, he missed the many *Juden Verboten* signs. He missed the Nuremberg Laws officially implemented during his trip. He missed the fact that Jews were prohibited from employment. He missed the yellow stars painted on Jewish storefronts, declaring those stores off limits to German nationals. How did he ignore all of this? Avery Brundage did not speak German. Forced to rely on interpreters, he heard the party line. He missed the underlying meaning. Brundage also never met alone with representatives of the Jewish sports clubs. Some of this undoubtedly was due to German regulations. On the other hand Brundage harbored a deep anti-Semitism. He was known as "a Jew hater and Jew baiter." Brundage believed that the boycott movement was a product of Jewish intervention. Criticism of his position he rejected as "obviously written by a Jew or someone who has succumbed to Jewish propaganda." Such an explanation was furthered by Brundage's chief assistant, Brigadier General Charles Sherrill, one of three Americans on the International Olympic Committee and a former Ambassador to Turkey. In a press conference, he said that "about 5,000,000 Jews in this country are using the athletes representing 120,000,000 Americans to work out something to help the German Jews."

After Brundage returned from Germany, he met with Max Schmeling, the German boxing champion, in New York. "What about this, Max?" Brundage asked. "A good number of black and Jewish athletes will be on the American team. Who is going to guarantee us that they won't be abused?"

German athletes, Schmeling replied, would guarantee the integrity of the games and would not allow any discrimination. Later, according to boxing historian Patrick Myler, Schmeling wondered if he "had been too presumptuous. After all, how could he be sure that what he said would be honored by Hitler?" Schmeling was not a member of the Nazi Party. His advice, however, further steered Brundage into taking the position for American participation.[4]

As for Avery Brundage, he allowed himself to be duped by the Nazis. In Emanuel Celler's words, he "prejudged the situation before he sailed from America. The Reich Sports Commissars have snared and deluded him." The Nazis, for instance, assured him during his tour of Germany that Jewish athletes would be included on their team. To that extent, Rudi Ball was invited to play on the hockey team (for the winter games in Garmisch). Helene Mayer, who had won a gold medal in fencing in 1928, was brought back to Germany from Los Angeles (she would win the silver medal in fencing in Berlin). The German record holder in the high jump, Gretel Bergmann, received an invitation from the Reich Sports Office to participate in the Berlin Olympics. She returned to

Germany from England. Two weeks before the games began, however, she received a letter disinviting her. Instead of an Olympics invitation, Gretel Bergmann received tickets to the games, in the standing room only section.

In December of 1935, the American Olympic Committee, in a close vote, decided to send American athletes to Berlin. President Roosevelt did not overrule, as President Jimmy Carter did in 1980 in response to the Soviet invasion of Afghanistan.

Of course, had Roosevelt acted in support of a boycott, the superlative feats of Jesse Owens would not have occurred. In the 1936 Olympics, Owens won four gold medals. According to the American newspapers, after one of Owens' gold-medal-winning performances, Adolf Hitler spurned the victor and stormed out of the stadium. "I wasn't invited to shake hands with Hitler," Owens responded to questions regarding Hitler's snub, "but I wasn't invited to the White House to shake hands with the President either."[5]

As for President Roosevelt and the proposed boycott, he never directly addressed the issue. Avery Brundage called the result a "great victory for Olympic principles."

By participating in the Berlin Olympiad, America played into the hands of Adolf Hitler and his propaganda festival. America, with a chance to condemn the Nazi regime, instead fostered its legitimacy. What would the effects of a boycott have been? By taking action, might a message have been sent to Hitler and the Nazis? Might that message have influenced Western Europe and its coming policy of appeasement? The answers aren't clear. However, by not boycotting the Berlin games, the United States became a pawn of Hitler's grand illusion. An illusion best summarized by Hitler himself, as he proclaimed on the eve of the Olympics, "We are, and always will be, at peace with the world."[6]

Another story must be told concerning Avery Brundage. A week before the Berlin Olympics were set to begin, Marty Glickman and another American sprinter named Sam Stoller continued their preparations for the 400-meter relay race. On the eve of the race, however, the American track team replaced Glickman and Stoller with Jesse Owens and Ralph Metcalfe. Both Glickman and Stoller were Jewish, the only Jews on the American track team.

"Something terrible had happened," Glickman later said, "and I wasn't even sure what the hell it was."[7] Avery Brundage and Dean Cromwell, the U.S. Olympic track coach, made this decision. One based on anti-Semitism, according to Glickman.

As Jesse Owens and the rest of the relay team stood on the victory stand and received their gold medals, Glickman was shocked and outraged. "I ought to be out there," he thought to himself, "and I'm not."

To make matters worse, when Glickman returned to the United States, he went to the New York Athletic Club in Manhattan with a track friend. In the lobby the club's Athletic Director turned Marty Glickman away. Club policy mandated that Jews could not use the facilities.

Fifty years later, as a tribute to Jesse Owens, American athletes returned to the Olympic Stadium in Berlin. Marty Glickman told historian Peter Levine, "As I walked into the stadium, I began to get so angry. . . . Not about the German Nazis . . . that's a given. But the anger at Avery Brundage and Dean Cromwell for not allowing an eighteen-year-old kid to compete in the Olympic games just because he was Jewish."

I can attest to the keenness of Marty's sense of betrayal. I was fortunate to meet and befriend Marty Glickman later in life. Although he'd gone on to a very successful career as the voice of the New York Knicks and the football Giants, he still smoldered with the events of long ago. Those scars were evident.

Chapter 9

◄ ►

Quarantine

The middle years of the decade witnessed the advance of dictators. The forces of the Italian dictator Benito Mussolini marched into Ethiopia, with only scant attention paid by the League of Nations. General Francisco Franco's revolt in Spain escalated into the Spanish Civil War. The Japanese raided the Chinese city of Nanking, savagely torturing and murdering over three hundred thousand people whose sole crime was being Chinese. In Germany, Hitler's rearmament intensified. On March 7, 1936, the Nazis crossed the Rhine and entered the demilitarized zone. Had the French reacted then to Nazi belligerence, they could have marched all the way to Berlin. That's how ill prepared Nazi defenses were at that point.

If anyone further denied Nazi belligerence, Adolf Hitler's proclamation made his motivations clear. In his address to the Reichstag of January 30, 1937, commemorating the fourth anniversary of his rise to power, he declared "the withdrawal of the German signature" from the Treaty of Versailles.

Meanwhile, hostilities toward the Jews increased. An additional thirteen decrees further defined the Nuremberg Laws, including a new edict outlawing Jewish children from attending public schools. The decrees not only took away the right to work (half of the Jewish population was without means of livelihood) but made survival a cruel task. "In many a town the Jew found it difficult if not impossible to purchase food," William L. Shirer, an eyewitness, wrote. "Over the doors of the grocery and butcher shops, the bakeries and the dairies, were signs, 'Jews Not Admitted.' In many communities Jews could not procure milk even for their children. Pharmacies would not sell them drugs or medicine. Hotels would not give them a night's lodging."[1] And then there were the signs. "Jews Strictly Forbidden in This Town." "Jews Enter This Place at Their Own Risk." On the road near the town of Ludwigshafen, "Drive Carefully! Sharp Curve! Jews 75 Miles an Hour!"

Meanwhile, the neutrality and isolation of America increased. In May of 1937, Congress passed, and the President signed, yet another Neutrality Act. This one called for a series of restrictions: a mandatory arms embargo toward belligerents; a mandatory travel ban on belligerent ships; a mandatory loan ban to belligerents; a mandatory ban on arming of American merchant ships trading with belligerents. Among the general populace, a Gallup poll revealed that two-thirds of the population had no interest concerning global events.

This sentiment continued to hold sway all the way until Pearl Harbor. The war in Europe had only reinforced American isolationism. Consider, for instance, the invocation given by Rabbi Michael Aransohn of Cincinnati at the 1940 Republican Convention. "Of what will it avail us if we offer up our sons and daughters on the altar of Moloch? Is it not better to fight in our own land against the more hideous Huns and fiercer vandals in our own midst—the bands of gangsters and racketeers who flourish everywhere. Let us not let ourselves be sucked into the maelstrom of war."[2]

While Roosevelt publicly supported neutrality, he worked behind the scenes to stem the advance of the dictators. Specifically, the President pushed for the selling of nonmilitary goods to his European allies (and as a carrot to American business, he okayed the selling of the same goods to belligerent nations). The isolationists in Congress, with the disturbing images of the First World War in mind, fought Roosevelt's strategy vociferously. Roosevelt's reaction: "I am walking a tight rope," he admitted to Democratic

Party Chairman James Farley. "I realize the seriousness of this from an international as well as a domestic point of view."[3]

Roosevelt, at this point in his second administration, was reeling from a major miscalculation. In early 1937, he introduced legislation which permitted the President to appoint one additional Justice to the Supreme Court, up to a total of six new appointments, for every sitting Justice who declined to retire at age seventy. The Supreme Court then comprised six Justices seventy or over, including the moderate Louis Brandeis (eighty years of age) and the arch conservative "Four Horsemen"—James McReynolds (seventy-five), George Sutherland (seventy-four), Willis Van Devanter (seventy-seven) and Pierce Butler (seventy).

Roosevelt, upset that the Supreme Court had struck down the heart of his New Deal legislation, labeled the Justices "nine old men" who set the Constitution back to "horse and buggy days." His innuendo concerning senility set off a fury around the country. In a Gallup Poll taken in February of 1937, 53 percent of those polled opposed the President's Supreme Court proposal. In addition, the proposal suddenly gained a deleterious name: "Court Packing."

In a *Time* Magazine interview Roosevelt reacted, "When I retire to private life on January 20, 1941, I do not want to leave the country in the condition Buchanan left it to Lincoln." President Roosevelt took his Supreme Court proposal directly to the people, campaigning against those who had fought the legislation, particularly powerful Senators and Congressmen from the South. The country saw his actions, however, as vindictive and menacing.

In addition, the economy, built on Roosevelt's confidence as much as anything else, took a downturn. During "Roosevelt's Recession," two million workers received layoff notices, expanding the ranks of the unemployed to ten million, or 19 percent of the work force.

Roosevelt, at this point in time, couldn't buy a vote. His political clout was at its lowest point. Still, he recognized the troubling international scene and he fought for a more international foreign policy. That led to a compromise with Congress. The provision, eventually known as Cash-and-Carry, stipulated that raw materials and other items not military in nature could be purchased, as long as the buyer paid in cash and carried the goods away from American ports in their own ships. Cash-and-Carry began Roosevelt's emphasis on building up American military production. As decreed by the Treaty of Versailles, the American armed forces ranked seventeenth in the world, behind Portugal. What would become an all-out priority on war production in the coming years began here, with a way of aiding allies in the face of growing belligerent nations and deep American isolationism. Cash-and-Carry, though a necessary first step, nearly bankrupted the British. Fortunately, Roosevelt conceived of and implemented the brilliant policy known as Lend-Lease.

In October of 1937, at the low point of his Presidency, a prescient Franklin Roosevelt appeared in Chicago and took a stab at warning both the isolationists in America and the belligerents of the world. In the Quarantine Speech, he said:

> The peace, the freedom, and the security of ninety percent of the population is being jeopardized by the remaining ten percent who are threatening a breakdown of all international order and law. Surely the ninety percent who want to live in peace under law and in accordance with moral standards that have received almost universal acceptance through the centuries can and must find some way to make their will prevail. It seems to be unfortunately true that the epidemic of world lawlessness is spreading. When an epidemic of physical disease starts to spread, the community approves and joins in a quarantine of the patients in order to protect the health of the community against the spread of the disease.

The press response to the Quarantine Speech was immediate and quizzical, enough in fact to push the World Series off the front pages (the Yankees, led by DiMaggio and Gehrig, in his last year although he did not yet know it, beat my beloved Giants, led by my favorite player, Mel Ott, four games to one). The press sought clarification. The day after the speech, President Roosevelt held a press conference in Hyde Park.

Q: I had two major things in mind. One was what you had in mind with reference to quarantining—what type of measure? Secondly, how would you reconcile the policy you outlined yesterday with the policy of neutrality laid down by the Act of Congress?

Roosevelt: Read the last line in the speech. That gives it about as well as anything else. [Roosevelt had ended the speech with, "Therefore America actively engages in the search for peace."]

Q: But you also said that the peace-loving nations can and must find a way to make their wills prevail.

Roosevelt: Yes?

Q: Is anything contemplated? Have you moved?

Roosevelt: No, just the speech itself.

Q: Yes, but how do you reconcile that? Do you accept the fact that that is a repudiation of the neutrality—

Roosevelt: Not for a minute. It may be an expansion.

Q: Doesn't that mean economic sanctions anyway?

Roosevelt: No, not necessarily. Look, "sanctions" is a terrible word to use. They are out of the window.

Q: Is there a likelihood that there will be a conference of peace-loving nations?

Roosevelt: No, conferences are out of the window. You never get anywhere with a conference.

Q: Foreign papers put it as an attitude without a program.

Roosevelt: That was the *London Times.*

Q: Would you say that that is not quite it, that you are looking toward a program as well as having an attitude?

Roosevelt: It is an attitude, and it does not outline a program, but it says we are looking for a program.

Q: Wouldn't it be almost inevitable, if any program is reached, that our present Neutrality Act will have to be overhauled?

Roosevelt: Not necessarily. That is the interesting thing.

Q: You say there isn't any conflict between what you outline and the Neutrality Act. They seem to be on opposite poles to me and your assertion does not enlighten me.
Roosevelt: Put your thinking cap on, Ernest [Lindley].

Q: I have been for some years. They seem to be at opposite poles. How can you be neutral if you are going to align yourself with one group of nations?
Roosevelt: What do you mean, "aligning"? You mean a treaty?

Q: Not necessarily. I meant action on the part of the peace-loving nations.
Roosevelt: There are a lot of methods in the world that have never been tried yet.

Q: Do you agree or disagree with what apparently amounts to the conclusion of the British, that sanctions mean war?
Roosevelt: No. Don't talk about sanctions. . . .

Q: Is a "quarantine" a sanction?
Roosevelt: No.

Q: Are you excluding any coercive action? Sanctions are coercive.
Roosevelt: That is exactly the difference.

Q: Better, then, to keep it in a moral sphere?
Roosevelt: No, it can be a very practical sphere.[4]

The press conference continued in its roundabout and evasive manner. The President's Quarantine Speech, however, remains open to interpretation. What was Roosevelt attempting? Was he warning his isolationist colleagues within the government? Was he cautioning the world? Was he trying to suggest a system of collective security? Was he putting forth the concept to see how the world would react? What if the world had listened? Would Neville Chamberlain and Edouard Daladier have gone to Munich and agreed to Hitler's demands? Would Hitler have then marched on the Sudetenland? Would the world community have tolerated *Kristallnacht*, or Japan's butchery in Nanking, or General Franco's (estimated) execution of two million Spaniards?

The Quarantine Speech appeared to fall on deaf ears. To the President's speechwriter and special counsel, Sam Rosenman, Roosevelt said, "It is a terrible thing to look over your shoulder when you're trying to lead—and find no one there."

However, soon after the speech, the President requested a billion-dollar appropriation for expansion of the Navy. A reluctant Congress obliged. And the priority toward military production began to take shape.

Chapter 10

◄►

"An Orgy of Sadism"

O n March 12, 1938, German troops marched into Austria. No Austrian troops defended their land. No soldiers put up a brave but losing battle. Instead, the Austrians responded with instantaneous celebration and sheer adulation for the Nazi leader. An eyewitness in Vienna, the reporter William L. Shirer, then working for the Columbia Broadcasting System (CBS), and Edward R. Murrow, its chief correspondent in Europe, called the welcoming of the arrival of Adolf Hitler, "tumultuous. . . . At every village, hastily decorated in his honor, there were cheering crowds. During the afternoon he reached his first goal, Linz, where he had spent his school days. The reception there was delirium and Hitler was deeply touched. . . ."

The Austrian people lost no time in instigating a pogrom. "For the first few weeks the behavior of the Vienna Nazis was worse than anything I had seen in Germany," Shirer wrote. "There was an orgy of sadism. Day after day large numbers of Jewish men and women could be seen scrubbing the sidewalks and cleaning the gutters. While they worked on their hands and knees with jeering storm troopers standing over them, the crowds gathered to taunt them. Hundreds of Jews, men and women, were picked off the streets and put to work cleaning public latrines and the toilets of the barracks where the SA and the SS were quartered. Tens of thousands more were jailed. . . ."[1]

In under a month, Austrian authorities arrested 34,000 Jews. That led to a Masada-like suicide pact; some two hundred Jews committing suicide per day. Propaganda Minister Joseph Goebbels responded, "There is talk of mass suicides of Jews in Vienna. It is not true. The number of suicides remains unchanged; the difference is that whereas Germans committed suicide before, it is now Jews. We cannot protect every Viennese Jew with a special policeman to prevent him from committing suicide."[2]

Many Austrian Jews were able to purchase their freedom. The Nazis in fact set up an agency, the "Office for Jewish Emigration," just for this lucrative trade. Baron Louis de Rothschild, for instance, bought his freedom by turning over his steel mills to the Hermann Goering Works. Perhaps half of Vienna's 180,000 Jews managed in this way to leave Austria.

Others could not. At first, the Gestapo would not permit the emigration of Sigmund Freud and his family. The Gestapo made an example of Freud, searching his house and headquarters (at the Vienna Association of Psychoanalysis) and arresting and interrogating his daughter, Anna. Under pressure from President Roosevelt, however, the Nazis relented. But not before Sigmund Freud signed a document stating that he had not been mistreated. In the postscript, the document read, "I can most highly recommend the Gestapo to everyone." The Freuds moved first to Paris, then to England. Freud's four sisters, however, remained in Vienna. All perished in concentration camps. Freud himself committed suicide three weeks after the Nazis invaded Poland. On September 23, 1939, after a long bout with maxillary (jawbone) cancer, he had his personal physician administer twenty-one milligrams of morphine. A lethal dose.

In Vienna, three thousand Jews per day applied for American visas. In Stuttgart, there was a stampede at the American Consulate. A backlog of nearly 110,000 visa applications quickly accumulated.

One survivor of the Holocaust, Ernest Michel, discovered the near impossibility of visa acquisition in Stuttgart. As a young teenager, Michel, a citizen of Mannheim, Germany, met an American businessman named Robert Lindsay from Wilmington,

Delaware. That chance meeting led to a pen-pal relationship between Michel and Lindsay's son, Bob. In 1938, desperate to flee Germany, Michel's father wrote to Robert Lindsay asking for any kind of assistance. Lindsay, in an act of remarkable generosity, not only offered to sponsor Ernest Michel in America, but to take him into his family and to see to his education.

Ernest Michel thought he was heading for freedom. Six months passed with no word from the American Consulate. The required affidavit hadn't come through. Meanwhile in Germany, laws banning Jews from employment and from contact with non-Jews were strictly enforced. Ration cards were distributed to the Jews, denying butter, permitting meat once a week. A Nazi edict assigned the middle name of Israel to all Jewish males, the middle name of Sara to all Jewish females.

Finally, in June of 1939, the American Consulate contacted the Michel family with the news of the affidavit's arrival. Ernest Michel and his father took a train down from Mannheim. From the Stuttgart train station, father and son walked to the Consulate. Fear of riding the streetcar necessitated that walk.

Long lines greeted their arrival. The lines moved slowly. Hours passed. Eventually, they met a Consul representing the government of the United States. In his memoirs, Ernest Michel wrote, "He said something about making sure we were not Communists. I tried not to laugh. . . . How could a Jewish 16-year old boy in Germany be a Communist?"[3]

The Consul was in the midst of granting Ernest Michel a quota number when he said, "If everything goes as expected, your number should be called some time in 1942."

Ernest Michel's heart sank. His father couldn't believe his ears. "Why three years?" he asked. "How can we last for another three years? Don't you know what is happening to the Jews in Germany?"

The Consul's response was typical bureaucracy, "You have to wait, just like everybody else." One wonders now: Was Michel's story typical? And if so, how many others, with an affidavit literally in hand, were denied visas? Three months after Michel's incident at the Consulate, Germany invaded Poland. Ernest Michel went to Auschwitz. His father and his mother died there.

In response to the various voices within the United States calling for action, including columnist Dorothy Thompson and Congressman Emanuel Celler, Undersecretary of State Sumner Welles went to President Roosevelt. "Get out in front and attempt to guide" on refugee issues, Welles recommended. President Roosevelt took Welles' advice to heart. On March 22, 1938, ten days after the *Anschluss*, Roosevelt called a press conference. The scene wasn't the Oval Office or Hyde Park or even Washington, D.C., but rather, the side of the road in Warm Springs, Georgia. From the back seat of a Ford Roadster, Roosevelt announced the merging of the German/Austrian immigration quota (which went in direct violation of Congressional law), raising the German quota by some two thousand entry spots. At the same time, he invited thirty-two nations to join in a conference to address the refugee problem in Germany and to facilitate emigration. His invitation specified that no country "would be expected or asked to receive a greater number of emigrants than is permitted by existing legislation."[4] And so a conference on refugees was born.

Governor Herbert Lehman of New York responded to Roosevelt's conference with a single-word cable: "Splendid." Roosevelt's return cable read, "I only wish I could do more."

Two weeks before the Evian Conference, a prominent boxing match in New York City exposed the fierce antagonism and relentless propaganda between Nazi Germany and the United States of America. In one corner stood the heavyweight champion of the world, the American Joe Louis, nicknamed the "Brown Bomber." In the other corner stood the former heavyweight champion and top-rated challenger, the German Max Schmeling. Unshaven and with his black hair slicked back, Schmeling waited calmly for the bell. The Brown Bomber shadow-boxed, his energy aggressive and percolating.[5]

Joe Louis, since he'd won the heavyweight championship one year earlier, considered his title incomplete. The only loss on his record, by knockout, had come at the hands of Max Schmeling back in 1936. "Ah'm not champion until I beat Schmelin'," Louis declared in his Alabama drawl. In that fight Schmeling, an underdog in the betting by 8-1, had detected a flaw in Louis's style. The

Brown Bomber had a tendency to drop his left hand after jabbing. This played right into Schmeling's strategy; a short, straight right was Schmeling's best punch. The German knocked out the American in the twelfth round.

Following Schmeling's victory, the Nazi government adopted Schmeling as their favorite son. "Congratulations," Minister Goebbels cabled. "I know you won it for Germany. We are proud of you. *Heil Hitler.*" Adolf Hitler sent his own message: "Most cordial felicitations on your splendid victory." Hitler then invited Schmeling and his wife, the Czech actress Anny Ondra, to the Reich Chancellery for lunch. There, Hitler and Goebbels asked for and received a full recapitulation of the fight.

To Hitler and Goebbels, Schmeling's victory proved Nazi ideology. The German had beaten the American. The Aryan had knocked out the "negro." Racial superiority had ruled the day.

When the lunch at the Chancellery became public knowledge, the American press identified Schmeling as a Nazi supporter. In 1936, columnist Westbrook Pegler wrote, "At no time during the months when Schmeling was preparing to fight Louis did the Nazi government accept any responsibility in the matter. Schmeling did not then enjoy the status of official patriot and representative of Nazi manhood. . . . But before the night was over Schmeling had become a great German patriot, and his unexpected conquest of the colored boy had been taken over as a triumph for Adolf Hitler and his government."

By 1938, the Nazi propaganda machine had created a hailstorm. "The swastika hugged Schmeling like flypaper," Chris Mead, a biographer of Joe Louis, aptly wrote. "Whether I wanted it or not," Schmeling responded in his autobiography, "I was a showpiece for the Nazis."

Americans could not dissociate Schmeling from his fascist homeland. That led to protests everywhere Schmeling went. When he arrived in America six weeks before the fight, a crowd lined the pier and shouted abuse. Banners proclaimed: "Schmeling Go Home" and "Boycott Nazi Schmeling". On the eve of the fight, when Schmeling arrived at the St. Moritz Hotel, he was greeted by protestors chanting, "Nazi, Nazi."

Even the American President got into the act. Roosevelt invited Joe Louis to the White House. During a brief conversation, attended by the press, Roosevelt said to the champ, "Lean over, Joe, so I can feel your muscles." With Louis playing along, Roosevelt continued, "Joe, we need muscles like yours to beat Germany." The American press exaggerated Roosevelt's words. "Joe," the newspapers quoted the President, "beat Schmeling to prove we can beat the Germans."

Adolf Hitler, in turn, sent a cable to Schmeling. "To the coming World's Champion, Max Schmeling," the cable read. "Wishing you every success." The cable became public knowledge.

The Louis-Schmeling rematch took place on the humid night of June 22, 1938. The scene was Yankee Stadium. Over seventy thousand fans jammed the place. Ringside seats went for forty dollars. Scalpers charged as much as two hundred. Millions of people throughout the world heard the fight over the radio. The fight was broadcast in four languages: English, Portuguese, Spanish, and German. In Nazi Germany, an estimated twenty million Germans listened to the fight despite the time differential. The restaurants and cafes, in fact, stayed open until six a.m. One Schmeling fan who did not stay up was Max Schmeling's wife, Anny Ondra. Barred by Goebbels from traveling with her husband to America (Goebbels feared that Schmeling and his wife might defect), she slept the night away at home.

When the bell sounded, Louis attacked. Determined, hungry, with a rage of intensity, Joe Louis was vicious. He knocked Schmeling down three times. Nearly two minutes into the first round, he threw a punch that would provoke a controversy, with the Schmeling camp claiming an illegal kidney punch. The punch paralyzed Schmeling. Louis later said, in his Alabama drawl, "I just hit him, tha's all. I hit him right in the ribs and I guess maybe it was a lucky punch, but man, did he scream! I thought it was a lady in the ringside cryin'." Schmeling later replied of the punch, "It was a right swing that caught me on the left kidney. It absolutely paralyzed me. I could not feel anything. I could not straighten up, or even think. It was a foul blow, absolutely. It was the worst punch I have ever received."

At this point in the fight, Max Machon, Schmeling's trainer, threw a white towel into the ring. The towel, of course, signified surrender. The referee picked up the towel and flung it away. That wouldn't happen today, but New York State boxing then did not recognize the gesture. The towel caught the rope marking the perimeter of the ring and swayed there.

After Louis knocked Schmeling down for the third time, the referee stepped in, ending the fight at the count of five. The fight lasted two minutes and four seconds, the quickest knockout ever recorded in a heavyweight fight in America. The crowd, according to 1930s reporter and writer Damon Runyon in his article "Louis Was Truly Great," was "so stunned by the sudden ending that it sits a full half-minute in silence before breaking into a tremendous roar of admiration for Louis." Joe Louis showed no emotion as he was proclaimed winner and still heavyweight champion of the world. Schmeling spent ten days in a hospital.

In Germany, the reaction was confusion and disbelief. Those listening believed that the announcer, in his excitement, had made a mistake. "It's impossible" was the general response. Minister Goebbels, after hearing about the supposed kidney punch, claimed that not only had Louis landed an intentional foul blow but that his gloves were padded with lead. The Nazi newspaper, the *Völkischer Beobachter*, alleged that boxing in America was "controlled by Jews."

To a certain degree, history portrays Max Schmeling as a Nazi sympathizer. And there is some validity to the charge. When Hitler came to power, Schmeling welcomed the changes. Hitler's promises—to end unemployment, to re-energize German patriotism, to re-institute the typically precise and orderly German way of doing things—seemed in sharp contrast to the previous era's chaos. Hitler, as the saying goes, promised to make the trains run on time. Schmeling celebrated the new Germany. At the same time, Schmeling never joined the Nazi Party. He never acted as a spokesman for the Party either in Germany or America. And regarding the treatment of Jews, Schmeling took an anti-Nazi attitude. His manager, Joe Jacobs, was an American Jew. That led to a continuing argument with Nazi officials. On numerous occasions, including a face-to-face confrontation with Adolf Hitler, Schmeling refused to fire his manager. "I thought the world of Jacobs," Schmeling said years later. "He was very religious, and every Friday night he would go to the synagogue. Many times I went with him. I sat right next to him through the whole service."

Schmeling was also instrumental in aiding and perhaps saving the lives of two Jewish boys during the *Kristallnacht* pogrom. When the violence of November 9–10, 1938, swept over Germany, Max Schmeling opened his apartment to the Jewish brothers, whose father ran a clothing store where Schmeling bought his suits. The boys stayed in the Schmeling apartment for two days. Then Schmeling escorted the brothers to their house. Schmeling never spoke about the incident. Only fifty years after the fact did one of the brothers go public with the story.

Regarding the Louis-Schmeling fight, Schmeling wrote in his autobiography, "Every defeat has its good side. A victory over Joe Louis would perhaps have made me into the toast of the Third Reich."

"Looking back today," Patrick Myler wrote in *Ring of Hate*, "it is hard to escape the conclusion that Schmeling was an opportunist. Undoubtedly, he was in a difficult position. His home, his family, and his roots were in Germany, while his boxing interests could not flourish without American support. The logical thing was to keep a tentative foot in both camps." Certainly, Schmeling followed that path. He fought in the Second World War. Under heavy fire, he parachuted onto the island of Crete during a German offensive. Later, he acted as an envoy for the Nazi government with Pope Pius XII. All the while he worked behind the scenes to help Jews. He intervened on behalf of a Jewish friend who was sentenced to death; he arranged to have another Jewish friend's records at Gestapo headquarters switched from one file to another, removing the man from a most wanted list; and he literally helped another Jewish friend sneak off a truck bound for a concentration camp.

As the propaganda of the Louis-Schmeling fight faded, President Roosevelt's conference on refugees commenced in the town of Evian on the shores of Lake Geneva. The date was July 6, 1938. Prospects for success were immediately discouraging. Even before the Evian Conference began, the posturing portended failure. Switzerland originally refused to host, then reconsidered. Britain announced it would attend only if Palestine was not discussed as an emigration destination. Panama, Honduras, Nicaragua, and Costa Rica, all regarded as possible sites for Jewish resettlement, released a joint statement. "Traders or intellectuals," an anti-Semitic euphemism, would not be accepted.[6]

President Roosevelt appointed Myron C. Taylor to lead the American delegation. Taylor, the Chairman of the Board of U.S. Steel, was unfamiliar with refugee issues. He also had no connection to the government, other than a friendship with the President. What message was Roosevelt sending by appointing an unelected outsider to such an enormous and important mission? Why didn't Roosevelt appoint a knowledgeable insider, such as Congressman Emanuel Celler or Undersecretary Welles or James McDonald, who in 1938 became the Chairman of the President's Advisory Committee on Political Refugees?

In Berlin, Propaganda Minister Goebbels ranted, "If there is any country that believes it has not enough Jews, I shall gladly turn over to it all our Jews." Adolf Hitler claimed he was "ready to put all these criminals at the disposal of these countries, for all I care, even on luxury ships."[7]

The Evian Conference quickly showed world opinion. Country after country came forward with a reason for not accepting Jewish immigration. The French delegation claimed that they had accepted 200,000 refugees (reputedly from the Spanish Civil War) and could accept no more. Argentina, with a population one-tenth the size of the United States, stated that it had accepted almost as many refugees as the United States and could not be included in large-scale immigration. Peru observed that the United States had given an example of "caution and wisdom" regarding immigration restriction and it would follow America's lead.[8] Australia, advertising for settlers in the United States and Britain, declined to open its borders. "As we have no real racial problem," the Australian delegation announced, "we are not desirous of importing one."[9]

As for the United States, its major concession was to fulfill the legal quota of 27,370 refugees per year. According to George

Warren, the assistant to Myron Taylor, Roosevelt was "terribly embarrassed because, having called the conference, he couldn't do anything about taking refugees into the United States himself. All he could do was to exhaust the quotas, which he did. But he did that with Congress growling at him every day of the week."[10]

Statistics, however, proved Warren's assertion incorrect. In 1938, the year of the *Anschluss* and the merging of the quota and the Evian Conference, America accepted 17,868 refugees. Ten thousand less than the legal limit.

One reason for the unfulfilled quota was a fear of saboteurs. Communists, anarchists, Fifth Columnists (defined as any clandestine faction or group attempting to undermine a nation's solidarity), the list of possible subversive agents was long and, in Congressional perspective, fearsome. That fear ascended to the highest level of government. Roosevelt would make policy and appoint officials with the fear of Fifth Columnists in mind. Breckinridge Long, who would stultify Jewish immigration during the war years, was one of those appointments.

In 1938, however, Breckinridge Long was not on the national scene and the refugee quagmire was growing exponentially. The Evian Conference did nothing to offset the tide. In fact, Evian ended in a whimper. The Conference, according to Emanuel Celler, "did not even have the dignity of announcing its failure; it merely fizzled out."[11] There would be no mass refugee resettlement following Evian. There would be no condemnation of Nazi policy. In fact, the Evian Conference justified Germany's Jewish policy. "If this is coming to the help of the refugees," Britain's *Daily Herald* editorialized, "then what would the nations do if they meant to desert them?"[12]

Chapter 11

◄►

A "Dangerous People to Have Around in Large Number"

The aftermath of the Evian Conference saw more activity than the Conference itself. In London, the Intergovernmental Committee on Refugees (IGC) was formed. The IGC, under the directorship of Roosevelt ally George Rublee, spent the next couple of months conferring with Hjalmar Schacht, the President of the Reichsbank, and Schacht's successor, Helmuth Wohlthat, over the ransom price for Jews. Two plans came out of those negotiations. Both plans attempted to finance the emigration of German Jews. The Schacht Plan called for the German government to receive a payment of three billion marks ($1.2 billion) and an intricate system for forcing the émigrés to buy German goods (going against the international boycott) in exchange for fifty thousand Jews of working age to be released per year for three years. The Rublee Plan called for the same emigration numbers. Both plans were rejected. Sumner Welles objected to the Plans' bargaining "human misery for increased exports."[1] *The Nation* denounced the Plans as "refugee barter, extortion and blackmail."[2]

Meanwhile, the Dominican Republic confidentially made an offer to the IGC, welcoming 50,000 to 100,000 refugees as agricultural colonists. The strongman of the Dominican, General

Rafael Trujillo, offered an estate on the north shore called Sosua. The site included some 5,000 acres of arable land, good timber, sufficient water, and a harbor ten miles from a deep-sea port. The site never amounted to much. The first five hundred refugees arrived in March of 1940. By June of 1942 only 472 refugees had settled at Sosua and the total never expanded much beyond. A shortage of ships limited the transportation of refugees from Europe. Also, the colony was beset with administrative and disciplinary problems and many of the refugees used Sosua as a stepping-stone to immigration to the United States.[3]

Meanwhile, in the Philippines, a U.S. protectorate at the time, the High Commissioner Paul McNutt cabled the State Department with a proposal. "President Quezon [the elected leader of the Philippine government] has indicated his willingness to set aside virgin lands in Mindanao for larger groups of Jewish refugees who wish to engage in agricultural enterprises or related activities in the development of community life in undeveloped and practically uninhabited areas."[4] Under President Quezon's offer, two thousand Jewish refugee families could be allowed to settle in Mindanao in 1939 and five thousand families a year thereafter, reaching a peak of thirty thousand families.

The State Department responded immediately, calling the plan "utterly impractical." Joseph Jacobs, the director of the State Department's Office of Philippine Affairs, questioned the proposal on a series of levels. How would Europeans respond to hard labor in the tropics, he wondered? Could Europeans compete against the cheap native labor? And on a foreign policy level, if Jews were settled in Mindanao, wouldn't they then appeal to their brethren in America for assistance, in effect hindering the independence movement of the Philippines? "Do we want to add another troublesome group to our stay-in-the-Philippines advocates?" he wrote to his colleagues at State. A final point killed the proposal, at least from a State Department perspective. If the Jewish settlement failed, Jacobs wrote, "We would have to allow and fund their entry into the United States."

President Manuel L. Quezon, through the assistance of Paul McNutt, submitted an alternative plan. One thousand refugees would be welcome in the Philippines per year up to ten thousand total. As these deliberations continued, small groups of European Jews reached the Philippines. The first wave of 125 refugees reached Manila in October 1938. The second wave left Germany shortly after *Kristallnacht*. By the end of the year, there were some 300 Jewish refugees in Manila and enough Jewish children to establish a Sunday school in the city's synagogue, Temple Emil.

The plan for ten thousand immigrants never made it through the deliberation stage. The reasons were varied. The State Department stalled out negotiations for two years. General Emilio Aguinaldo, the Filipino revolutionary leader, declared that "millions" of Filipinos from other areas wished to settle in Mindanao and their welfare should be the country's priority. World events also conspired against the settlement. Once the war began, Hitler ended his Jewish expulsion policy, essentially imprisoning the Jews within the German Reich. By June 1940, the Axis powers had closed off the Mediterranean shipping route. In June 1941, Germany invaded the Soviet Union, cutting off the escape route across Siberia. By July, the Japanese were in a position to attack the Philippines, endangering the lives of all in the archipelago. The Japanese attack on Pearl Harbor essentially ended the settlement plan. In all, fewer than 1,200 European Jews reached the Philippines.

Meanwhile in Washington, as High Commissioner McNutt cabled the State Department with the first Mindanao proposal, Interior Secretary Harold L. Ickes began to push for settlements. First came Alaska. The Interior Department commissioned a nine-month study. The Slattery Report (named after the Undersecretary of the Interior, Harry Slattery) identified a sparse population in Alaska (60,000 inhabitants) and noted the uneven makeup of Alaska's economy. Fishing and mining accounted for 95 percent of employment. The report called for colonists, or "hundreds of thousands of pioneers," to industrialize the territory, most of whom, the report assumed, would be unemployed Americans. Thousands of skilled refugees, however, would be needed. On March 13, 1940, Senator William King of Utah and Representative Franck Havenner of California introduced Alaskan colonization legislation. The King-Havenner Bill welcomed the immigration of male refugees (in other words, laborers) between the ages of sixteen and forty-five. Each immigrant could bring his wife and children and none of the immigrants would count against the quota system. King-Havenner immediately ran into opposition, both in the Congress and from native Alaskans. Senator Robert Reynolds of North Carolina, in the vanguard of isolationist Senators, condemned the legislation as "just a smoke screen" for refugees "to get in the back door." Taking up where Reynolds left off, an editorial in the *Alaska Weekly* identified the real purpose of the King-Havenner legislation as "colonizing Alaska with refugees, financed by private capital. That it is Jewish capital and that the refugees to be poured into Alaska if this bill is passed will be Jewish is obvious." The Bill never made it to the floor of either the House or the Senate.[5]

The Interior Department, however, had predicted such a conclusion and turned its settlement ideas elsewhere, specifically the Virgin Islands. The Department of the Interior found a loophole within the quota system. The category "temporary visitors seeking asylum" was not subject to quota restrictions in the Virgins. A small influx of refugees (at most 2,000 people) could "visit" without immigration visas, Ickes argued. Those refugees could then wait in safety until their quota numbers were called. Once that occurred, a new population of refugees could "visit" the Virgins, facilitating a cycle of immigration. Under Interior Department pressure, a resolution was brought before the Virgin Islands legislative assembly. The resolution passed. The Governor of the Islands then agreed to the plan. At this point the State Department stepped in, arguing that the resolution required Congressional approval. In effect, the State Department stalled the plan for months. In November of 1940, Assistant Secretary of State Breckinridge Long entered the negotiations. He argued, directly to Roosevelt, that if the plan went into effect the Virgin Islands would be open to Fifth Columnists. Roosevelt, calling the matter foreign policy and therefore the exclusive province of the President and the State Department, ordered Ickes to drop the matter.[6]

Nobody wanted the Jews. Hitler's policies during the 1930s suggested it. The world's response corroborated it. "The Jews are dangerous people to have around in large number," General Emilio Aguinaldo, the Filipino revolutionary leader, declared. And so the world believed.

Chapter 12

◄►

"Chased Like an Animal"

In September of 1938, British Prime Minister Neville Chamberlain averted war by surrendering to Hitler's demands at Munich. That agreement cut the heart out of the Czechoslovakian nation. Ceding the Sudeten territory disrupted the Czechoslovakian infrastructure, including rail, road, telephone, and telegraph systems. Czechoslovakia lost 70 percent of its iron and steel, 80 percent of its textiles, 40 percent of its timber, 66 percent of its coal. The gutting of Czechoslovakia, Chamberlain hoped, would halt Hitler's advances. The day after the Munich Conference he met secretly with Hitler and presented an agreement, the essence of which can be found in the last sentence. "We [the leaders of Germany and Britain] are determined to continue our efforts to remove possible sources of difference, and thus to contribute to assure the peace of Europe."

Hitler signed the agreement, in the words of his interpreter, "with a certain reluctance . . . only to please Chamberlain."[1] Neville Chamberlain flew home to London. He received a triumphant welcome. Outside the Prime Minister's residence on Downing Street, the crowd shouted, "Good old Neville!" and sang, "For He's a Jolly Good Fellow."

"My good friends," Chamberlain addressed the crowd, "this is the second time in our history that there has come back from Germany to Downing Street peace with honor [Disraeli returned from the Congress of Berlin in 1878]. I believe it is peace in our time." The next day, Hitler's army marched into the Sudetenland. Within six months, Czechoslovakia would be obliterated.

In Britain, one voice understood the consequences. On the floor of the House of Commons on October 5, 1938, Winston Churchill declared, "We have sustained a total and unmitigated defeat." He was heckled at this point in his speech; he had to stop to let the jeering subside. "We are in the midst of a disaster of the first magnitude," Churchill continued. "The road down the Danube . . . the road to the Black Sea has been opened. . . . All the countries of Mittel Europa and the Danube valley, one after another, will be drawn in the vast system of Nazi politics . . . radiating from Berlin. . . . And do not suppose that this is the end. It is only the beginning. . . ."[2]

Have truer words ever been spoken? In another kind of beginning, one month later, the largest pogrom in the history of Germany (up to that point) occurred. On the night of November 9–10, the Nazis looted Jewish homes, burned synagogues, smashed Jewish shops, killed dozens of Jews, and arrested some twenty thousand "criminals." On the morning of the 10th, Germans awoke to broken glass littering their streets. That scene of destruction gave the pogrom its name: the Night of Broken Glass, or *Kristallnacht*. The pogrom extended from Germany to Austria and beyond.

The road to *Kristallnacht* began on October 27, 1938, when the German government rounded up eighteen thousand Jews throughout the Reich and transported them by train to the Polish border. Zindel Grynszpan was one of those expelled. In a letter to his oldest son Herschel, living in Paris, Grynszpan recounted his family's travails. The arrests in Hanover. The train ride through the night in a cattle car. No food or water. On the border, SS guards forced the Jews into a run. Those who didn't respond were whipped. Once in Poland, Zindel Grynszpan wrote, "The Jews were put in stables still dirty with horse dung. At last a lorry with bread arrived from Poznan, but at first there was not enough bread to go round."[3]

In Paris, Zindel's son Herschel bought a gun. With letter in hand, he went to the German Embassy. The date was November

6, 1938. Herschel Grynszpan sought retribution for his family. "Being a Jew is not a crime," he would declare. "I have a right to live and the Jewish people have a right to exist on this earth. Wherever I have been I have been chased like an animal."[4]

Herschel Grynszpan intended to murder German Ambassador Johannes von Welczeck. He was greeted at the German Embassy, however, by Ernst vom Rath, the Third Secretary, and he fired a bullet into vom Rath's belly.

Vom Rath, at that very moment, was under suspicion from the Gestapo. He apparently did not share in his party's anti-Semitic philosophies. Neither did vom Rath's father. A corollary story: in 1940, the Gestapo hired Ernst vom Rath's father, believing that since the son had been murdered by a Jew, the father would be antagonistic and vengeful toward the entire religion. That wasn't the case. According to Heinrich Grüber, a Protestant pastor in Berlin who was eventually jailed for aiding Jews, the senior vom Rath "helped us clandestinely on many occasions."[5] In Gestapo headquarters, for instance, vom Rath would let the latest orders sit on his desk, available for many, including Pastor Grüber, to view. Grüber would then describe the orders to his contacts in the Underground.

In Paris in the split second when Herschel Grynszpan shot Ernst vom Rath, the Embassy's Third Secretary went from suspect to martyr. As vom Rath lay dying in a Parisian hospital, Hitler denounced the deed as part of a Jewish-inspired world conspiracy against Germany. Behind the scenes, Adolf Hitler gave the go-ahead for the pogrom that was later known as *Kristallnacht*.

Ernst vom Rath died on November 9. That evening the violence began. The burning of synagogues. The looting and smashing of Jewish-owned businesses. In Berlin, according to a young boy, "what seemed like hundreds of men, swinging great truncheons, jumped from lorries and began to smash up the shops all around us."[6]

"In thousands of streets," Martin Gilbert wrote in *The Holocaust*, "Jews were chased, reviled and beaten up. In twenty-four hours of street violence, ninety-one Jews were killed. More than thirty thousand (ten percent of the overall population) were arrested and sent to concentration camps."

Eight thousand Jews went to Dachau. Aaron Pozner, a former Hebrew teacher, was among them. His head was shaved, his body stripped. He received the coarse uniform with the yellow star. In his diary, he wrote about "the public hangings after morning roll call . . . the public floggings before afternoon roll call, and the drownings in vats after the evening count. In between there were crucifixions, garrotings, and, the specialty of one guard, castration by bayonet."[7]

One hundred and ninety-one synagogues burned that night. In Vienna, all twenty-one synagogues were set on fire. In the German town of Baden-Baden, the Nazis rounded up the Jewish men and marched them to the synagogue. There, the Jews were ordered to read passages from Hitler's autobiography, *Mein Kampf*. "I read the passage quietly," a member of the Baden-Baden Jewish community reported, "indeed so quietly that the SS man posted behind me repeatedly hit me in the neck." The reading went on for an interminable time. Eventually the synagogue was burned while the Jews were made to stand and witness. "If it had been my decision," one of the SS men told the Jewish congregation, "you would have perished in that fire."

In the town of Mannheim, the synagogue was set on fire in the morning. "The entire building was engulfed," Ernest Michel wrote. "The brownshirts of the SA had taken out the prayer books, the prayer shawls, the Torah scrolls, everything they could get their hands on. They'd dumped them in a pile on the street and, laughing boisterously, were trampling on them, enjoying themselves. . . . 'Burn the Jews!' they kept chanting. 'Burn the Jews!'"[8]

In the United States, the response to *Kristallnacht* was deep outrage. Condemnations were issued by almost every major public figure, from former President Herbert Hoover to former presidential candidate Alfred Landon to Interior Secretary Harold Ickes. Bibb Graves, the Governor of Alabama, wrote to President Roosevelt that "it is time for America to stand four-square for humanity."[9] (Graves, ironically, was also the Grand Dragon of the Alabama Ku Klux Klan.) Father Charles Coughlin proved to be the exception to the rule. He called Germany's behavior "a defense-mechanism" against Jewish-sponsored Communism.

At the Vatican Pope Pius XI, three months away from his death, did not voice outrage at the German-promulgated pogrom. Rather, he remained mute. According to Vatican scholar Peter Godman, the Vatican considered breaking off diplomatic relations with Nazi Germany. That action was not taken. A month after Pius XI's death (March 1939), the new Pope, Pius XII, gave the reason. "If the government [of Germany] breaks off relations, good—but it would not be clever if the break comes from our side." Cleverness, according to Pius XII, implied "doing one's best" to improve relations. "The world should see that we have done everything to live in peace with Germany," Pius announced.[10] Had the Vatican reacted differently, with a formal and vociferous protest, would the world have followed? Was the Vatican's silence a clear message to Hitler's government that the appeasement policies of the West would continue?

The same question could have been asked of President Roosevelt. In the immediate aftermath of *Kristallnacht*, he proceeded with caution. He did not comment on events in Germany and he told reporters to take their questions to the State Department. Five days later, public response pushed Roosevelt to act. He extended the tourist visas of nearly fifteen thousand German-Jews who were here in the United States. He recalled the American Ambassador from Germany. During a press conference, he issued a statement. "The news of the past few days from Germany has deeply shocked public opinion in the U.S. Such news from any part of the world would inevitably produce a similar profound reaction among American people in every part of the nation. I myself could scarcely believe that such things could occur in a twentieth century civilization. . . ."

His outrage was clear. How far did the indignation go? *Time* Magazine believed that due to public opinion the President had been given a "mandate" which he could "translate into foreign policy." Shockingly, nothing changed in foreign policy. No move was made to liberalize the quota system. Nor did the President instigate an intervention-based coalition of nations. And so, without any serious international interference, Hitler's government continued along its chosen path.

Chapter 13

◄►

"No Cause for Alarm"

The year 1939 was the city of Hamburg's 750th anniversary and as May commenced, signs of festivities were everywhere. Flags decorated the main avenues. Hamburg's official seal mingled with the superabundance of swastikas. Banners advertised a victory parade, with a special guest of honor, the Führer himself.

At the city's port, a different sort of parade commenced. On a Friday afternoon, shortly before sundown, nearly thirty Orthodox Jews passed through the Gestapo checkpoint and stepped up the gangway. The following day, a line of some 900 Jews continued the parade. They too passed through the Gestapo inspection shed before experiencing the most extraordinary sight: one of Germany's most luxurious ships, the S.S. *St. Louis*.[1]

The swastika flag flying high above the stern brought the passengers back to reality. Yes, the Jews had purchased tickets. (At exorbitant rates. Eight hundred *Reichsmarks* for first-class, six hundred for tourist class. In addition, each passenger needed a permit, at a cost of three thousand *Reichsmarks* for a family of four. Three thousand *Reichsmarks* translated into around twelve hundred dollars.) Yes, the ship was bound for Havana, Cuba. Still, this was a German ship, under Nazi rule.

A photographer representing the Propaganda Ministry and its chief, Joseph Goebbels, snapped photos of passengers moving up the gangway. The Propaganda Ministry would later publish these photos with captions calling the passengers "subhuman savages" and "furtive-looking fugitives."

A photographer for *Der Stürmer*, the Nazi propaganda publication guided by Julius Streicher, snapped a photo of two Jewish men. Both men perched their elbows upon the ship's railing. Both men wore tailored suits and hats. Both men wore huge smiles, the kind that could light up the Atlantic from Cherbourg to Ellis Island. *Der Stürmer* termed these men "happy Jews" and reminded its readers of the mythical Jewish "tradition" of the Middle Ages, murdering gentile children and using the blood to bake Passover matzah. *Der Stürmer* reminded its readers to protect all belongings, children included. *Der Stürmer* accused the Jews on board the *St. Louis* of fleeing with stolen goods.

The *St. Louis* passengers were limited to carrying ten *Reichsmarks* (about four dollars) each, as per Nazi regulations. Jews could leave Germany during the 1930s; they just couldn't take anything with them. Nazi policy, up to this point in time, was Jewish emigration. To that end, German ships like the *St. Louis* sailed from Hamburg to all parts of the globe. In the two previous years, for instance, fifteen thousand German Jews had sailed to Shanghai.

On May 5, a week before the *St. Louis* sailed, the tickets sold out. On that same day, President Laredo Brú of Cuba issued Decree 937, forbidding the entry of all refugees into his country. Officially, he blamed the country's financial status for the decree, specifically the rising unemployment and the dearth of economic growth. He neglected to explain another concern: Fulgencio Batista, the Commander of the Army at that point in time, threatened Brú's political power. Brú felt obligated to take a stand. Refugees, and specifically Jews, were easy targets.

On that same day, just outside Brú's window, the largest anti-Semitic demonstration in the history of Cuba occurred. The originator of the demonstration was not Cuban but in fact German. Under the authorization of Joseph Goebbels, propaganda agents had infiltrated Cuba a month earlier. Using the radio and Havana newspapers, they revved up the anti-Semitic rhetoric. Forty thousand demonstrators participated. Among them was former Cuban

President Grau San Martin. His associate, Primitivo Rodriguez, urged the demonstrators to "fight the Jews until the last one is driven out."

Two hours after leaving port, Gustav Schroeder, the Captain of the *St. Louis*, received a cable from his superiors at the Hamburg-American Shipping Company (Hapag), mentioning two other refugee ships (the British *Orduna* and the French *Flandre*) bound for Havana. "Imperative you make all speed Havana," the cable asserted. "Have confirmation that whatever happens your passengers will land." The cable ended with a four-word encouragement: "No cause for alarm."

"Imperative you make all speed Havana" had a double meaning. Otto Schiendick, a courier for the German secret service, was a member of the crew. He had orders to disembark in Havana and meet with Robert Hoffman, an Abwehr (German military intelligence) agent and manager for Hapag. The purpose of his voyage was to receive espionage secrets (information regarding secret American military installations as well as detailed drawings of the dams at Lake Gatun and Lake Pedro Miguel, the source of all water for the Panama Canal locks). He was to return to Germany with these in hand. The mission had a code name: Operation Sunshine.

Four days into the *St. Louis's* voyage, the British government published the McDonald White Paper on Palestine. The document, named after Colonial Secretary Malcolm McDonald, limited Jewish immigration in Palestine to a total of seventy-five thousand over a five-year period, with the number of Jews in the country not to exceed one-third of the total population. In repudiating the Balfour Declaration of 1917, the White Paper limited immigration to the one place seemingly most logical.

"This White Paper," Rabbi Stephen Wise would later write, "issued shortly before Hitler was to begin his mass annihilation of European Jewry, was in effect a death sentence for scores of hundreds of thousands of Jews who could have found life and safety in Palestine rather than death in Maideneck [sic] and Auschwitz."[2]

Worldwide reaction to the White Paper was mixed. The Arabs threatened a revolt, claiming the document did not offer enough restriction. On the other hand, Adolf Hitler agreed with the White Paper. That document validated his government's Jewish policy. The British, put off by Hitler's support of the White Paper, began to identify other possible areas of Jewish settlement. Forty thousand square miles of land in British Guiana were initially identified. That resettlement suggestion instigated a round of counter-suggestions. President Roosevelt wrote to Rome concerning Ethiopia as a possible resettlement area. Benito Mussolini, responding to Roosevelt, favored "the open areas of Russia." Responding to that suggestion, the Kremlin proposed Alaska. The United States government countered with Angola. Even Hitler entered the fray, suggesting Madagascar. Proposals and counter-proposals substituted for any real policy. Who wanted the Jews? The answer to the question became increasingly clear

The passengers on board the *St. Louis* knew nothing of this drama. Crossing the Atlantic took two weeks. In that time the passengers settled in and took advantage of the ship's luxuries: a live orchestra, a first-class restaurant, a full social calendar. Passenger Vera Hess remembered the amusement. "We danced and we had music and we were young people and we had a wonderful time," she reflected.[3] Consider the confusion of the then fifteen-year-old from a small town close to Frankfurt: from the severe restrictions of Nazism, from watching the Gestapo remove her father from the family home on *Kristallnacht*, to a sudden liberty, a festive sailing.

In his journal, passenger Aaron Pozner wrote about "a feeling of anticipation, of release from the Nazi horror. People laughed and prayed, and the crew smiled, pretending to understand."

The *St. Louis* dropped anchor in the Havana harbor early on a Saturday morning. Captain Schroeder ordered the ship's siren sounded. The passengers gathered on the decks and looked out at the sleeping city. In her diary, passenger Rosemarie Bergmann wrote, "It's like a dream. I have never jumped out of bed so quickly. The sky is dark blue but I can make out a few white buildings stark against it. There are still stars in the sky."

Morning light brought a hubbub of activity and chaos. Thousands of people gathered on the docks: some tourists, some small-time entrepreneurs (tea and cookie vendors, for instance),

FDR and Henry Morgenthau Jr. The inscription from
Roosevelt reads: "For Elinor [Morgenthau's wife] from
one of two of a kind." (Courtesy of the Franklin D. Roosevelt
Presidential Library and Museum)

FDR, Eleanor and Mayor Fiorello La Guardia,
May 31, 1934. (Courtesy of the Franklin D. Roosevelt
Presidential Library and Museum)

FDR and Churchill during the Atlantic Charter
Conference, with Harry Hopkins over Roosevelt's
right shoulder. (Courtesy of the Franklin D. Roosevelt
Presidential Library and Museum)

FDR signing the Declaration of War against Japan, Dec. 8,
1941. (Courtesy of the Franklin D. Roosevelt Presidential
Library and Museum)

Meeting of the American Bund in Madison Square
Garden under the disguise of George Washington's
Birthday, Feb. 20, 1939. (Courtesy of the
Franklin D. Roosevelt Presidential Library and Museum)

A breadline during
the Great Depression,
New York, Feb. 1932.
(Courtesy of
the Franklin D.
Roosevelt Presidential
Library and Museum)

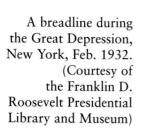

A breadline during the Great Depression, New York. (Courtesy of the Franklin D. Roosevelt Presidential Library and Museum)

A run on the People's Trust and Savings, Chicago, Illinois, June 1932. (Courtesy of the Franklin D. Roosevelt Presidential Library and Museum)

Hooverville, New York, Feb. 16, 1932. (Courtesy of the
Franklin D. Roosevelt Presidential Library and Museum)

Hooverville, Seattle, Washington, June 10, 1937. (Courtesy of the
Franklin D. Roosevelt Presidential Library and Museum)

Apple stands during the Great Depression, New York. (Courtesy of the Franklin D. Roosevelt Presidential Library and Museum)

Pope Pius XII with Myron C. Taylor, U.S. Representative to the Vatican, Aug. 11, 1944. (Courtesy of the Franklin D. Roosevelt Presidential Library and Museum)

Dwight Eisenhower, Omar Bradley, and George
Patton view the charred bodies of prisoners burned
in a concentration camp, Gotha, Germany, April
1945. (Courtesy of the Franklin D. Roosevelt
Presidential Library and Museum)

Meeting of the heads of the War Refugee Board.
From left to right, Secretary of State Cordell Hull, Secretary
of Treasury Henry Morgenthau Jr. and Secretary of War
Henry Stimson, March 21, 1944. (Courtesy of the
Franklin D. Roosevelt Presidential Library and Museum)

FDR and King Ibn Saud of Saudi Arabia on board the USS
Quincy, Great Bitter Lake, Suez Canal, Feb. 14, 1945.
(Courtesy of the Franklin D. Roosevelt Presidential
Library and Museum)

FDR with familiar hat and
cigarette holder. (Courtesy of
the Franklin D. Roosevelt
Presidential Library and
Museum)

John McCloy, Assistant Secretary of War. (Courtesy of the Franklin D. Roosevelt Presidential Library and Museum)

Eleanor Roosevelt visits the Refugee Center at Fort Ontario, Oswego, New York, Sept. 20, 1944. (Courtesy of the Franklin D. Roosevelt Presidential Library and Museum)

Devastation during the battle of London. (Courtesy of the Franklin D. Roosevelt Presidential Library and Museum)

Albert and Elsa Einstein with Stephen Wise, 1934. (Photograph by Pere Lamiere. Courtesy of the Leo Baeck Institute, New York)

Peter Bergson in 1948. (Courtesy of the Jabotinsky Institute)

Aerial reconnaissance photograph of Auschwitz, taken on June 26, 1944. (United States Holocaust Memorial Museum, courtesy of the National Archives and Records Administration)

The broken shop window of a Jewish-owned business, destroyed during Kristallnacht. (USHMM, courtesy of the National Archives and Records Administration)

Jan Karski in 1943. (USHMM, courtesy of Jan Karski)

Apartment buildings burn during the Warsaw ghetto uprising.
(USHMM, courtesy of Instytut Pamieci Narodowej)

Chiune Sugihara in 1940.
(USHMM, courtesy of
Hiroki Sugihara)

Beckinridge Long in 1943.
(USHMM, courtesy of the
National Archives and Records
Administration)

Corpses of murdered victims in Auschwitz. (USHMM, courtesy of
the Leopold Page Photographic Collection)

Gerhart Riegner in 1950.
(USHMM, courtesy of the
Jacob Rader Marcus Center of
the American Jewish Archives)

A member of the SA throws confiscated books into a bonfire, Berlin, May 10, 1933. (USHMM, courtesy of the National Archives and Records Administration)

Per Anger, Raoul Wallenberg's assistant in Budapest, poses in front of a portrait of Wallenberg, 1985. (USHMM, courtesy of Per and Ellena Anger)

The Warsaw ghetto in ruins. (USHMM, courtesy of the National Archives and Records Administration)

Passengers on board the S.S. *St. Louis*. (USHMM, courtesy of Fred Buff)

Jews during a deportation from the Warsaw ghetto. (USHMM, courtesy of the Leopold Page Photographic Collection)

Varian Fry in Marseilles, 1941. (USHMM, courtesy of Annette Fry)

Cuban officials, relatives of those on board. Some of those relatives chartered crafts to take them closer to the *St. Louis*, close enough to throw fruit to their families. The going rate for a craft was twenty-five cents, round trip.

The harbor quickly filled with vessels of all sorts, from rowboats carrying loved ones within shouting range of the ship to a flotilla of police boats to ferries carrying reporters who bombarded the passengers with their questions. A police detail guarded the gangway.

Throughout the day, immigration officers boarded and exited. A few passengers were processed, receiving an *R* (for refugee) next to the red *J* (for Jew) in their passports. Only one Jewish family disembarked. The Bonné family carried official visas, not just landing permits. Those permits were issued by a Cuban named Manuel Benitez, who had opened an unofficial and illegal office in Havana. He gave his office an official name: the Bureau of Immigration. In early 1939, when President Brú drew a distinction between tourists and immigrants, Benitez circumvented the system by offering landing permits to anyone who paid one hundred and fifty dollars. That spring, he signed over four thousand landing permits. He pocketed nearly six hundred thousand dollars. These were the documents the vast majority of *St. Louis* passengers carried.

As that first day in Havana passed, both the *Orduna* and the *Flandre* entered the harbor. None of the passengers on either ship disembarked. The *Orduna* departed that same afternoon, in search of a more hospitable port.

The American reaction was inertia. The American Consul General in Havana, Coert du Bois, cabled Secretary of State Cordell Hull in Washington. "There appears to be no action that the embassy or Consulate general could properly take at present," he wrote. This statement would become American policy.

The next morning, several hundred Jewish residents of European heritage gathered at the harbor. Nobody said a word. Not a shout of encouragement to the *St. Louis* passengers. Not a scream of anger at the immigration officials. Not even a prayer. Celina Zylberglat, then in the second grade, remembered "just standing there. No one said anything."[4] Among the activities that day—the vendors selling their wares, relatives traveling as close to the *St. Louis* as possible, tourists viewing the spectacle—the Cuban Jewish community stood in silent allegiance. Looking shipward, Celina Zylberglat thought to herself, "I could not understand why they could not come ashore." Looking cityward, some nine hundred refugees wondered the same thing.

Meanwhile, a ferry transported the crew of the *St. Louis* to Havana for a little rest and relaxation. Nazi courier Otto Schiendick seemed at first to join his fellow crew members. His first stop, after passing through a thorough search conducted by Cuban officials, was a newsstand. There, he bought a number of English-language magazines. Then he entered a gift shop and bought walking sticks for the entire crew. The gifts came as quite a surprise. Schiendick was a notoriously gruff man.

In town, the crew separated. Alone, Schiendick made for the Hapag office. Nobody followed him. Not a fellow crew member. Not anyone from American intelligence. Not even one of the many reporters lurking around the pier.

Robert Hoffman, the Abwehr agent in Havana, greeted his colleague. They exchanged walking sticks and magazines. The walking stick Schiendick held contained, in its tube, the espionage secrets.

Back on the pier, the Cuban police offered a rudimentary search of the crew. With the use of his new cane, Otto Schiendick stepped onto the ferry, which returned him to the *St. Louis*.

For the passengers on board, the mood soon began to deteriorate. One passenger, Max Loewe, attempted suicide by slitting his wrists and jumping into the bay. His rescue, by a crew member who followed him into the water together with the police patrol in the bay, landed him in a Havana hospital. His suicide attempt introduced a surprising consequence. If you jumped and survived, you ended up on land, in the safety of a hospital. If you died, well, wasn't that better than returning to Germany?

The story of Max Loewe was not uncommon. In the pre-Nazi era, he had been a successful lawyer. Even during the 1930s, his practice prospered. In September of 1938, when the Reich enacted a law prohibiting Jews from practicing law, Loewe considered emigration. He even purchased visas to Britain for his family, but then reconsidered. He thought Britain was too close in proximity to Germany. Plus, his wife did not want to move. But she changed her mind after *Kristallnacht* and Loewe bought the permits to Cuba. In the interim months, he made his living by preparing briefs for trials, then handing them over to sympathetic German lawyers. The practice was illegal and in the winter of 1939 he was discovered. He went underground. After that experience, paranoia pervaded his psyche. By the time he jumped, Loewe had taken on the mentality of the hunted. He thought Gestapo agents were everywhere. He lived in terror.

Sensing the deteriorating mood on board and fearing a mass suicide, Captain Schroeder went to the Passenger Committee for advice. He implemented their suggestions immediately. They included: crew members and able passengers would patrol the ship as a suicide watch; the ship's hull should be lit by floodlights at night (to help identify jumpers); lifeboats should be prepared for instant launching in case of further jumps. With these suggestions in place, the *St. Louis*, according to passenger Aaron Pozner, "now resembled a floating concentration camp."

Passenger Babette Spanier wrote in her journal, "There was no real news. We had done all the waving, the calling of greetings, the chasing after rumors . . . and we were still on board. We did not know why—and that was the worst thing."

Passenger Vera Hess said, "We packed our things but we couldn't get down. We thought," slipping into the Spanish of Havana, "*mañana* and *mañana* and *mañana*, but tomorrow never came."[5]

As negotiations between the Jewish Distribution Committee (JDC) and the Cuban government commenced, the ship's Passenger Committee began a writing campaign. The first cable reached the wife of President Brú. "Over 900 passengers, 400 women and children, ask you to use your influence and help us out of this terrible situation," read the telegram. "Traditional humanitarianism of your country and your woman's feelings give us hope that you will not refuse our request."

At a mid-week Cabinet meeting, President Brú reiterated his stance on the *St. Louis* and Decree 937. In his mind, the German shipping company was responsible for the state of affairs. Hapag had, after all, gone ahead with the voyage even after the declaration of 937. In addition, another Hapag ship, the *Orinoco*, carrying two hundred Jews, had set sail for Havana. Brú accused Hapag of "bringing these passengers here with documents obtained through bribery."

Brú ordered the *St. Louis* to move out of Cuban waters. Once that occurred, he announced, he would be willing to negotiate. Captain Schroeder responded to Brú's order by dressing in civilian clothes and boarding a ship-to-shore transport. From the pier, he traveled by car to the Presidential Palace. At the Palace, he demanded an audience with the President. An envoy interceded. In quiet desperation, Schroeder launched into an account of the state of affairs on board the *St. Louis*. He spoke of the threat of further suicide attempts, the general sense of despair, the plight of the women and children. He pleaded for landing rights.

The envoy echoed Brú's statement: negotiation would commence once the *St. Louis* entered international waters. The envoy added a threat. If the *St. Louis* didn't leave Havana's harbor, the Cuban Navy would be forced to act.

His desperation mounting, Schroeder tried another tactic. He claimed the *St. Louis* needed to take on provisions. The envoy granted a single day. At that point the Captain lost his cool. He threatened Brú's envoy with prosecution, claiming that the Cuban government was legally bound to accept the passengers, as per the agreement with Hapag. The envoy responded by threatening a counter-lawsuit. He claimed the original agreement was a product of coercion and bribery. A day before the *St. Louis* set sail, never again to anchor in Cuban waters, negotiations had deteriorated to lawsuits and counter-lawsuits.

In America, the *New York Times* carried an account of Max Loewe's suicide attempt. A protest march was held in Atlantic City. Other demonstrations followed in New York, Washington, and Chicago. Messages supporting the *St. Louis* passengers were sent to President Roosevelt, Interior Secretary Harold Ickes, and Cardinal Spellman of New York, among others. In addition, an avalanche of telegrams bombarded President Brú, all of them asking him to repeal Decree 937. Perhaps affected by the telegrams, President Brú agreed to a meeting with the JDC's head negotiator, Lawrence Berenson. News of that meeting made the front page of the *Havana Post*. The headline read, "Hope is seen for homeless on *Saint Louis*."

The *New York Times* carried a different headline, "Cuba orders liner and refugees to go." The *St. Louis* headed north at a deliberate pace. The seaman's term is "dead slow ahead."

To Lawrence Berenson and the JDC, President Brú made his price clear: a one hundred and fifty thousand dollar bond to guarantee the passengers sustenance on the Isle of Pines (an old prison establishment), plus five hundred dollars per passenger, returnable once the refugees settled outside of Cuba. In addition, Brú set a deadline for meeting his demands. Forty-eight hours.

Berenson went back to his hotel room and crunched numbers. He subtracted the one hundred and sixty-two children on board the *St. Louis*. He figured five hundred a head for the rest of the passengers. He estimated the passenger count at nine hundred and thirty-three, twenty-six more than in fact were on board. The total came to three hundred and seventy-three thousand dollars. He then took into account the passengers on board the *Flandre* and the *Orduna*. He discounted those children. The total came to an additional seventy thousand dollars. The total for all three ships came to four hundred and forty-three thousand dollars. He submitted this proposal to the Brú government.

Meanwhile, off the coast of Miami, an array of vessels escorted the *St. Louis*, from deep-sea fishing yachts to press boats to a Coast Guard Cutter. The Cutter was under orders to keep the *St. Louis* out of U.S. waters, according to both Lawrence Berenson and Captain Schroeder. However, according to official Coast Guard history, Treasury Secretary Henry Morgenthau, Jr. wanted to keep the ship under serveillance. Concerned for the welfare of the passengers on board, Morgenthau therefore contacted the Coast Guard, which was then under Treasury Department jurisdiction.

After a long, tense weekend, the *St. Louis*'s radio picked up a news flash from a Miami radio station. The passengers on board the *St. Louis*, according to President Brú, could disembark on the Isle of Pines. Captain Schroeder immediately turned the ship southward. At present course and speed (twelve knots) he estimated his arrival to be the next morning by nine.

Relief and excitement filled the corridors. "We are no longer wandering Jews," passenger Babette Spanier wrote in her journal.

At six the next morning, the *St. Louis* received a cable from Havana. The five words stunned Captain Schroeder. "Isle of Pines not confirmed." The next announcement further stunned him. "The Cuban government could not except [*sic*] the [JDC's] proposal," President Brú declared, "and having passed excessively the time allowed, the government terminates the matter." In between Florida and Cuba, Captain Schroeder decided to idle. He hoped, perhaps naively, that the United States government would offer sanctuary. Toward that end, the Passenger Committee sent out telegrams. One reached the State Department. Another reached the Oval Office. In that telegram, the Committee implored the President to act on behalf of the passengers "of which more than 400 are women and children." The White House received the telegram. Did Roosevelt read it? Certainly he never responded. He never clarified his position. He never offered even a word of sympathy. Vera Hess, speaking from the passenger's perspective, called Roosevelt "anti-Jew."[6]

A few minutes before midnight on June 6, some three weeks after departing Hamburg and a little over a week after leaving Havana, the *St. Louis* set course for Europe. Captain Schroeder had no choice. He'd received another cable from the home office. "Return Hamburg immediately," the cable read. In addition, the ship had just enough provisions on board to make the transAtlantic crossing.

During those weeks, Morris Troper, the JDC's European director, held furious negotiations with Western European countries. King Leopold III of Belgium was the first to open his borders, permitting the landing of two hundred passengers. Queen Wilhelmina of Holland followed, granting temporary asylum to one hundred and ninety-four passengers. The British accepted two hundred and eighty-eight passengers. The French accepted two hundred and fifty. Otto Schiendick, the Abwehr agent, disembarked in Antwerp.

The story of the *St. Louis*, however, did not end with the passengers' disembarkation in Western Europe. The story of the *St. Louis* ended in death camps like Auschwitz and Treblinka. The story of the *St. Louis* passed through transit camps like Westerbork and Drancy. Those passengers who disembarked in England were the fortunate few. None of them died in concentration camps. Of those who disembarked on the continent, an estimated 30 percent died in camps. Passenger Aaron Pozner was among them. He disembarked in Holland. The Nazis sent him to the transit camp Westerbork. Shortly before being shipped to Auschwitz, Pozner gave his diary to a friend. The diary survived.

Max Loewe's family (without husband) settled in Britain. Max Loewe spent six months recovering in Havana. Then he made his way to London. He died of a heart ailment in 1942, at the age of fifty-one.

Vera Hess and her family went to France. She and her siblings were hidden in a Catholic children's home. In 1941, her family made the overland trek into Spain. Ironically, the Hess family caught a ship to Cuba. Not a luxury liner, however. This time the family disembarked in Havana.

Captain Schroeder, never a member of the Nazi Party, took a desk job once the war started. His actions on board the ship speak to a deep-seated humanitarianism. He never, for instance, divulged his steward's secret. Leo Jockl was half-Jewish and, by Nazi law, not allowed to work. He concealed his Jewish identity. He told only a few trusted allies. Captain Schroeder was one of them. At the risk of great personal harm, Schroeder preserved Jockl's secret.

Also, later in the drama, when the *St. Louis* was sailing seemingly back to Nazi Germany, Captain Schroeder developed an alternate plan. Rather than return to Germany, he told his first officer, he would run the *St. Louis* close to Beachy Head on the Sussex coast of England, set fire to the ship and evacuate the passengers ashore. That plan did not become necessary.

After the Nazis' defeat, many Germans stood trial during the process of de-Nazification. Captain Schroeder was among them. He gained his acquittal thanks to *St. Louis* passengers, who testified on his behalf. In 1957, the West German government awarded Gustav Schroeder a medal for the part he played during the voyage. He died two years later.

Who failed the passengers of the *St. Louis*? That question, many decades after the ship's sailing, remains. There is plenty of blame to go around. Start with Cuba. President Brú could have opened his port, or designated the Isle of Pines as a haven. Other countries came forward with offers (Honduras, Panama, the Dominican Republic). Why weren't these options examined more strenuously? Which brings up the JDC. Why did that organization pin all of its hope on Cuba? And why didn't other Jewish-American organizations come forward? In the spring of 1939 one Jewish organization (the anti-Zionist American Jewish Committee) could not hold Sunday meetings because "so many of the members went to the country for weekends."[7] Apparently, not even crises stop vacation plans.

In America, where was the persistent public outcry? That spring, for instance, I was finishing my junior year in college. I was, if I remember correctly, a follower of current events. And yet I don't recall reading about the *St. Louis* in the newspapers (even though in fact the story dominated the headlines). I don't recall discussing the situation in classes. I don't recall chatting about it with my friends. I certainly don't recall a movement on campus, a demonstration. Why didn't we demand asylum for those German Jews? What does our silence say about our humanity? Were we indifferent?

A few Americans did speak out. Philanthropist Bernard Sandler urged Congress to grant asylum. Singer Eddie Cantor promised to help fund the refugees' welfare. Why wasn't there a whole battalion of Bernard Sandlers and Eddie Cantors? In Congress, where was the voice of compassion? In the State Department, where was the outcry? Undersecretary of State Sumner Welles informed the American Consul in Cuba that the State Department was "distinctly against making representations" to the Cuban government concerning the refugees. But once the Cubans rejected the *St. Louis*, why didn't the State Department seize the opportunity and find some kind of sanctuary? Where was Secretary Cordell Hull during the ordeal? In telephone conversations between Secretary Hull and Treasury Secretary Henry Morgenthau, Hull was remote and ambiguous. This would become his persona throughout the refugee crises of the 1940s.

Finally, the question must be asked: Where were the Roosevelts? Why didn't Eleanor Roosevelt, one of the great humanitarians of the day, undertake a vociferous campaign, as she did in so many other refugee crises? On June 8, she received a letter from an eleven-year-old. "Mother of our Country," the child wrote, "I am so sad the Jewish people have to suffer so. . . . Please let them land in America. . . . It hurts me so that I would give them my little bed if it was the last thing I had because I am an American let us Americans not send them back to that slater [sic] house. We have three rooms we do not use. Mother would be glad to let someone have them."[8] The decision not to fight harder for the admission of refugees, in the case of the *St. Louis* and later, would cause Eleanor Roosevelt the "deepest regret at the end of her life."[9]

She did, one year later, come to the aid of another boatload of Jewish refugees. In September of 1940, the *Quanza*, a Portuguese vessel carrying eighty Jewish refugees fleeing from France, arrived at Veracruz, Mexico. The passengers carried official transit visas. The Mexican government would not let them disembark. The ship, on its way back to Europe, stopped at Norfolk, Virginia, ostensibly for coal. While the *Quanza* took on provisions, Eleanor Roosevelt applied such pressure on the State Department that Secretary of State Cordell Hull eventually yielded. The refugees received their visas.

During the ordeal of the *Quanza*, President Roosevelt took a passive stance. As Assistant Secretary of State Breckinridge Long wrote, "It was apparent that he [Roosevelt] did not want to talk to me on the subject, and I inferred—and it now seems correctly so—that he would leave the matter entirely in my hands."[10]

Regarding the *St. Louis*, Roosevelt left the matter entirely in the hands of others. He took no action. He offered no words of declaration. His reaction reflected the government's at large. In a letter to the *Richmond Times-Dispatch*, Bishop James Cannon, Jr., of Richmond, Virginia, condemned the government's silence. "During the days when this horrible tragedy was being enacted right at our doors," he wrote, "our government in Washington made no effort to relieve the desperate situation of these people. Why did not the President, Secretary of State, Secretary of the Treasury, Secretary of Labor and other officials confer together and arrange for the landing of these refugees who had been caught in this maelstrom of distress and agony through no fault of their own? The failure to take any steps whatever to assist these distressed, persecuted Jews in their hour of extremity was one of the most disgraceful things which has happened in American history and leaves a stain and brand of shame upon the record of our nation."[11]

Bishop Cannon wrote these words during another monumental disgrace: the failure of the government to pass the Wagner-Rogers Bill.

Chapter 14

◄ ►

"Fear of the Hordes"

How deep was the anti-Semitism in the United States as the 1930s turned into the 1940s? "Slightly below the boiling point," according to sociologist David Riesman.[1] There were thirty million unemployed Americans. There were labor leaders claiming saturation of the work markets due to foreigners accepting minimum wages. There was the Ku Klux Klan swelling to nearly five million people and serving to highlight anti-Jewish culture. There was Father Charles Coughlin, spewing over the radio his hate-filled rhetoric. There was Preacher Gerald L. K. Smith, launching his anti-Semitic magazine *The Cross and the Flag*, running for U. S. senator in the state of Michigan and forming the America First Party. There was the One Hundred Percent American movement and its call for Anglo-Saxon purity, excluding all others of "doubtful origin." There were opinion polls, taken from 1938 to 1945, in which 15 percent of the population voiced approval for a possible large-scale anti-Jewish campaign and 35 to 40 percent would have gone along with one.[2] There was another opinion poll, taken in the aftermath of *Kristallnacht*, asking if this nation should "allow a large number of Jewish exiles from Germany to come to the United States to live." Seventy-seven percent of those polled responded in the negative.[3] There was Montana Republican Jacob Thorkleson, on the floor of the House of Representatives, calling a segment of liberal Jews an "obnoxious tribe" which "prefers the Protocols of the Learned Elders of Zion to the Constitution of the United States." (*The Protocols of the Learned Elders of Zion*, a document asserting a plan to achieve Jewish global domination, was actually produced by the Imperial Russian Secret Police to blame the Jews for Russia's troubles during the revolutionary period.) There was Mississippi Democrat John Rankin, on the floor of the House of Representatives, calling the news columnist Walter Winchell "that little kike." Neither Congressional censorship nor public rebuke followed his comments.

This then was the climate when New York Senator Robert F. Wagner and Massachusetts Representative Edith Nourse Rogers, in the spring of 1939, introduced the Wagner-Rogers Bill. The Child Refugee Bill, as it was also known, sought to admit German children for a temporary period, or "until safe living conditions were re-established." The bill called for ten thousand children, most of them Jewish and all of them under the age of fourteen, to be admitted in 1939 and another ten thousand in 1940. The children would be admitted outside the quota system. This provision was necessary, according to Senator Wagner, because admitting the children within the quota would push out German adults in despair. Wagner's fears were justified. From July 1932 to July 1938, according to statistics compiled by the Quakers, only 26 percent of the German quota had been filled.[4]

To make the Child Refugee Bill more palatable to the mainstream, the legislation included two key provisions. The children would not be allowed to work, and the children under no circumstances would become "public charges." In 1930, President Hoover, seeking to curb immigration in the face of rising unemployment, signed an executive order mandating that an immigrant had to possess either enough money to support himself or he had to produce affidavits showing that relatives in the United States would provide for him. The Child Refugee Bill, to satisfy the requirement, stipulated that all financial arrangements regarding the shipping and care of these children would be paid for privately. To that end, the American Friends Service Committee (the Quakers) called on families to open their homes. Within 24 hours, four thousand American families did so. Radio stations and newspapers were swamped with offers. Jewish agencies promised to subsidize in-home costs. In short, the immediate response to the Child Refugee Bill was enormous.

Appearances of course are deceiving. A series of patriotic organizations lined up in opposition to the legislation, including both the Daughters and the Sons of the American Revolution. Nor was the general populace convinced. A public opinion poll taken in January of 1939 read: "It has been proposed to bring to this country 10,000 refugee children from Germany—most of them Jewish—to be taken care of in American homes. Should the government permit these children to come in?" Of those polled, 61 percent were against entry, with 9 percent voicing no opinion.

Meanwhile, members of the German-American Bund filled Madison Square Garden. The German-American Bund was not a bastion of liberalism celebrating the likes of Einstein, Mann, and the Weimar Republic but rather a front for Nazi activity. The rally seemed to celebrate the birthday of George Washington. A huge picture of President Washington rose from stage to ceiling. On one side of the image of the first President, the Stars and Stripes suggested American patriotism. On the other side of the image, the reason for the rally became apparent. On a flag, the United States Coat of Arms was imposed upon a swastika. The stage was awash in light.

Around the Garden, enormous slogans in red and black read: "Wake up America" and "Smash Jewish Communism" and "Stop Jewish Domination of Christian America."

Posters of local baseball players generating optimism for the coming season juxtaposed the slogans. Mel Ott of the Giants in his home-run stance. The greatest Yankee Joe DiMaggio swinging for the fences.

At eight p.m. precisely, an orchestra in full dress played *Lied der Deutschen* as amended by Horst Wessel. Then a boy's drum and bugle corps in brown shirts and trousers marched from the mezzanine level to the stage. Bund members carrying the red and gold swastika, the American flag, and the Italian flag followed the drum and bugle boys. Next came the Storm Troopers: hundreds of goose-steppers parading down the aisles, with their arms raised in the *Heil Hitler* salute. Those in the arena, filled to capacity, stood too in the *Heil Hitler* salute.

Eventually, the "Führer" of the Bund, Fritz Kuhn, took the stage. He went on an anti-Roosevelt rant, calling the President "Rosenfeld" and his policies the "Jew Deal," as his superiors in Nazi Germany regularly did, and attacking the President for being part of the Bolshevik-Jewish conspiracy. Kuhn ended his speech by boasting about becoming, "America's Hitler."

In contrast to Kuhn and his movement, a series of influential Americans came forward to voice their support for the Child Refugee Bill. They included former President Hoover, former presidential candidate Alfred Landon, New York Governor Herbert Lehman, Cabinet members Harold Ickes, Frances Perkins, and Francis Biddle, comedian Joe E. Brown, entertainer Eddie Cantor, actress Helen Hayes, and actors Don Ameche and Henry Fonda.

Eddie Cantor tried to gain presidential support for the bill. "For generations to come," Cantor wrote to Roosevelt's secretary, "if these boys and girls were permitted entry into this country, they would look upon our leader as a saint—they would bless the name of Franklin D. Roosevelt."5

The bill had the support of the First Lady. In fact, Eleanor Roosevelt became one of the legislation's sponsors. In a mid-February press conference, she stated that the bill "seems to me the humanitarian thing to do."6

Did the President agree? In a telegram to his wife while vacationing on board the *USS Houston*, Roosevelt wrote, "It is all right for you to support the bill, but it is best for me to say nothing."7

In her memoirs *This I Remember*, Eleanor Roosevelt wrote, "Franklin frequently refrained from supporting causes in which he believed, because of political realities." The President's political realities in 1939 included a Neutrality Act inhibiting international action, a Europe about to explode, and the growing need to arm the British.

In *This I Remember*, Eleanor Roosevelt quoted her husband on his policies. "When I would protest, he would simply say: 'First things come first, and I can't alienate certain votes I need for measures that are more important at the moment by pushing any measure that would entail a fight.' "

In fact, Eleanor pushing for a cause and the President holding back his support was an old story, begun early in Roosevelt's first term. Back in 1933, a series of lynchings—twenty-eight in all—spread from South Carolina to California. On October 18, according to the *New York Times*, "a frenzied mob of 3,000 men, women and children . . . overpowered 50 state troopers" and removed a prisoner from his cell. Accused of attacking a white woman, George Armwood was stripped naked, tortured, and hanged. His body was then dragged "half a mile on Main Street to a blazing pile in the centre of the thoroughfare."[8]

Eleanor Roosevelt joined the anti-lynching movement. Alongside the NAACP, she campaigned vociferously for federal anti-lynching laws. Her crusade influenced Senator Robert Wagner, who proposed legislation. The Wagner-Costigan bill endeavored to hold local officials accountable for failure to protect its citizens. President Roosevelt refused to either speak out on lynching or endorse the bill. "I did not choose the tools with which I must work," he told Walter White, the president of the NAACP. "Had I been permitted to choose them I would have selected quite different ones. But I've got to get legislation passed by Congress to save America. The Southerners by reason of the seniority rule in Congress are chairmen or occupy strategic places on most of the Senate and House committees. If I come out for the anti-lynching bill, they will block every bill I ask Congress to pass to keep America from collapsing. I just can't take that risk."[9] Considering the coming years and such controversial legislation as the Wagner-Rogers Bill, these would be prophetic words.

The fight for the legislation began on April 20 when Subcommittees for the House and Senate Immigration Committees convened jointly. Through a letter, Secretary of State Cordell Hull expressed his opposition to the Child Refugee Bill. Providing twenty thousand German visas in addition to "an estimated 30,000 immigration visas now being issued annually in that country," Hull wrote, "will inevitably necessitate increased clerical personnel, unfamiliar with the law and regulations, as well as additional office accommodations." Below the surface, Hull's words were clear. The Child Refugee Bill presented a sharp departure from the quota system.

Senator Robert Wagner followed the reading of the Secretary's letter. In his many years in the Senate, Wagner had fought for predominantly liberal causes. A strong supporter of the New Deal, which earned him the nickname, the "Legislative Pilot of the New Deal," he helped to draft a series of acts, including the Social Security Act and the National Labor Relations Act. He also cosponsored the anti-lynching Costigan-Wagner Bill and in the 1940s, he became a staunch supporter of Zionism.

In his speech before the Subcommittees advocating for Wagner-Rogers, Wagner listed a set of essential points:

1. The idea for the legislation was a product of prominent Catholic and Protestant clergymen.
2. The Quakers and other organizations had raised finances to support the legislation in full.
3. The spontaneous support by thousands of American families had been tremendous, overpowering even.
4. Other nations had already offered sanctuary to German children. (In fact, the United States dragged behind other nations in bringing in German children following *Kristallnacht*. The Dutch received two thousand German Jewish children. Belgium received one thousand, five hundred. England received nine thousand. Sweden received two hundred and fifty. The United States received two hundred and forty.)
5. The admission of twenty thousand children could be of little economic consequence to a nation of 130 million. Even organized labor had come out in support of the bill.
6. Many of the youngsters added would not be Jewish, an important point considering the essential prejudice of the Congress and the country.

Following Wagner, a series of hostile witnesses came forward. Mrs. Agnes Waters, representing the Widows of World War I

Veterans, said, "I am the daughter of generations of patriots. This nation will be helpless to guarantee to our children their rights, under the Constitution, to life, liberty, and the pursuit of happiness if this country is to become the dumping ground for the persecuted minorities of Europe."

An opinion poll taken in April 1939 asked, "If you were a member of Congress would you vote 'yes' or 'no' on a bill to open the doors of the United States to a larger number of European refugees than now admitted under our immigration quotas?" Eighty-three percent of those polled answered in the negative.

"The refugees have a heritage of hate," Mrs. Agnes Waters continued. "They could never become loyal Americans." But couldn't the same sort of rhetoric be heard in Nazi Germany? How different was the Nazis' "Aryan race" from Mrs. Waters' verbiage?

Next came Francis Kinnicutt, who represented the Allied Patriotic Society (thirty organizations united to press for and preserve patriotism). "This is just part of a drive to break down the whole quota system—to go back to the condition when we were flooded with foreigners who tried to run the country on different lines from those laid down by the old stock," he said. "Strictly speaking, it is not a refugee bill at all, for by the nature of the case most of those admitted would be of the Jewish race." According to the Quakers' Clarence Pickett and Senator Wagner, 31 percent of the children were non-Jewish.

Next came Colonel John Taylor, the main lobbyist for the American Legion. Not only did Taylor voice his opposition to Wagner-Rogers, but he threw his loyalty to the Reynolds Bill. That legislation, echoing the virulent isolationism of its sponsor, Senator Robert Reynolds of North Carolina, called for the abolition of all immigration to the United States for ten years. "If this bill passes," Colonel Taylor warned, referring to Wagner-Rogers, "there is no reason why we should not also bring in twenty thousand Chinese children. Certainly they are being persecuted too."

The Reynolds Bill was not the only anti-immigration legislation introduced in the immediacy of Wagner-Rogers. In fact, some sixty pieces of legislation were proposed. One of them, sponsored by Representative Stephen Pace of Georgia, suggested that "every

Alien in the United States shall be forthwith deported."

The line of hostile witnesses continued with John Trevor, the head of the American Coalition of Patriotic Societies. He rebuked the Child Refugee Bill by arguing that the nation contained "a mountain million of neglected boys and girls, descendants of American pioneers, undernourished, ragged and ill." Trevor called for protests "to protect the youth of America from this foreign invasion."

In a private conversation, Mrs. Laura Delano Houghteling, wife of the Commissioner of Immigration and cousin of the President, claimed the trouble with the Wagner-Rogers Bill was that "20,000 children would all too soon grow up into 20,000 ugly adults."

Such rhetoric reflected the isolationists' central theme: fear. Fear of Jews. Fear of immigrants. Fear that the inclusion of 20,000 German children might eventually mean the inclusion of those children's parents. Fear that the passage of the bill might undermine the entire immigration system. Or in the words of Congressman Leonard Allen of Louisiana, "fear of the hordes."

The Subcommittees adjourned on April 24, 1939. A second round of hearings was due to commence on May 24. In that month both sides of the legislation went on publicity campaigns. Those against the bill argued on patriotic grounds. Congressman Martin Dies of Texas (the first Chairman of the House Un-American Activities Committee) pushed for a series of bills aimed at easing the deportation procedures. Senator Robert Reynolds played the espionage card. In the event of a war, he claimed, today's German immigrants would become tomorrow's spies. "The danger is from within," he declared in an address to the American Defense Society. Americans were "asleep at the switch" and should beware of "certain minorities."

In the audience that day, the German-American Bund leader Fritz Kuhn responded enthusiastically. Asked about the Senator's speech, he replied, "I liked it very much. I would underline everything."

Those for the Child Refugee Bill argued its political merit. Frank P. Graham, the President of the University of North Carolina, lobbied southern Congressmen, hoping to win a few votes and give the impression of nationwide support. Dr. Henry Smith Leiper, Secretary of the Federal Council of Churches, suggested that refugees stimulated economic development. Industries that had never before been to American shores suddenly developed with the inclusion of foreigners, he asserted. According to a British study, eleven thousand refugees created fifteen thousand new jobs. The Quakers published a booklet entitled *Refugee Facts*. According to their statistics: from July 1, 1932 to July 1, 1938, a total of 241,962 immigrants entered the United States. During those same six years, 246,000 persons departed. A net loss of over four thousand.

The American Legion countered these arguments by making a case for family values. According to traditional American policy, Colonel Taylor asserted, "home life should be preserved" and Wagner-Rogers proposed "breaking up of families. . . ." Did the American Legion understand that the alternative to bringing German children to freedom was Dachau?

The second round of Congressional hearings commenced at the end of May (as the *SS St. Louis* approached the port city of Havana). The antagonism began immediately, as Congressman Leonard Allen grilled Joe E. Brown. Would the entertainer personally adopt a child? the Congressman asked. Brown responded that he and his wife had already adopted two baby girls, and a Serbian boy had been living with them for years. Rather than mollify the Congressman, Brown's statement provoked him further. "Would the gentleman advocate bringing the hordes of Europe here when the record shows we have thousands of poor people in this country who are in want?" he thundered.

That led, yet again, to hostile witnesses testifying against the legislation. James Wilmeth of the Junior Order United American Mechanics took an isolationist's position. "We are afraid to lift the quota . . . ," he said. "We don't know where it will end."

Representative John Z. Anderson of California argued the "Charity begins at home" theme, claiming there were a "million and a half people wandering around our own country at the present time without shelter, without necessary food, without proper clothing." The fact that Americans offered homes to foreign children when American children were in need struck Representative Anderson as "a rather sad commentary on our country."

Representative Edward Rees of Kansas echoed Anderson's theme and wondered how America's poor would feel if the country admitted 20,000 refugee children. What message, Rees asked, would that send to the "hundreds of thousands of these children and parents of these children that don't have just even a meager supply of food, shelter, and clothing"?

At this point in the proceedings, Representative William Poage of Texas presented a compromise. Each of the refugee children would be issued a temporary visitor's visa, valid until six months after the child's twenty-first birthday. Upon reaching the age of twenty-one, the refugee could then apply for citizenship and receive preference under the German quota.

The Poage compromise did not generate significant support. As the second round of hearings began to wane, the Wagner-Rogers Bill appeared on the verge of collapse. Those who supported the bill tried one last campaign. The Quakers' Clarence Pickett described eyewitness accounts of Nazi atrocities. Frank P. Graham argued that the Child Refugee Bill was consistent with the American tradition of providing a haven for religious and political refugees. "This is the form of our government," New York Congressman Samuel Dickstein, the Chairman of the House Immigration Committee, replied to Graham, "but as a matter of fact, we have never done the things we preach. So far, during my time here, I do not think we have done that. We talked about it."

Only a vigorous campaign by the President might have saved the bill. Congresswoman Caroline O'Day of New York, in fact, wrote a letter to Roosevelt, asking for assistance. The President's attention, however, was focused on defense. Publicly, he sought half a billion dollars to construct Naval bases and to expand the Air Corps, which he prophesized would win the next war. Secretly, he was in the midst of finding a way to arm the British and the French with aircraft and ships. Eventually, his agenda led to the sale of fifty over-age U.S. destroyers to the British in exchange for British military bases in the Americas (September 1940). That sale generated condemnation both within an isolationist-minded

Congress and an under-equipped military. Roosevelt, however, knew he had to keep Britain afloat.

At the same time that he pressed for the destroyer deal, Roosevelt knew that he had to build up America's Armed Forces. This led to the unpopular Selective Service Act. In the general election of 1940 Republican nominee Wendell Willkie called the President "a War Monger" and charged that if Roosevelt won reelection, America would be at war by April 1941. Roosevelt countered with the words, "I hate war." Again, Roosevelt was willing to go against the grain of American isolationism. Yes, he took a step back and did not push for the Selective Service Act, which passed in the House by a single vote, 203 to 202. Yes, he compromised and agreed to limit a draftee's period of service to one year. But in an America adamant on maintaining its neutrality, Roosevelt pushed as far as he thought he could.

Would a similar endorsement have paid off with the Child Refugee Bill? Could Roosevelt have found a way to support both his war aims and this humanitarian effort? He suggested an answer with a note scribbled in the margin of Congresswoman O'Day's letter. "File. No Action," he wrote.

On June 30, the Senate Immigration Committee amended Wagner-Rogers. The 20,000 children would be given preference within the German quota. Senator Wagner responded to that amendment with outrage and frustration, judging the bill "wholly unacceptable." Permitting the entry of twenty thousand children would sign the death warrants for twenty thousand adults. "The proposed change would in effect convert the measure from a humane proposal to help children who are in acute distress to a proposal with needlessly cruel consequences for adults in Germany who are in need of succor . . . ," Wagner said. The Senator withdrew the bill before a floor vote could take place.

A year later, on August 27, 1940, Congress passed the Hennings Bill. The legislation, named after Congressman Thomas Hennings of Missouri, permitted the evacuation of children from Britain who were endangered by Nazi air raids. To my knowledge, none of those children were Jewish.

Chapter 15

◄ ►

"With a Determined Resolve"

In the spring of 1940 an American code clerk named Tyler Kent was caught turning American-British diplomatic correspondence, including Roosevelt-Churchill exchanges, over to Axis sympathizers. The information, relayed to the Nazi government, helped the Germans crack the American code. The effects on Roosevelt were considerable. "From this point on," historian Richard Breitman wrote, "FDR could hardly overemphasize the fifth column danger."[1] Roosevelt in fact appointed a point person on issues relating to national security. He chose Breckinridge Long.

A descendant of the notable Breckinridge family of Kentucky and the Long family of North Carolina, Breckinridge Long became acquainted with Franklin Roosevelt during the Presidency of Woodrow Wilson. Long, who was born in Missouri and active in local politics, became a Third Assistant Secretary of State. Roosevelt at the time served as Assistant Secretary of the Navy. The two men became friends. Later, during the election of 1932, Breckinridge Long made a sizable contribution to FDR's campaign. Also, at the Democratic Convention in Chicago, Long's work as a floor manager assisted FDR in his attempt to gain the Democratic nomination. Roosevelt, after winning the election, rewarded Long with an Ambassadorship in Italy. At first Long was in awe of the Fascisti of Italy. "Mussolini is an astounding character . . . ," he wrote. "The Fascisti in their black shirts are apparent in every community. They are dapper and well dressed and stand up straight and lend an atmosphere of individuality and importance to their surroundings."[2] Eventually, Long soured on the Fascisti, calling the movement, "deliberate, determined, obdurate, ruthless and vicious." But throughout his stay in Italy (1933 to 1936), he impressed the man in the White House. "I do not need to tell you how proud I am of the splendid record you made in Rome . . . ," Roosevelt wrote to Long. "You are a grand fellow—and you know my devotion to you. . . . After November [the election of 1936] I shall want you again to be part of the Administration."[3] That promotion came after Germany invaded Poland in September of 1939. Roosevelt asked Long to serve as Special Assistant Secretary of State. In January of 1940 Roosevelt promoted Long to Assistant Secretary of State. In that policy-making position, Long oversaw twenty-three of the forty-two divisions, including passports and visas.

In June 1940, Breckinridge Long formulated a new visa policy. In a memorandum distributed within the State Department he wrote, "We can delay and effectively stop for a temporary period of indefinite length the number of immigrants into the United States. We could do this by simply advising our Consuls to put every obstacle in the way to require additional evidence and to resort to various administrative advices which would postpone and postpone and postpone the granting of the visas." Long's policy decisions were sent to diplomatic and Consular officers on June 29. A terse but satisfied Long wrote in his diary, "The cables practically stopping immigration went!"

The new policy, for Europeans, created a sense of desperation. "Our future had come to depend on three new guidelines," the Berlin-born journalist Peter Wyden wrote, " 'The quota'—the total number of German refugees permitted to enter the United States under the miserly immigration laws; 'the affidavit'—the document from an obscure umpteenth cousin . . . guaranteeing that he would support us if we became destitute; and 'the visa'—which would be our stamped admission ticket into the promised land."[4]

And so immigration to the United States during Breckinridge Long's tenure, already significantly below legal limits even before his appointment, underwent a drastic reduction. For example, the

German-Austrian quota in the years 1939 and 1940 basically had its allocation filled. In 1941, immigration dropped below 50 percent of the legal limit. In 1942, immigration dropped below 18 percent of the legal limit. From 1943 to the end of the war, immigration dropped below 5 percent.[5]

President Roosevelt, according to Breckinridge Long, supported the policy. "The whole subject of immigration, visas, safety of the United States, procedure to be followed; and all that sort of thing was on the table," Long wrote in his diary following a meeting with the President on October 3, 1940. "I found that he was 100% in accord with my ideas." Roosevelt even complimented Long's service. "Good job, Breck," the President commended.

What motivated Long to pursue his policies of immigration reduction? He seemed to suffer from a kind of paranoia. He saw enemies in a multiplicity of places. That included, as he wrote, "my colleagues in the Government." David Wyman wrote, "Long was certain that some of them disliked him intensely, interfered with his work, and conspired against him." That led to Long's declaring that he bore "the brunt of the worst attack made against *any* officer in this Government."

Long wrote that he was also under attack from "the Communists, extreme radicals, Jewish professional agitators, refugee enthusiasts" as well as "the radical press" and "Jewish radical circles." He claimed, "They all hate me."

Regarding refugees, Breckinridge Long was an extreme nativist. In his diary, Long wrote that immigrants, particularly from Eastern Europe, were "lawless, scheming, defiant—and in many ways unassimilable."

"Hostile to foreigners and particularly Jewish refugees," Henry Morgenthau, the son of the Treasury Secretary, wrote, "Long, in the name of national security, seemed to be doing everything he could to impede immigration of all kinds."[6] Breckinridge Long saw himself as the first line of defense against Fifth Columnists. Unquestionably, he believed that such spies and saboteurs infiltrated the ranks of refugees. And so his view of protecting the country left him with one option: to do everything in his power to severely tighten the flow of immigration. Had Secretary of State

Cordell Hull, or President Roosevelt, placed a priority on the Jews of Europe, Long's attitudes might have been mitigated. Certainly the threat of saboteurs is one every nation at war recognizes. Without supervision, however, Long's mind-set and tendencies had free range.

In the same month that Breckinridge Long was reconceptualizing immigration policy and implementing his "postpone and postpone and postpone" tactics, a conference took place at the Commodore Hotel in New York. Two hundred guests gathered to discuss the refugee crisis in France. For the nations fighting Hitler, June of 1940 was a tumultuous time. The British, driven to Dunkirk and the edge of the continent by the Germans, were rescued by an extraordinary endeavor. Destroyers, cargo and fishing boats, yachts, ferries, motorboats, and tugs answered a general call throughout Britain for ships, no matter the size. The unusual flotilla spent days transporting troops across the Channel. In all, the evacuation included 212,000 British soldiers, 113,000 French soldiers, and 13,000 wounded.

Meanwhile, the situation in France was deteriorating. On June 9 the government fled Paris. On June 15 the *New York Times* printed the headline, "Germans Occupy Paris." The undertitle read, "Reich Tanks Clank in the Champs-Elysee." A week later, the French agreed to an unconditional surrender. Article 19 of the agreement declared: "The French government is obliged to surrender on demand all Germans named by the German Government in France as well as in French possessions, colonies, protectorate territories and mandates."

The implications were clear: hundreds, if not thousands, of political refugees who had fled Germany for France during the rise of the Nazi Reich were suddenly in horrific danger. Many of those refugees, after the Nazis carved up France, creating an occupied zone in the north and a French-led government in the south, fled to the ports of the Mediterranean.

During the conference at the Commodore, eloquent speakers, from radio commentator Raymond Gram Swing to German theologian Reinhold Niebuhr to Erika Mann, the daughter of exiled

German author Thomas Mann, spoke on the plight of the refugees. From these roots an organization called the "Emergency Rescue Committee" (ERC) arose. In the course of the one-day conference, the ERC raised 3,500 dollars. Erika Mann, however, warned the audience, "We musn't forget that money alone is not going to rescue those people. Most of them are trapped without visas, without passports that they dare use. They can't just get on a boat and leave. Somebody has to be there who can get them out."[7]

Only one man volunteered for the job. His name was Varian Fry. To Paul Hagen, one of the ERC's organizers, Fry wasn't qualified. Rescuing refugees called for "someone who was tough and nerveless, clear thinking under pressure, adaptable to illegality and those who commonly practiced it." Fry was a 32-year-old journalist, an idealist, an intellectual with a degree in the classics from Harvard.

Why did Fry take on this daunting task? There were sentimental reasons. Among the refugees stuck in France were many famous writers and authors. "For some of these men," Fry wrote, "although I knew them only through their work, I had a deep love; and to them all I owed a heavy debt of gratitude for the pleasure they had given me. Now that they were in danger, I felt obliged to help them, if I could; just as they, without knowing it, had often in the past helped me."[8]

There were also Fry's political convictions. "Most of all," Fry wrote, "it was a feeling of sympathy for the German and Austrian Socialist Parties which led me to go to France in the summer of 1940, a sympathy born of long familiarity with their principles and their works. . . . I had not always agreed with their ideas or their methods, but I knew . . . that their hearts were in the right place."

There was also Fry's first-hand knowledge of what Nazi brutality meant. At age twenty-seven, Fry witnessed the Brownshirts raiding Berlin's *Kurfürstendamm* and battering anyone who looked Jewish. One moment would haunt Varian Fry for the rest of his life. In a café sat a man, clearly Jewish, trying to blend in to the scene. When two Brownshirts approached, the man, trying to act like a regular customer, reached for his beer. Suddenly one of the Germans flaunted a knife. In a swift strike, the Nazi nailed the man's hand to the table. And the two Brownshirts laughed.

A day later Varian Fry, so disgusted by the scene, asked for and received permission to speak to the Nazi in charge of the Foreign Press. That man's name was Ernst Hanfstängl. During the interview, Hanfstängl identified a group of Jews who had jeered at a pro-Nazi movie. Their hissing, according to Hanfstängl, set off the storm of brutality that flowed on to the *Kurfürstendamm*. Hanfstängl then went on to talk about the struggle within the Nazi Party. On the Jewish issue, there were the moderates and there were the radicals.

What did the radicals (including Hitler and Goebbels) want to do with the Jews? Fry asked. Exterminate them, Hanfstängl answered matter-of-factly. Hanfstängl saw himself as a civilizing influence on the volatile Hitler. In that, he underestimated his boss's capacity for evil (as did the entire world).

Varian Fry arrived in Marseilles in August 1940. Along with $30,000 with which to support his cause, Fry carried the list of some two hundred refugees identified by the ERC, many of them artists, writers, and scientists. The list included the writer Heinrich Mann, the brother of Thomas Mann and an outspoken critic of Nazism. Mann, whose books were scorched during the book-burnings of 1933, was the first prominent German to be stripped of his citizenship. The list included Lion Feuchtwanger, who blasted the Nazis in his historical novel, *The Oppermans*. The list included Franz Werfel, whose best-selling novel, *The Forty Days of Musa Dagh*, denounced the Nazi movement. All of these men were living under a death sentence.

Fry had access to emergency visas. Two months earlier, delegates of the ERC had met with Eleanor Roosevelt and explained their mission. In their presence, she phoned the President. For twenty minutes, she tried to convince her husband to grant visas to those on the ERC's list. When she couldn't produce that result, she ended the conversation with a threat. "If Washington refuses to authorize these visas immediately," Eleanor Roosevelt said, "German and American émigré leaders with the help of their American friends will rent a ship, and in this ship will bring as many of the endangered refugees as possible across the Atlantic.

If necessary the ship will cruise up and down the East Coast until the American people, out of shame and anger, force the President and the Congress to permit these victims of political persecution to land." Within a month President Roosevelt authorized emergency visas for prominent foreigners.

In France, Fry had three goals to carry out, according to the job description composed by the ERC. He "was to prepare a full report on the conditions affecting the refugees." He "was to try to find the people on his list and help them get to Lisbon and Casablanca, so they could more easily find their way to the United States." Finally, he "was to find and designate individuals who could in the future act as agents for the Emergency Rescue Committee." Fry thought his mission would last three weeks. He stayed thirteen months.

At first, Fry sought out the names on his list. But he quickly realized that multitudes were in need of aid. Using a room in the Hotel Splendide as his base, Fry put out the word that he could be of service to refugees. Long lines formed immediately. Desperate people gathered on the stairwell. "Most of the refugees were eager to get away," Fry wrote in his memoirs. "I sat in my little room on the back of the fourth floor of the Hotel Splendide and they came to me. I gave them money and advice and tried to give them hope. Those who already had visas I instructed how to cross the frontier [into Spain and eventually on to Portugal]. When they were ready to leave, I shook their hands, and said, 'I'll see you in New York.' Many of them were incredulous, hardly daring to hope. But that short sentence, spoken with conviction, seemed to do more than anything else to restore their faith in the future. If the American is so sure he will see us soon in New York, they must have thought, then maybe there is some hope."

Fry hired a series of people—mainly inexperienced relief workers, wealthy socialites, a student or two, and the refugees themselves —to aid in his endeavors. Together, they did the extraordinary: engaging black-marketers to forge papers, organizing a network of smugglers, setting up escape routes both by land and sea, and, on many occasions, guiding refugees across the mountains. "The crossing cost a minimum of $5,000 per person," a member of Fry's team later recalled. "And you must imagine how difficult it was, in a city full of informers, patrolled by the Vichy police. . . . It was dangerous."[9]

Varian Fry was constantly under surveillance. Both the Gestapo and the Vichy police wanted to arrest him. The ERC thought he'd overstepped his duties and wanted to recall him. The American Consulate wanted to deport him. The State Department continuously tightened visa applications while ignoring Fry's requests for assistance, terming Fry's frequent appeals "more Fryanna." To Fry, the Americans seemed as heartless and anti-Semitic as Vichy and the Germans. He called the State Department "America's open scandal."[10]

Still, he went about his business outwardly unfazed. He raised money from various sources, including the heiress Peggy Guggenheim, the movie studio Metro-Goldwyn-Mayer, the American Book of the Month Club. He distributed funds to countless refugees to keep them afloat. He provided a sense of optimism to the seemingly stranded refugees. And he saved lives. In the case of artist Marc Chagall, for instance, the Vichy police arrested him at his hotel on April 9, 1941. While her husband was being taken to jail, Chagall's wife called Fry in a panic. Fry then phoned the police precinct. In an icy tone he said to the officer in charge, "Do you know that Monsieur Chagall is one of the world's greatest living artists? If, by any chance, news of his arrest should leak out, the whole world would be shocked, Vichy would be gravely embarrassed and you would probably be severely reprimanded." Fry then threatened to report the incident to the *New York Times* if Chagall continued to be imprisoned. A half-hour after the conversation, Vichy released the artist.

Fry also received help from surprising sources. In the case of Lion Feuchtwanger, the Vichy police arrested him in the summer of 1940. He'd then been interned at a concentration camp near Nimes. An American Consulate worker named Myles Standish drove to the camp in a red Chevrolet belonging to his boss Harry Bingham, the American Vice-Consul in Charge of Visas. Standish met Feuchtwanger at the swimming area (where the prisoners were permitted to exercise), quickly produced some women's clothing, and with the writer disguised as Standish's mother-in-law, drove to Bingham's villa outside of Marseilles. Feuchtwanger lived there until he escaped Vichy France.

Harry Bingham, who behind the scene masterminded the Feuchtwanger rescue, "went out of his way and took a personal risk and a personal initiative to help refugees." In addition to Feuchtwanger, for instance, Bingham secretly sheltered Thomas Mann's children at his villa. The State Department reacted to Bingham's tactics by transferring him to Buenos Aires.

Throughout Fry's stay in France, the State Department plotted against him. Outwardly, State claimed that Fry was in danger. The position was summarized by Assistant Secretary of State Adolf Berle. Fry "has got to get home as soon as he can. . . . I should not be surprised to find that he . . . is now in considerable danger of arrest." Covertly, the Department worked to revoke Fry's visitor visa while applying pressure on the ERC to recall their envoy. Fry continued to stay. His reasoning was heroic. "I must stay as long as I can," he thought to himself, "even if it means saving only one more human being." He stayed until the late summer of 1941, and only under the deportation orders of the Gestapo and the Vichy police did Fry leave Marseilles.

How many refugees did Varian Fry and his group rescue? Varian Fry, who never had the time to count actual cases, estimated that he reviewed the files of 15,000 refugees. In all, he was able to financially aid some 4,000 people. Between 1,200 to 1,800 of these refugees found their way to safety.

As for the fear of Fifth Columnists, Fry wrote, none of those who made their way to America "has ever had his loyalty questioned. All of them know, perhaps even better than we, the true value of democracy. For they once lost it, and only after much suffering found it again."

In 1940, as Varian Fry arrived in Marseilles to begin his rescue operation, another was taking place many miles to the east. Thousands of Jews had congregated outside the Japanese Consulate in Kaunas (Kovno), Lithuania. Word had spread. Japanese Consul-General Chiune Sugihara was issuing transit visas. With that documentation, a Jewish refugee could obtain a Soviet exit visa and travel across the length of the Soviet Union to freedom in Japan. Consul Sugihara, in fact, wasn't just issuing transit visas; he was writing them by hand. He began on July 9, as the Soviet army, in a grab for territory, invaded the Baltic states. By July 29, he had issued sixty-eight handwritten visas. By August 14, he'd written 1,711 visas. By August 24, the total reached 2,135. He wrote visas into September. According to his wife, Yukiko, Sugihara wrote visas even after permanently closing the Consulate. He wrote them from his hotel room. He wrote them in the train station, as his family awaited transportation to his new posting in Berlin. He wrote them from the train window as the train pulled away.

A year earlier, the Kaunas Jewish population totaled 30,000. When Germany invaded Poland on September 1, that number drastically increased. Waves and waves of Polish Jews streamed into Lithuania. The country's Jewish population swelled to over a quarter of a million. Meanwhile, the Molotov-Ribbentrop Nonaggression Pact between the Soviets and the Germans seemed to initiate a peace. The Jews in Lithuania apparently had found a haven.

That lasted less than a year. The Molotov-Ribbentrop agreement (actually signed on August 20, 1939, before Germany invaded Poland) secretly carved up Eastern Europe. Poland and Rumania would become German territory. The Baltic states, Lithuania included, would fall under the domain of the Soviets. In July 1940 the Soviets invaded Lithuania. The Jews were caught in a vise, between two horrific anti-Semitic forces: the Nazis and the Soviets.

Once in control of Lithuania, the Soviet Union closed all foreign Consulates, as Moscow became the center of operations. Only two Consuls kept their offices open in Kaunas: Chiune Sugihara and Jan Zwartendijk, the Dutch Consul.

Crowds of frantic Jews suddenly appeared at the Japanese Consulate. "Men with desperate eyes continued trying to climb over fences," Yukiko Sugihara wrote in her memoirs. "They overtook the maid as she tried to go out of the gate to go shopping for food. They were desperately trying to get access into the Consulate to speak with Chiune."[11]

Chiune Sugihara decided to meet with five Jewish representatives. Consul Zwartendijk also attended the meeting. For two hours, the Jewish representatives told their harrowing stories, from escaping the Nazis in Poland to crossing the border to fearing now both the Soviets and the Nazis. Sugihara listened. He might not have known then about the terror the Jews related, but he knew about Soviet and German troop movement. Chiune Sugihara, in fact, was a spy for the Japanese Empire. An expert on Russia, he had been strategically placed in between Moscow and Berlin to uncover military secrets on each.

At the end of the meeting the Jewish representative said, "We came here because we heard that we might be able to get transit visas from the Japanese Consulate. We are asking you to issue us visas." And indeed Consul Sugihara had issued a few transit visas up to this point, mainly to wealthy Jews.

At the meeting Consul Zwartendijk claimed he could issue entry visas into Curacao, a Dutch territory in the Caribbean. To get to Curacao, however, the refugees needed transit visas through the Soviet Union. Consul Sugihara asked himself a difficult question: Should he issue these visas? "That night was one of the most upsetting of Chiune's life," Yukiko wrote in her memoirs. "With the heavy burden that lay before him—should he or should he not issue the visas—it was impossible for Chiune to sleep. I knew . . . because I heard the unceasing sound of his bed squeaking. He tossed and turned, while contemplating the situation and thinking about the decision he had to make. It was a long and sleepless night for both of us."

He wasn't the only one losing sleep. The Jews "all seemed very tired and exhausted," Consul Sugihara later commented. "I did not know whether they had any place to sleep in Kovno in those days, maybe they just slept in the station or on the street."[12]

Sugihara decided to consult with his government. He cabled his superiors three times for permission to issue entry visas into Japan. In one cable he wrote, "Hundreds of Jewish people have come to the Consulate here in Kaunas seeking transit visas. They are suffering extremely. As a fellow human being, I cannot refuse their requests. Please permit me to issue visas to them."[13] Each time he was denied. Sugihara and his wife Yukiko decided to disobey their government's orders. "We knew—and it was insupportable—that they were killing the Jews, and the massacres were going on and on!" Yukiko remembered. "So we gave out the visas on our own authority. All of August, my husband never stopped giving out visas. Right up to the time the Russians ordered us to close the Consulate. When we had to go, I remember, there were still twelve people standing in the street: they had a lost look, completely bewildered, and we could do nothing more for them. It was heartrending."

With a Curacao stamp as an entry visa and a Japanese transit visa, a Jewish refugee became eligible for a Soviet exit visa. Why were the Soviets issuing such documentation? Money. The Joint Distribution Committee paid the costs of travel. (In addition to the visas themselves, the train trip across the Soviet Union cost about $200.)

Chiune Sugihara promised the refugees outside his door that he'd issue visas for each and every one of them. His goal was to write three hundred visas a day. "Each day's work left him drained and exhausted," Yukiko wrote in her memoirs. "Each visa was a lengthy document, comparable to writing two or three paragraphs. After a long day, he went straight to bed. As he fell asleep, I massaged his arm, which was stiff and cramped from writing. Throughout this ordeal he continued his routine of rising early in the morning. Many people stood outside the Consulate from morning until night waiting for visas. It was freezing at night, but many people slept in the adjacent park to ensure a spot near the front of the line. Chiune continued to write out visas with a determined resolve. . . ."

The refugees used the visas to travel by train to Moscow and then by Trans-Siberian Railroad to Vladivostok. From there, the refugees went to Kobe, Japan. Some 1,400 refugees made the trip to Curacao. After Pearl Harbor, those in Kobe were sent to Shanghai.

How many Jewish refugees did Sugihara save? The exact numbers aren't known. His wife believed that he simply lost count during the writing fury. Consul Sugihara suggested that he wrote some

3,500 visas. That number was corroborated by the Joint Distribution Committee representative in Lithuania. However, a family needed only one visa, so far more than 3,500 people might have been a part of Sugihara's rescue scheme.

One fact is clear: Consul Sugihara continued to write visas after he left Kaunas. He wrote them from Berlin. He wrote them from Prague (after another transfer). From September 1940 to the end of February 1941, Sugihara wrote sixty-nine transit visas to German Jews.

Why did Sugihara respond so heroically? He wrote in an unpublished memoir that he "just acted according to [his] sense of human justice, out of love for mankind." His son commented, "You know, there were these thousands of people cramped around the Consulate begging someone to give them visas. . . . Whatever they were, Jews or non-Jews, he had to help them in some way. I am sure that would have been his answer. Jews, in our eyes, what are they? Just strangers. That is to say: people who aren't Japanese. Jews, Christians, for us it is all the same thing. . . ." Yukiko Sugihara based her husband's actions on his "strong moral convictions." In her memoirs, she recalled his reasoning in his own words. "'I have to do something,'" Chiune Sugihara told his wife. "'A young man comes into my home for protection. Is he dangerous? No. Is he a spy? No. Is he a traitor? No. He's just a Jewish teenager who wants to live.'" The choice was clear. "'I may have to disobey my government,'" Chiune Sugihara told his wife, "'but if I don't, I will be disobeying God.'"[14]

After the war, after returning home to Japan, Chiune Sugihara was dismissed from the foreign ministry. His decision to disobey his government and issue the visas ended his career. In the years that followed, he tried to support his family through a series of odd jobs. For instance, in 1951 he worked in the Ponve Department store, a Jewish-owned store in Tokyo. A colleague of his remembered Sugihara as "dour and depressed" at that time. "A difficult man to approach," the colleague continued, "he felt himself above others but had lost face."[15] He died in 1986, essentially forgotten for his courage and bravery during the war years. Only posthumously has the name Sugihara gained distinction.

The same can be said for the name Varian Fry. After the war, Fry too bounced around. He returned to his trained vocation: journalism. However, he couldn't hold a job for either the *New Republic* or *Common Sense*. Later, he took a job teaching Latin in a high school in Connecticut. But by then, both of his marriages had ended. In 1967, Fry failed to show up for class and the school asked the police to investigate. A policeman found Fry dead in his bed. He died of a cerebral hemorrhage.

The name Varian Fry now is celebrated. Yad Vashem, the Holocaust Memorial Museum in Israel, recognizes Fry as the only American to have saved Jews during the Holocaust. As such, he is known as a "Righteous Among the Nations." The same can be said for Chiune Sugihara, the only Japanese with that honor.

As for Breckinridge Long, he resigned his government position on December 2, 1944. The next day he wrote in his journal, "So, I am out of office—and a free man again—free to rest a little, readjust my life and plan for the future at the age of 63 1/2. My record in the State Department speaks for itself. I am satisfied and happy. . . ." He returned home to Laurel, Maryland, and devoted the rest of his life to breeding racehorses. Breckinridge Long died in 1958.

Chapter 16

◄ ►

"The Crime of the Bureaucrats"

" A cheerful little station," prisoner Tadeusz Borowski once wrote about Auschwitz, "very much like any other provincial railway stop: a small square framed by tall chestnuts and paved with yellow gravel."[1] That railroad station, on March 26, 1942, saw its first wave of prisoners, nearly 1000 Jewish women from Slovakia. On April 2, a second wave of 965 Slovakian Jews arrived. On April 17, another 973. On April 19, another 464. In fact, 8,000 Slovakian Jews arrived in a single month.

On May 12, 1,500 Polish Jews from Sosnowiec arrived. Not one of these Jews was subjected to a selection on the train platform. Not one of these Jews was marked for a work camp. Not one of these Jews was stripped of hair or belongings. Not one of these Jews received an ill-fitting uniform or a number stamped onto a wrist. All of these Jews, instead, were transported to a building on the edge of the camp. There, they were gassed.

The trains continued to pull into the station, many of them originating from Western Europe. On July 17, 2000 Dutch Jews arrived. On July 19, 1000 Parisian Jews. On August 4, 1000 Belgian Jews. During the month of August, 30,000 Jews reached Auschwitz.

Early autumn saw the deportations increase and the gassing intensify. On September 23, 806 French Jews died. On September

25, another 481. On September 27, another 897. On September 29, another 685. The lists of deportations and deaths went on and on and on.

The Summer of 1942

Telegrams detailing Nazi atrocities arrived almost daily at the World Jewish Congress in Switzerland. Some of these telegrams described the relentless deportations throughout Western Europe to someplace east. Some of these telegrams described the movement and action of the *Einsatzgruppen* in Poland and Russia, murdering Jews in massive numbers. Some of these telegrams described the degrading conditions of the ghettos. All of these telegrams found their way to one man in particular, Gerhart Riegner, the representative of the Congress in Geneva.

Riegner struggled with an almost impossible task: maintaining contact with as many Jewish communities in Europe as possible. In Riegner's words, he was a "listening post." He recalled, "I felt I had to report the facts, and try to make suggestions. But the responsibility lay outside. Our freedom of information was limited. We were in the trap, albeit on a little island. But we had to do what we could do. . . ."[2]

In his position, Riegner had been receiving reports for many months. He passed on some of the information to his superiors in New York. In one letter dated October 27, 1941, he told of the "horror of deportation" from Germany and Czechoslovakia to Poland and of the terrible conditions within Poland itself. He wrote, "An eyewitness told me recently that there are currently 2,000 cases of typhus in the Warsaw ghetto."

The number of reports intensified during the summer of 1942. Their content pointed toward the Nazis' horrifying objective: the Final Solution. At the end of July, one message came from Dr. Arthur Sommer. "In the East," wrote Sommer, an economist working with the Nazis' Army High Command and a secret anti-Nazi, "camps are being prepared where all the Jews of Europe and a great part of the Russian prisoners-of-war will be exterminated by gas. Please relay this information immediately to Churchill and Roosevelt personally. If the BBC [British Broadcasting Company] comes out every day with a warning against lighting the gas ovens, then perhaps they may not be put into operation, for the criminals are doing everything to prevent the German people from finding out what they are planning to do and will certainly carry it out."

August of 1942 brought a deluge of reports to Riegner's office. He called the month a "great agony." In one report, the Polish government-in-exile (in London) detailed the massacre of 700,000 Jews since the German invasion three years earlier. Another report documented the first use of mobile gas vans, at Chelmno, in which carbon monoxide was used to asphyxiate 90 Jews at a time. In this manner, the Nazis exterminated 1000 Jews a day. Another report verified the suicide death of Adam Czerniakow, the Elder of Warsaw (the leader of the *Judenrat*, or Jewish council). Czerniakow killed himself rather than submit to the Gestapo the names of 100,000 Jews, all of whom would be sent east. Czerniakow realized "that the 100,000 would most probably be massacred."[3] In fact, the 100,000 became 250,000 and they all died at the death camp Treblinka. Another report told the story of Szmul Zygielbojm. A Polish Jew who had fought in the defense of Warsaw before escaping across the full expanse of the Third Reich to England, Zygielbojm went on the BBC and called for immediate action. "It will really be a shame to live on, a shame to belong to the human race, if means are not found at once to put an end to the greatest crime in human history," he announced. "The governments of Great Britain and America must be compelled to put an end to this mass murder. For if we do not try to find means of stopping it we shall bear part of the moral responsibility for what is happening."[4]

Szmul Zygielbojm couldn't have known it, but the British had knowledge of the mass murders at an early stage. Beginning in 1939 and escalating in 1940 and 1941, British intelligence services decoded the messages of the German police and the SS. For instance, according to a British report in 1941, a German police battalion "liquidated 1,059 Jews at or near Slavuta [Ukraine] on August 19–22." Another police battalion "participated in killing 367 Jews on August 23 and another 468 Jews the next day around Kowel [Ukraine].

The German police suffered no losses." On August 25, another police battalion killed 1,342 Jews in a "cleansing action," while the First SS Brigade shot 85 prisoners and 283 Jews."[5]

The British reaction was to seal away the reports under the warning "Most Secret" and "Never to Be Removed from This Office." Some fifty years later, the British government declassified the files.

Gerhart Riegner, of course, had no access to this information. He reacted to the grisly reports reaching his desk. His response was to search for more information, to seek corroborative evidence. Riegner recognized a fundamental flaw in his material. All of it derived from either Polish or Jewish sources. In order to convince the Allied governments of the Nazis' extermination campaign, Riegner realized that he needed a corroborating source within Nazi circles.

Gerhart Riegner was not a man of spontaneous action. He could have panicked. After all, here he was, tipped off to the greatest mass murder ever undertaken. In addition, he had personally witnessed Nazi brutality. In 1933, he had sat in a bath in the family home in Berlin, overwhelmed by terror. Outside, the Nazis shouted, "Jews out! Jews out!" The Riegner family soon moved to France. In 1942, Gerhart Riegner had every reason to react impulsively. He didn't. Gerhart Riegner was a thoughtful, thorough man.

On July 29, 1942, he received a phone call from a Jewish friend. A leading industrialist in Germany, a man with access to Hitler's inner circle, reported that Hitler had ordered the extermination of European Jewry. In the report, the industrialist identified the way in which the Jews would be eradicated: prussic acid, the lethal ingredient in Zyklon B gas.

Doubt crossed Riegner's mind at first. He and his friend "discussed it for five or six hours, walking along the lake shore. Did we have to take it seriously?" Riegner wondered. "Was it conceivable to kill millions of people? Was it credible?"[6]

Who was Riegner's informant? The industrialist, to protect his identity, remained anonymous and, for many years thereafter, the mystery went unsolved. Historians Richard Breitman and Walter

Laqueur eventually identified the man as Eduard Schulte. In *Breaking the Silence*, Breitman and Laqueur detailed Schulte's life. From the earliest days of the Nazi regime, Schulte believed that Germany was headed for self-destruction. When the war broke out, he began to pass on information to the Allies by traveling to Switzerland. He made numerous trips. After the Riegner episode, he continued to relay information. In May of 1943 he came in contact with Allen Dulles and the Office of Strategic Services (the precursor to the Central Intelligence Agency). As an OSS agent, his assignment was to outline conditions in Germany and make recommendations for postwar reconstruction. In December of 1943, Schulte learned from friends in German Military Intelligence that the Gestapo had begun to investigate him. He fled to Switzerland, where he remained for the duration of the war, working with Dulles in an effort to gather and analyze data.

After "the industrialist" gave him the information, Riegner, in his thorough manner, searched for verification. He found it in two ways, two details he later recalled which "gave a sense to the whole thing." First and foremost, he had Hitler's own words. On many occasions, Hitler had warned the world that the war would end with the annihilation of the Jews. And secondly, the pattern of deportations taking place all over Western Europe seemed to confirm the worst.

In a state of "great agitation," Riegner contacted the American Consulate in Geneva. There, he met with Vice-Consul Howard Elting, whose response to Riegner's report was, at first, incredulity. "When I mentioned that this report seemed fantastic to me," Elting later wrote, "Riegner said that it had struck him in the same way."[7]

Riegner asked Elting to send his report to the State Department and Rabbi Stephen Wise in New York. Elting sent the report to the State Department on August 8. He also included a personal note endorsing Riegner as "a serious and balanced individual." That same day, Riegner went to the British Consulate in Geneva. He asked that the same report be cabled to the Foreign Office and to Sydney Silverman, a Member of Parliament and Chairman of the British chapter of the World Jewish Congress. In the cable to the Foreign Office Riegner included an extra line not found in the State

Department telegram. The very last sentence read, "Please inform and consult New York." Meaning: send this cable to Rabbi Wise. Riegner's telegram to the State Department read:

> Received alarming report stating that in Führer's headquarters plan discussed and under consideration according to which all Jews in countries occupied or controlled by Germany numbering 3 1/2 four million should after deportation and concentration in east be exterminated at one blow to resolve once and for all the Jewish question in Europe stop action reported planned for autumn methods under discussion including prussic acid stop we transmit information with all necessary reservation as exactitude cannot be confirmed stop informant stated to have close connections with highest German authorities and his reports generally speaking reliable.

Within the British Foreign Office, a debate raged. How should the office handle the telegram? Finally, after nine days of internal squabble, the Foreign Office contacted Sydney Silverman, who immediately sent the cable to Rabbi Wise. Wise's first glance at the Riegner cable occurred on August 28. By then, the State Department had suppressed the cable for twenty days.

September

On September 2, Rabbi Wise cabled Riegner's telegram to Undersecretary of State Sumner Welles. Wise, of course, did not know that Welles had been in possession of the telegram for nearly a month. The two men met in Washington. Wise made two requests: that Riegner further substantiate the report, and that the State Department inform President Roosevelt. Welles made a request of his own: that the Rabbi not go public with the information, ostensibly to give the State Department time to confirm its veracity. As for informing the President, there's no evidence that Welles took that step.

Did Rabbi Wise anticipate this? On September 3, Rabbi Wise sent word to Supreme Court Justice Felix Frankfurter, suggesting he inform the President. Frankfurter did. "Most of the deportations of Jews were for forced labor rather than extermination," Roosevelt responded.[8]

Did Roosevelt believe his own rhetoric? "He must have known this to be untrue," Conrad Black wrote in *Champion of Freedom*, "and was either trying not to disconcert his old friend or was inexplicably reluctant to take the issue on fully."

Stephen Wise trusted Sumner Welles. In his autobiography, he wrote that the Undersecretary was "as always, deeply understanding and sympathetic."[9]

Although Rabbi Wise did not release the information to the public, he did "devise some means for countering the extermination plan." The Rabbi's plans included: forming a temporary committee of American Jewish leaders to try to help European Jewry; meeting with the President's Advisory Committee on Political Refugees (led by the sympathetic James McDonald); urging Myron Taylor, President Roosevelt's representative to the Vatican, to appeal to Pope Pius XII; and meeting with key, and like-minded, members of the Roosevelt Administration in order to obtain their support. Wise, through the autumn, met with Vice President Henry Wallace, Assistant Secretary of State Dean Acheson, and Interior Secretary Harold Ickes, among others.

Another report surfaced during a meeting of Wise's temporary committee. According to Isaac Sternbuch (the Agudath Israel World Organization's representative in Switzerland), 100,000 Jews within the Warsaw ghetto had already been murdered and "similar fate is awaiting the Jews deported to Poland from other occupied territories. Suppose that only energetic steps from America may stop these persecutions. Do whatever you can to cause an American reaction to halt these persecutions."[10]

The temporary committee sent a telegram to the State Department to check into Sternbuch's information. That led to a meeting between the committee and Sumner Welles, who promised an investigation. Confirming the Sternbuch report took less than a month.

Agudath's president in New York, Jacob Rosenheim, went beyond the State Department. He cabled Sternbuch's report to President Roosevelt. He also met with James McDonald, who had close ties to the First Lady. Neither Roosevelt nor his wife reacted publicly.

Meanwhile, Gerhart Riegner added two substantive reports to his earlier telegrams. In one document, a German informant, an officer attached to the high command of the Wehrmacht, claimed that there were factories processing Jewish corpses for the manufacture of soap, glue, and lubricants. Scientific studies had established the value of one corpse at 50 *Reichsmarks*. Another document contained two letters, written in code by Jews to pass through German censorship. The letters suggested that the Jews of the Warsaw ghetto were being deported to their deaths. The State Department squelched both reports.

Years later, in his memoirs, Riegner wrote, "Never did I feel so strongly the sense of abandonment, powerlessness and loneliness as when I sent messages of disaster and horror to the free world, and no one believed me."

Those same feelings afflicted an important Congressman on this side of the Atlantic. In his memoirs, Emanuel Celler of Brooklyn wrote, "It is difficult to describe the sense of helplessness and frustration which seized one when streams of letters poured in from constituents asking help for a sister, brother, mother, child caught up in the Nazi terror. . . ." And then Celler relayed a story. In response to the mass deportations from France to some place in the east, a rabbi came into Celler's office. "Trembling and enfeebled," Celler wrote, "he had traveled from Brooklyn to Washington to talk to his Congressman. Not once did he seem conscious of his tears as he pleaded. . . ." The rabbi beseeched his Congressman to do something. " 'Don't you see,' " Celler quoted the rabbi, " 'can't you see, won't you see that there are millions—millions—being killed? Can't we save some of them? Can't you, Mr. Congressman, do something?' "11

Celler responded by writing a letter to President Roosevelt, asking how to relieve the persecution and suffering of refugees. He also introduced legislation in Congress to ease quota restrictions. The Celler bill would have opened America's doors to refugees in France (who were, at that time, foremost in the news) so long as they could prove they were facing persecution at the hands of the Nazis or the Vichy regime.

The legislation went nowhere. The Chairman of the House Committee on Immigration and Naturalization, Samuel Dickstein promised to hold hearings on the bill, but only after mid-term elections. Those mid-term elections pushed a conservative Congress further to the right. The hearings were never held.

September ended with a speech from Adolf Hitler. ". . . If Jewry should plot another world war in order to exterminate the Aryan peoples of Europe, it would not be the Aryan peoples which would be exterminated, but Jewry. . . . At one time the Jews of Germany laughed about my prophecies. I do not know whether they are still laughing or whether they have already lost all desire to laugh. But right now I can only repeat: they will stop laughing everywhere, and I shall be right also in that prophecy."

October

On October 21, Congressman Celler received a response from the President. "You have raised a question in your letter that for some time has given me deep cause for thought," Roosevelt wrote.[12] The President then went on to list the actions the United States was currently involved in. They included: repeated protests against inhumane treatment; threatening judgment against both the general populace and the ringleaders after the war; a program caring for as many refugee children as possible; bringing to America as many refugee children as possible. "These are the positive actions which we are pursuing as diligently as we can," the President wrote.

And yet, evidence suggested otherwise. The State Department, for instance, described to the Congressman the near impossibility of aiding refugees. "We cannot," the State Department told Celler, "divert shipping for the transportation of war materials and troops for the refugees, and if we could, how could we reach them? How could they get to us? . . ."

The State Department led by Breckinridge Long routinely claimed that a lack of shipping curtailed effective rescue policy. "In

December 1941," Long summarized, "most neutral shipping disappeared from the seas. . . . There is just not any transportation."13

Was there truth to this statement? David Wyman, in *The
Abandonment of the Jews*, called the unavailability of shipping "a
fraud." He wrote, "When it was a matter of transporting Jews,
ships could almost never be found. This was not because shipping
was unavailable but because the Allies were unwilling to take the
Jews in."

According to Wyman, neutral ships crossed the Atlantic
throughout the war. Three Portuguese vessels made the trip every
six weeks. Another two dozen Portuguese and Spanish ships
crossed the Atlantic less frequently, but still routinely. In addition,
American troop ships and Lend-Lease ships could have carried
thousands of refugees across the Atlantic.

Personally, I saw many ships return to the United States during my duties at Gourock and other ports in Scotland. At first,
they went back with empty loads. Later, they carried the wounded.
Certainly, there was space for refugees. Those refugees, of course,
were not located in Great Britain. Did the troop ships landing in
Mediterranean ports have the same kind of room to transport
refugees back to the States? If Great Britain was any indication,
the answer was an unequivocal yes.

November

President Roosevelt opened the month by submitting legislation
to Congress. According to the Third War Powers Bill, the
President would have been given the power to suspend laws hindering "the free movement of persons, property and information
into and out of the United States." According to David Wyman,
Roosevelt submitted such legislation to "bypass the maze of complicated forms and procedures required by the tariff, customs,
and immigration laws." Those laws, in Wyman's estimation,
encumbered war production.

So why was the word "persons" written into the bill? That
single word instantly generated a commotion. Congressman Roy
Woodruff of Michigan believed the bill would "make the President

a virtual dictator." Congressman Harold Knutson of Minnesota declared, "As I read it, you throw the door wide open on immigration." The *Chicago Tribune* was mystified by the attempt "to flood this nation with refugee immigration from Europe and other nations."[14]

What was the President's objective? Was it strictly war-production related or was he also responding to the many reports of Nazi atrocities that must have crossed his desk? Was Roosevelt, in fact, trying to somehow circumvent immigration law?

In his diary, Breckinridge Long wrote, "The entire trouble and the cause of the whole opposition was simply because of the word 'persons'—for that meant immigration and that meant that the President *could* (but he would not) throw open the doors."[15] (Both the italics and the parentheses were his.) David Wyman agreed. He wrote that "Roosevelt had no intention whatever of using the proposed legislation to increase that trickle" of immigration.

That may be so. But the fact remains: Roosevelt added the word "persons." Why? Roosevelt had watched Congress take an intense anti-immigration stance repeatedly. In fact, he'd seen it on display a month earlier when Congressman Celler introduced his bill. And yet he added the word. Roosevelt believed that the best way to help the Jews of the Holocaust was to defeat Nazi Germany. He would not detract from the war effort. And yet he added the word. Roosevelt rarely addressed the massacre of European Jews. In his press conferences, for instance, his first words on the subject weren't spoken until November 5, 1943. And yet he added the word. Was this legislative effort his way of addressing the subject?

The question became one for the historians. The House Ways and Means Committee rejected the bill twenty-four to zero.

On November 24, Rabbi Wise met with Sumner Welles at the State Department. Rabbi Wise brought along his son, James Waterman Wise, a member of the World Jewish Congress. "We took our places," Rabbi Wise wrote of the meeting, "and I shall never forget the quiet but deeply moving way in which he [Welles] turned to us and said, every word etching itself into my heart, 'Gentlemen, I hold in my hands documents which have come to me from our legation in Berne. I regret to tell you, Dr. Wise, that these confirm and justify your deepest fears.'"[16]

The State Department, nearly four months after first receiving Gerhart Riegner's telegram, now authenticated it. "For reasons you will understand," Welles continued, "I cannot give these to the press, but there is no reason why you should not. It might even help if you did."

In the next few days, Wise held press conferences in Washington and New York. Using State Department intelligence, he revealed the horrible truth. Two million Jews had been killed in an extermination campaign. Only one hundred thousand of the nearly half a million Warsaw Jews remained alive. All of European Jewry was at risk.

The purpose in going public, Wise announced, was "to win the support of a Christian world so that its leaders may intervene and protest the horrible treatment of Jews in Hitler Europe." America's response, according to Rabbi Wise, was "what might have been expected. There was general horror throughout the country, wherever the press dispatches carried, and heartbreak everywhere in American Jewry."

The State Department assumed a policy of detachment. When questioned by the press, the Department offered neither confirmation nor further information. As for Rabbi Wise, the State Department only offered that he had "visited the Department in connection with certain material in which he was interested" and that the information Wise received was "told to the press in confidence and not for publication."[17] The man in charge of Jewish affairs for the European Division of the State Department, R. Borden Reams, even pressured Wise to "avoid any implication that the State Department was the source of documentary proof of these stories." Rabbi Wise did not abide by this pressure.

December

"Dear Boss," Rabbi Wise addressed Franklin Roosevelt in a letter, using his favorite familiar term for the President, "I do not wish to add an atom to the awful burden which you are bearing with magic and, as I believe, heaven-inspired strength at this time. But you do know that the most overwhelming disaster of Jewish history has befallen Jews in the form of the Hitler mass massacre." Wise called it an "indisputable" massacre. "It would be gravely misunderstood," Wise continued, "if, despite your overwhelming preoccupation, you did not make it possible to receive our delegation and to utter what I am sure will be your heartening and consoling reply." Wise concluded, "As your old friend, I beg you will somehow arrange to do this." The letter was dated December 2. That same day, a worldwide observation took place. From America to Western Europe to Auschwitz to Palestine, Jewish people recognized a day of mourning.

Roosevelt did not disappoint Rabbi Wise. At noon on December 8, a half-hour meeting took place between Roosevelt and the Jewish temporary committee. Roosevelt began by launching "into a semihumorous story about his plans for postwar Germany."[18] (Adolph Held, who represented the Jewish Labor Committee, would later say that Roosevelt monopolized the meeting by speaking 80 percent of the time.) The Committee then presented Roosevelt with a report. The Committee's *Blue Print for Extermination* analyzed the annihilation country by country. Meanwhile, Rabbi Wise read a two-page letter, emphasizing that "unless action is taken immediately, the Jews of Hitler Europe are doomed." The letter proposed a war crimes warning. The President agreed, but authorized the Committee to write the warning.

In the press conference following the meeting, and under authorization from the President, Wise revealed that Roosevelt "was profoundly shocked to learn that two million Jews had perished as a result of Nazi rule and crimes." Wise threatened that: "The American people will hold the perpetrators of these crimes to strict accountability in a day of reckoning which will surely come."

Roosevelt's shock was shared by many among the Allied nations. In fact, that shock factor led to a declaration condemning Nazi atrocities. The document, signed on December 17 by the Allied nations, exposed the German government's "intention to exterminate the Jewish people in Europe" and condemned "in the strongest possible terms this bestial policy of cold-blooded extermination." The document promised a "solemn resolution to ensure that those responsible for these crimes shall not escape retribution." Regarding the mass deportations, the declaration read, "None of those taken away are ever heard of again. . . . The infirm are left to die of exposure and starvation or are deliberately massacred in mass executions." Regarding the number of victims, the declaration estimated, "Many hundreds of thousands of innocent men, women and children."

In Britain's House of Commons a startling occurrence followed the reading of the declaration. In his diary, Sir Henry Channon, a Conservative Member of Parliament, described the session as "sublime. Anthony [Eden, Foreign Secretary] read out a statement regarding the extermination of the Jews in East Europe, whereupon Jimmy de Rothschild [liberal, Jewish member of Parliament] rose, and with immense dignity, and his voice vibrating with emotion, spoke for five minutes in moving tones on the plight of these people. There were tears in his eyes, and I feared that he might break down; the House caught his spirit and was deeply moved."[19]

For the next two minutes, the Members of Parliament stood in silence, their heads bowed in an expression of grief. In its lengthy history, Parliament had never before experienced such a show of silence. But, as touching as this was, British policy did not change.

In another declaration, this one emanating from the Vatican on Christmas Eve, Pope Pius XII attempted to give a "clear and comprehensive" condemnation of Nazi atrocities.[20] During the year 1942, the Vatican had received numerous reports detailing Nazi atrocities and, specifically, the annihilation of the Jews. In public, Pope Pius XII had not offered a condemnation. Rather, he had chosen the tactic of silence, despite pressure from many sides urging the Pope to censure the Nazis.

The Pope's traditional Christmas sermon centered on the Rights of Man and the problems of individuals in relation to the state. Midway through he came to the atrocities of war. He pleaded for a vow, according to papal scholar John Cornwell, "to be made by men of good will to bring society back to its immovable center of gravity in divine law, and for all men to dedicate themselves to the service of the human person and the service of a divinely ennobled human society."

"Humanity owes this vow," Pius said, "to those hundreds of thousands who, without any fault of their own, sometimes only by reason of their nationality or race, are marked down for death or gradual extinction." These few words marked the Pope's most significant protest. Notice, in his words, the lack of specific terminology. Not one mention of the specific victim, the Jews, or mention of the perpetrators, the Nazis. He also reduced the numbers—"hundreds of thousands" rather than millions—and therefore the magnitude.

According to Harold Tittman, a U.S. deputy representative to the Vatican, Pius's message did not "satisfy those circles which had hoped that the Pope would this time call a spade a spade and discard his usual practice of speaking in generalities." Tittman took his grievances to the Pope directly, asking why he had not mentioned the word *Nazi* in his sermon. Pius responded that he then would have had to mention the Communists too. Tittman, according to John Cornwell, did not ask the Pope why he hadn't mentioned the word *Jews*.

The Winter of 1943

The year opened with Gerhart Riegner sending another telegram to the State Department and Rabbi Wise. In his four-page cable, Riegner reported that the Germans were killing six thousand Jews per day in Poland. In addition, the message detailed the treatment of nearly 130,000 Jews in Rumania. Since their deportation to remote Transnistria, these Jews had been robbed of their belongings. Sixty thousand Jews had already perished and the remaining seventy thousand were slowly starving to death, Riegner reported.

The State Department, fed up with the flow of information from Riegner to Wise, tried, in the words of Treasury Secretary Henry Morgenthau, "to shut off the pressure by shutting off at the source the flow of information which nourished it."[21] The Department sent cable 354, dated February 10, to the United States Minister to Switzerland, Leland Harrison. The cable read, "It is suggested that in the future, reports submitted to you for transmission to private persons in the United States should not be accepted unless extraordinary circumstances make such action advisable. . . ."

Wise called the order, "The crime of the bureaucrats." The crime, however, went much deeper than a cable subverting information. Early in 1943, Gerhart Riegner submitted a cable to the State Department and Rabbi Wise revealing that 70,000 Jews in France and Rumania could be rescued and some Polish Jews moved to Hungary, which, to that point in time, had been spared Nazi atrocities. The rescue plan included paying bribes to Nazi officials. In order to facilitate the plan, Riegner explained, money needed to be deposited in the names of those officials.

The State Department procrastinated. Months passed without action. That July, in exasperation and frustration, Rabbi Wise went directly to the White House. He explained the plan to President Roosevelt. "Our armies will see to it that these Nazi mercenaries shall not live to reap the benefit of their hostage-holding, blackmailing plan," Wise suggested. ". . . The President's immediate answer astonished and delighted me. 'Stephen, why don't you go ahead and do it?' "22 Roosevelt immediately contacted Henry Morgenthau at the Treasury to begin the flow of money.

The State Department took an additional five months before signing off on the plan. What took so long? A mixture of State Department incompetence and sabotage combined with a policy of anti-immigration and anti-Semitism. At the top of the pyramid, Secretary of State Cordell Hull was an inefficient administrator. He was not an anti-Semite. In fact, he was married to a Jewish woman. He just didn't have the insight, the tenacity, and the strength to lead the State Department during such a challenging period. His subordinate, Breckinridge Long, called Hull "a sweet person and a fine character, but he lacks decision and executive ability and he lacks a great deal of knowledge of European politics and affairs. He is too idealistic."23

Undersecretary of State Sumner Welles was sympathetic to Jewish affairs. However, after a homosexual scandal, he was forced to resign. That took place at the most inopportune time for the Jews of Europe, August 1943. Without Welles, the Jews lost a key voice of support. Rabbi Wise was effusive to Welles in the aftermath of his dismissal. "Your vision and your wisdom, your courage and effectiveness cannot long be lost to the American people, which cherishes your service, as my fellow Jews in all free lands will, when the whole story can be told," Wise said, "bless your name."[24]

Thus State Department policy concerning the Jews of Europe fell on the desk of Breckinridge Long. For the Jews of Europe, there couldn't have been any worse news.

The Beginning of Spring

On March 1, 1943, thousands and thousands of sympathetic Americans flocked to Madison Square Garden. The occasion was the "Stop Hitler Now" rally, organized by Rabbi Wise in response to Nazi atrocities. An estimated seventy-five thousand people tried to fill a space built for twenty-one thousand. The overflow crowd gathered outside the arena. There, they remained, listening to the speakers through huge amplifiers.

Inside, the speechmakers called for action. Their demands could be found in the words of Dr. Chaim Weizmann, the president of the Jewish Agency for Palestine and the future President of Israel. "The democracies have a clear duty before them," he declared. "Let them negotiate with Germany through the neutral countries concerning the possible release of the Jews in the occupied countries. Let havens be designated in the vast territories of the United Nations which will give sanctuary to those fleeing from imminent murder. Let the gates of Palestine be opened. . . . The Jewish community of Palestine will welcome with joy and thanksgiving all delivered from the Nazi hands."

The "Stop Hitler Now" rally adopted a resolution, expressing "our solemn and reluctant protest against the continuing failure to act, against the strange indifference of the United Nations to the fate of five million human beings . . . who are captive in Nazi-occupied territories, who are unprotected by any code of human relations, who are unsponsored by any corporate state . . . and who are doomed to planned, unhuman torture and death."

Rabbi Wise sent this resolution to Secretary Hull. He added a cover letter. "It is a source of the deepest regret to me to have to underscore to you that despite the Declaration issued by the United Nations last December, little or nothing has been done to implement that Declaration and that the Nazi campaign of extermination has proceeded at an accelerated tempo . . . I ask you to take action which may aid in saving the Jewish people from utter extinction."[25]

Less than forty-eight hours later, the State Department responded, albeit in its oblique manner. In a press release, the State Department gave the false impression that the United States had initiated plans for a refugee conference to be held in Ottawa. In fact, the plans had been originated by the British. The December 17 Declaration had caused "intense public interest" in Great Britain over the fate of the Jews. Distinguished leaders had come forth with motions and warnings. One of those leaders, Rabbi Solomon Schonfeld, called for a series of propositions, including the temporary refuge of refugees in British colonies, specifically India; an appeal to those countries bordering Germany and German-controlled areas to allow temporary asylum and transit facilities; an offer to the governments of those bordering nations to help facilitate the movement of refugees; and an invitation to the other Allied governments to consider similar action.

Another leader, Archbishop of Canterbury William Temple, warned Parliament that European Jewry was confronted with "wholesale massacre." As a result, he called for "immediate measures on the largest and most generous scale" to permit "temporary asylum" in Britain to those Jews who managed to escape the clutches of Nazi-dominated Europe. Reacting to such public outcry, the Foreign Office suggested to the State Department a refugee conference.[26]

Meanwhile, Jews from Greece and Macedonia arrived at the Auschwitz railway stop. These southern Europeans were the first to be incinerated in the great crematoria. For Crematorium II began operation on March 13. The crematorium had taken eight months to complete. In fact, in the first few days of August 1942, as Gerhart Riegner was meeting with the American and British Consulates in Geneva and sending out his famous telegram, the Auschwitz authorities and the engineers at Toepf A.G. had finalized construction plans.

Chapter 17

◄ ►

Bermuda and Warsaw

The Canadians responded to the Ottawa Conference proposal with indignation. Not only had they not been asked to sponsor a conference by either the Americans or the British, but the Canadians knew that a conference on refugees would expose their own policies of immigration restriction.

Washington, D.C., was suggested as a replacement. The State Department, however, wouldn't hear of it. "To talk here," Breckinridge Long wrote, "would put *us* in a bad position."[1] (The italics were his.)

Finally, Britain and the United States settled on Bermuda. And, indeed, the island presented a perfect choice. Its isolation guaranteed that those in attendance wouldn't have to face the swarm of the press or the uproar of public opinion or the resentment of Jewish organizations. In fact, wartime regulations restricted all access to Bermuda.

The Bermuda Conference opened on Monday, April 19, 1943. The British delegation was led by Richard Law, the Parliamentary Undersecretary of State for Foreign Affairs and the son of former Prime Minister Bonar Law. The American side was led by Dr. Harold Dodds, the President of Princeton. A curious choice considering the subject of the Conference. "Princeton under Dodds," sociologist Jerome Karabel wrote, "was even more anti-Semitic than Harvard."[2] A rather damning indictment considering Harvard's history.

Others on the American delegation included Senator Scott Lucas of Illinois (one of President Roosevelt's possible running mates in the election of 1944) and Jewish Congressman Sol Bloom, the Chairman of the House Foreign Affairs Committee. Bloom's appointment was met with consternation by the Jewish community. According to Emanuel Celler, Bloom "was one of those who always hung on the coat tails of the State Department. He always wanted to curry favor with the State Department. He liked to attend the state dinners and he liked the diplomacy that the State Department would accord him. . . . And the State Department was always stroking Bloom the right way, never against his fur. And the result was that Bloom became more or less a sycophant of the State Department."[3]

When Bloom gained his appointment to the delegation, Rabbi Wise complained to Breckinridge Long that the Congressman was not an appropriate representative of American Jewry. Breckinridge Long's response was sharp. Congressman Bloom was a representative of the American people, he said.

On the morning of the 19th, while the Bermuda Conference convened, the message spread throughout the Jewish Underground in the Warsaw ghetto: the Germans, aided by Polish policemen, were encircling the ghetto wall. Some sixty thousand Jews had prepared for such an incident. They assumed their positions; those in the Underground set up in strategic locations, the rest of the inhabitants of the ghetto moved to previously prepared shelters in cellars and attics of buildings. "A deathly silence enveloped the ghetto," wrote Marek Edelman, a Warsaw ghetto survivor.[4]

At 4 a.m. German platoons attacked. Three hours later, tanks and armored vehicles rolled in. "Their triumph appeared to be complete," Edelman wrote. "It looked as if this superbly equipped modern army had scared off the handful of bravado-drunk men. . . ." And indeed the Germans were superbly equipped. Soldiers: 2100 for the Germans, 1200 for the Jews. Heavy machine guns: 13 for the Germans, none for the Jews. Submachine guns: 135 for the Germans, one for the Jews. Rifles: 1,358 for the Germans, 17 for the Jews.

"They did not scare us," Marek Edelman wrote, "and we were not taken by surprise. We were only awaiting an opportune moment." That moment occurred at the intersection of Mila and Zamenhofa Streets, when the Germans began their reconnaissance and the Jews began firing. "Strange projectiles began exploding everywhere (the hand grenades of our own make)," Edelman wrote, "the lone machine gun sent shots through the air now and then (ammunition had to be conserved carefully), rifles started firing a bit further away. Such was the beginning."

Meanwhile in Bermuda, the Conference immediately ran into impediments. "The humanitarian motive to aid individuals. . . ," Sol Bloom wrote in his memoirs, "had to be subordinated to the greater humanitarian motive of rescuing whole peoples. Any plan that might interfere with winning the war had to be rejected. We could divert no force, not a single ship, in direct use against the enemy to succor any of his victims."

In his opening speech, Richard Law reiterated his government's position. The refugees, he said "should not be betrayed . . . into a belief that aid is coming to them, when, in fact, we are unable to give them immediate succor." In his opening speech, Harold Dodds said, "The problem is too great for solution by the two governments here represented."[5] Both speeches were released to the press. They would be the only speeches released.

Meanwhile in Warsaw, the first evening of the uprising occurred on the first evening of Passover. One of the fighters, Tuvia Borzykowski, accidentally happened upon a rabbi leading a Seder. He remembered:

> The room looked as if it had been hit by a hurricane. Bedding was everywhere, chairs lay overturned, the floor was strewn with household objects, the window panes were all gone. It had all happened during the day, before the inhabitants of the room returned from the bunker.
>
> Amidst this destruction, the table in the centre of the room looked incongruous with glasses filled with wine, with the family seated around, the rabbi reading the

Haggadah. His reading was punctuated by explosions and the rattling of machine guns; the faces of the family around the table were lit by the red light from the burning buildings, nearby.[6]

Meanwhile in Bermuda, the Conference dissolved into a series of more denunciations. No direct appeal to the Germans would be considered, nor would a prisoner-for-refugee exchange, nor would the blockade of Europe be lifted for relief supplies. Richard Law voiced concern about "dumping" refugees on the Allies, "some of whom might be Axis sympathizers masquerading as oppressed persons."

In the face of so much hostility even Sol Bloom spoke up. He suggested that the United States and Britain make an effort to admit refugees in large numbers and that Britain's policy of restriction in Palestine be changed. In response to both options, Harold Dodds cut him off.

The World Jewish Congress, with an emissary at Bermuda, suggested rescue options, from opening up havens in the Allied nations to shipping food to imprisoned Jews to liberalizing immigration in the United States and Central America. These options, if they were considered by the conferees, were not discussed in public.

Only one definitive action came out of Bermuda. The twenty-one thousand refugees stuck in Spain would be moved to Allied-controlled North Africa. Only four to five thousand of those refugees were Jewish.

Meanwhile in Warsaw, on the third day of fighting (a day in fact when the Nazis had anticipated liquidating the ghetto) the Germans began burning structures, building to building, house to house, room to room. "The flames chased the people out from their shelters," Marek Edelman wrote. "Thousands staggered about in the courtyards where they were easy prey for the Germans who imprisoned them or killed them outright." According to German calculations, 7000 Jews died in the uprising, with fifty-six thousand Jews captured and deported to the death camp Treblinka.

The Bermuda Conference concluded on April 29. No report or conclusion was released to the press. Instead, a one-page bulletin stated that all possibilities of improving the refugee problem had been analyzed and "a number of concrete recommendations" would be made to the Allied governments, but since the recommendations involved "military considerations," confidentiality would be assured.[7]

Condemnation of the Conference was immediate and strident. Frank Kingdon, Methodist minister, President of the University of Newark and key member of the Emergency Rescue Committee, denounced the Bermuda Conference as "a shame and a disgrace." Emanuel Celler announced that the "results of the Bermuda Conference are a diplomatic mockery . . . and a betrayal of human instincts and ideals." After Bermuda, Celler committed himself to a long-term offensive concerning State Department policy. One of his plans was to form "an unofficial conclave of Representatives and Senators sympathetic to active and genuine rescue" that could put "extreme pressure" on the Roosevelt Administration to save Jews.[8]

The Bergson group (see Chapter 18) took out an advertisement in the *New York Times*, announcing, "To 5,000,000 Jews in the Nazi Death-Trap Bermuda was a 'Cruel Mockery.'" Congressman Samuel Dickstein said, "Not even the pessimists among us expected such sterility." Rabbi Israel Goldstein, the leader of the Synagogue Council of America, exposed the truth of Bermuda when he said, "The job of the Bermuda Conference apparently was not to rescue victims of Nazi terror, but to rescue our State Department and the British Foreign Office." Finally, years later, Richard Law remembered Bermuda as a "conflict of self-justification. . . . We said the results of the conference were confidential, but in fact there were no results that I can recall."[9]

The voice missing, the voice that could have pressed for action, belonged to the President. Roosevelt had almost nothing to do with the Conference. He did receive briefings. Breckinridge Long, for instance, told Roosevelt about the challenge of finding a Conference site, stating that both Washington and London should be avoided due to anticipated public pressure. Roosevelt agreed. He did receive final recommendations made at Bermuda. He never, however, followed the proceedings of the Conference (he repeatedly asked Secretary Hull about Bermuda's background and purpose), nor did he try to influence the results. He was silent.

"I cannot be silent," wrote Szmul Zygielbojm (the Polish Jew who went on the BBC and pleaded with the Allied governments to come to the aid of those in the Warsaw ghetto). "I cannot live while the remnants of the Jewish population of Poland, of whom I am a representative, are perishing. My friends in the Warsaw ghetto died with weapons in their hands in the last heroic battle. It was not my destiny to die together with them but I belong to them and in their mass graves. By my death I wish to make my final protest against the passivity with which the world is looking on and permitting the extermination of the Jewish people. I know how little life is worth today, but as I was unable to do anything during my life, perhaps by my death I shall contribute to breaking down the indifference of those who may now at the last moment rescue the few Polish Jews still alive."[10]

A few weeks after the Bermuda Conference concluded, and four days before the German commander in Warsaw declared the ghetto no longer in existence, Szmul Zygielbojm committed suicide.

Chapter 18

◄►

"We Shall No Longer Witness with Pity Alone"

C C ACTION—NOT PITY CAN SAVE MILLIONS NOW,"
shouted an advertisement on February 8, 1943 in the *New York Times.* "EXTINCTION OR HOPE FOR THE REMNANTS OF EUROPEAN JEWRY?—IT IS FOR US TO GIVE THE ANSWER."

Thousands of miles away in central Europe, fifteen trains reached Auschwitz throughout the month of February. The gas killed at least five thousand Jews. One train from France contained nearly one thousand Jews, including 123 children under twelve years of age. Less than two hundred Jews survived the selection process. All the children died in the gas.[1]

"What can be done?" the advertisement in the *Times* continued. The ad then answered its own question, calling for a change of policy, transforming the passivity of the Allies into a proactive and urgent plan. "The first dictate," the ad read, "would be the immediate approval of the demand for a Jewish Army of the Stateless and Palestinian Jews—an army 200,000 strong."

The Jews in Europe suddenly had a voice here in America, a crusader. His name was Peter Bergson.

Peter Bergson, or Hillel Kook as his birth certificate read, was born in Lithuania in 1915. Escaping the pogroms of Eastern Europe, his family migrated to Palestine in the 1920s. As a teenager, Bergson became a fervent follower of the Irgun Underground (a nationalistic organization dedicated to armed struggle against the Arabs and the British, after the publishing of the White Paper in 1939). The Irgun, Bergson believed, would eventually become "the liberation army of the Hebrew nation."[2]

In 1937, Bergson traveled to Poland. There, he met Vladimir (Ze'ev) Jabotinsky, the leader of the Zionist-Revisionists, the militant wing of the Zionist movement. Jabotinsky looked at Poland, in between Nazi Germany and Stalinist Russia, and saw Jews in danger. "We have got to save millions, many millions," he presciently advocated.[3] He envisioned an evacuation, transporting a million and a half Eastern European Jews to Palestine over a ten-year period. He was the only Jewish leader worldwide advocating such a position.

His plans met limited success. Prior to the outbreak of the Second World War, thousands of Polish Jews were shepherded overland and by ship to Palestine. The emigration took place in many covert forms, from bogus tourism (the visitors had no intention of leaving Palestine) to fictitious marriages (Jewish citizens of Palestine would go abroad, marry, return to Palestine, then divorce—the scheme worked because marriage to a Palestinian citizen guaranteed citizenship), to the first Maccabee Games in 1932 when thousands of visitors remained in the country. Between 1937 and 1940, the Irgun and other organizations, all presided over by Ze'ev Jabotinsky, "brought into Palestine successfully, on about forty ships, some 20,000 to 25,000 illegal immigrants."[4]

Those ships had to pass through harbors controlled and patrolled by the British. The task required guile and subterfuge. In *Lone Wolf: A Biography of Vladimir (Ze'ev) Jabotinsky*, Shmuel Katz gave one such example. A sailboat with an auxiliary engine carrying fifteen passengers arrived at night off the coast of Haifa. One passenger swam ashore and crossed the city to the house of Dr. Avraham Weinshall, a Jabotinsky contact. Weinshall sent word to Jabotinsky's nephew, Johnny Kopp, who worked for the electric company. The next evening, Haifa's electrical power grid was shut down and the fifteen passengers landed safely.

American Jewish leaders considered Jabotinsky a fascist. Rabbi Stephen Wise, for instance, referred to Jabotinsky as a "traitor."[5] Some of this had to do with Jabotinsky's organization's covert operations. Some of this had to do with Jabotinsky's antipathy toward the British. Some of this had to do with Jabotinsky's preaching the evacuation of Eastern European Jewry. Such an evacuation, the American Jewish leadership argued, actually supported and legitimized the expulsion policies of Nazi Germany in the era before the war. In other words, the American Jewish leadership argued, how was clearing Poland of Jews by Jews any different than clearing Germany of Jews by the Nazis? In addition, Rabbi Wise claimed that Jabotinsky's movement was directly responsible for bringing "unselected, unsuitable Jews to Palestine." Henry Montor, the director of the United Palestine's Appeal, went a step further. "I think it is fair to point out that many who have been brought into Palestine by the Revisionists [Jabotinsky's movement] have been prostitutes and criminals," he said.

Jabotinsky responded to Wise in the *Jewish Daily News Bulletin*. "Long ago an unkind American Jew told me this about Stephen Wise: 'He has one great quality, he says what he thinks; but he has one great defect, he doesn't think.' I now begin to see how such an opinion . . . could have arisen."[6] Such was the antagonism between the two leaders.

Jabotinsky's philosophies also included the notion of a Jewish army. During the First World War, he'd successfully petitioned the British to establish the Jewish Legion. As the Second World War began, Jabotinsky was at it again: pressing the British for a Jewish army. The British government rejected the idea, fearing both an Arab uprising and a Jewish army entrenched in Palestine.

Rebuffed by the British, Jabotinsky traveled to America. Knowing the influence Washington had on London, he planned on politicking the United States government. In order to facilitate a more effective campaign, he summoned his protégé, the charismatic and publicity-savvy Peter Bergson, to America. Bergson arrived from Poland in July of 1940. Jabotinsky died the next month.

Bergson quickly assumed the leadership role. He distilled Jabotinsky's movement down to one specific concentration: the Jewish army, creating the "Committee for a Jewish Army of Stateless and Palestinian Jews." Bergson explained: "We wanted to have a Jewish army because we felt we were a Jewish nation." Bergson told David Wyman in interviews conducted in 1973 and eventually published in *A Race Against Death*, "We're talking about survival, as a nation, not as individuals."[7]

The Committee for a Jewish Army held its first rally in June of 1941 at the Manhattan Center. Four thousand people attended. Media attention was high and endorsements poured in, from best-selling author Pierre van Paassen (the author of *Days of Our Years*, which touched on the dangers of Nazism) to theologian Reinhold Niebuhr to entertainer Eddie Cantor to Senator Claude Pepper of Florida. Pepper's support, in particular, had a major impact, knocking down the senatorial wall. Soon other Senators joined the Committee, including the former isolationists Guy Gillette from Iowa and Elbert Thomas of Utah, and the moderately conservative Edwin Johnson from Colorado. Even Secretary of War Henry Stimson sent a telegram of support.

Leading Jewish organizations, however, considered Bergson and his followers (known as the Bergson group) "irresponsible, unethical, and willing to edge very close to fraud in order to raise funds." What were the reasons for these condemnations? Bergson's tactics, specifically the concept of advertising, were used for a social cause. Prior to Bergson's campaign, Jewish organizations advertised specific events, not a crusade for political activism. "Full-page ads then was an unheard-of thing," Bergson said in *A Race Against Death*. "They [the Jewish establishment] thought this was obscene . . . they thought it was a disgrace." Historian David Wyman summarized the Jewish leaders' approach: "Don't be unconventional. Don't make a splash. Do it fairly quietly. We might have a boycott or a mass meeting. But to go beyond that to any loud, shrill kind of thing, such as some of these ads, would be provocative."

Bergson's tactics also went against the grain of the American Jewish perspective. Jews adhered to the Roosevelt line: the way to rescue the Jews of Europe was through the defeat of Nazi Germany. Samuel Merlin, Peter Bergson's right-hand man, explained:

> Jewish leaders identified themselves with Roosevelt and Churchill and everyone who said that nothing serious can be done during the war to rescue the Jews. They agreed that one could do nothing significant. They themselves said, how are you going to save so many people. You know what it means to save one person. They said, since it's impossible to do anything on an adequate scale during the war, one has to concentrate upon creating the best and most favorable conditions for the postwar period. And we said, the Jews who are being exterminated on such a scale cannot wait for postwar conditions.[8]

As evidenced by these words, the divisions between the American Jews and the Bergson group were deep and distrustful. American Jews feared in-your-face tactics. The message within the Jewish population was clear: assume a quiet, unobtrusive manner, work behind the scenes. The Bergson group saw it the other way, clamoring for attention.

In addition, Bergson was a Palestinian, an outsider in America, and a member of the Irgun, a terrorist organization according to the British. This generated skepticism and suspicion and, in the case of America's leading Jews, jealousy. "Stephen Wise," Samuel Merlin claimed, "will not tolerate any other Jewish organization working for Palestine and stealing honors and publicity from him."

Without question, Rabbi Wise was the most prominent American Jewish leader during the first half of the twentieth century. There were good reasons for this. He worked in the vanguard of the social justice movement, campaigning at various times in his life for free speech and black rights and, during the Great Depression, for unemployment insurance. Also, he held high office in many organizations and he served as the chief rabbi at the Free Synagogue in New York City (where my parents were members).

Wise was one of the supreme orators of his era, a close second to FDR. Thousands of Jewish families tuned in from their living rooms. My family was no exception. His Friday night sermons over the radio were riveting, mesmerizing. He could hold you in his thrall purely with the sound of his voice.

As a prominent figure, he certainly received his share of criticism. For instance, the rabbi was accused of vanity. According to the rabbi himself, when he met Sigmund Freud, Freud asked him to name, "the four greatest living Jews."

"Oh, that is easy," Wise replied. "Einstein, Ehrlich, Freud and Brandeis."

"And you," Freud said.

"No, no, no, no, you cannot include me," Wise answered.

"If you had said 'no' once," Freud said, "I would believe you, but four 'no's' leads me to suspect that you protest too much."[9]

Concerning the Holocaust, Wise put his faith in Roosevelt. Rabbi Wise, like all other Jews close to the President, deeply valued that relationship. Rabbi Wise had campaigned extensively for Franklin Roosevelt. In each of Roosevelt's elections, with the exception of one, Rabbi Wise pushed for the President "with boundless enthusiasm." The exception came early in Roosevelt's career during his gubernatorial campaign. Wise denounced the corruption and criminality of Tammany Hall. Roosevelt needed Tammany's support. But after FDR won the Presidency in 1932 and "faced the emergencies and human tragedies that dominated American life in 1933, he rewon my unstinted admiration," Wise wrote in his autobiography.

Wise became entranced with the President. "Thank God for Roosevelt," Wise wrote after a meeting in the White House. "We ought to distribute cards throughout the country bearing just four letters, TGFR, and as the Psalmist would have said, thank Him every day and every hour."[10] Did that closeness to Roosevelt harm the Jews of the Holocaust? Did his admiration affect his judgment? Wise himself touched on this very issue, in regard to other Jews within the Roosevelt Administration. "I sometimes felt that not a few of the Jews who had access to the President at this time did us a great disservice," he wrote in his autobiography. "They were so eager not to seem to plead the Jewish cause that they failed accurately to interpret . . . the tragic plight of their brother Jews in Hitler Europe."

Might a similar lens be pointed at the rabbi? Could he separate his personal esteem for the President from what should have been his paramount duty: agitating for the rescue of European Jews? The record suggests that Wise toed the Roosevelt line. For the most part, he adhered to the Roosevelt rescue-through-victory stance. He believed the President was sympathetic to the plight of Europe's Jews. He believed the President grasped the situation with, in his own words, "feeling and understanding." He believed the President would take any opportunity to rescue Jews. Regarding Roosevelt, Wise saw what he wanted to see. He was, in David Wyman's opinion, "unable to be critical of, or even objective about, the President" and "his total trust in Roosevelt was not an asset to American or European Jews."[11]

None of this, however, explains Wise's near obsession with the maverick and outsider Peter Bergson. Why would Wise, along with Nahum Goldmann (the powerful organizer and president of the World Jewish Congress), tell the State Department that Bergson "was as big a threat as Hitler to the well-being of American Jewry"?[12] Why would Wise threaten a young California Congressman named Will Rogers, Jr.? The Congressman recalled:

When it was known that I was becoming a member of the Bergson group, then there was a terrific amount of pressure from all sorts of areas. I went back to Beverly Hills and I remember meeting with Rabbi Stephen S. Wise in a synagogue. I had never been in a synagogue before. I didn't know quite what a synagogue was. And I put on that little funny hat and all the stuff and went down there. He took me aside and he said, "Now, young man. I knew your father very well. Now you are getting confused, you are getting mixed up with the wrong type of people. Let me tell you and steer you clear when you come on the Jewish people, or want to meet the right people, the responsible people." He put the heat on me very, very heavy and very,

very suave, very indirect. He was quite the diplomat. He didn't say, "If you do get mixed up with them, you are not going to be reelected." He wasn't that direct, but he certainly made every pressure that he could, and where he knew it would be effective.[13]

Why was Rabbi Stephen Wise so involved in breaking the Bergson movement? Perhaps it had to do with, in Congressman Rogers' words, Wise's fixation with "a bunch of upstarts, raising money, raising Cain. Getting readership and getting notice. Effective notice. And taking it away from the Jewish organizations."

At the end of November 1942, after meeting with Sumner Welles at the State Department, Stephen Wise went public with extermination news. The information instantaneously startled the Bergson activists. "The most traumatic day of my life," Bergson said in *A Race Against Death*. "We were hit with this thing by shock. . . . We felt something ought to be done."

The Bergson group responded to the extermination news by buying a series of advertisements in major newspapers. An advertisement appeared in the *New York Times* on December 7. "We shall no longer witness with pity alone. . . ," the headline read. The ad called for a Jewish army as "a vital contribution to victory and an immediate moral necessity for the cause of world freedom." The Jewish army campaign, however, soon turned into a call for rescue, with Bergson pressing for a governmental agency to specifically take on the task. The "magnitude of the slaughter wasn't anything that a charitable organization would handle," Bergson said in *A Race Against Death*. "Only a government could handle it. You had a government using all its power to do the murder. Only another government could oppose it."

An advertisement appeared in the *New York Times* on February 16. "FOR SALE to Humanity," the headline read, "70,000 Jews." The ad, written by Ben Hecht (a member of the Bergson group, a renowned reporter and screenwriter whose achievements included the scripts for *Wuthering Heights, Gunga Din*, and *Gone With the Wind*), publicized the suffering of the

Transnistria Jews, and then called on America and President Roosevelt to buy these people. "Guaranteed Human Beings at $50 a Piece," the ad read. "Attention Four Freedoms!!! Attention Humanity!!! Attention America!!! The Doors of Roumania Are Open! Act Now!" (The term "Four Freedoms" referred specifically to President Roosevelt, who, in one of his great speeches called for "four essential freedoms." They included: freedom of speech and expression, freedom of every person to worship in his own way, freedom from want, and freedom from fear. Roosevelt gave the Four Freedoms speech on January 6, 1941.)

American Jewry essentially rejected Bergson's call. The organization B'nai B'rith represented the general attitude: "There is only one way to stop the Nazi massacres, and this is by crushing the Nazis in battle."[14]

The Bergson group decided to further step outside convention. "What we were talking about was to have a very energetic, concentrated effort on rescue," Bergson said in *A Race Against Death*. "Something dedicated only to rescue."

One week after Stephen Wise held his "Stop Hitler Now" rally at Madison Square Garden (March 1943), a pageant filled the Garden for two nights. Forty thousand people attended "We Will Never Die," a drama in three acts. Financed by the Bergson group, written by Ben Hecht, with a score by Kurt Weill, and a cast that included Edward G. Robinson, Paul Muni, and Stella Adler, "We Will Never Die" focused on major events of Jewish history, Jewry's contributions to civilization, and the extermination in Europe.

In April of 1943, "We Will Never Die" moved to Constitution Hall in Washington, D.C. The audience consisted of hundreds of governmental officials, from members of Congress to Cabinet Secretaries to Supreme Court Justices to First Lady Eleanor Roosevelt. "One of the most impressive and moving pageants I have ever seen," Eleanor Roosevelt wrote in "My Day," her newspaper column. "No one who heard each group come forward and give the story of what had happened to it at the hands of a ruthless German military will ever forget those haunting words: 'Remember us.'"[15]

"We Will Never Die" then moved on to full houses in Philadelphia, Chicago, Boston, and Los Angeles. The pageant was effective in its core concept: disseminating information. Only through publicizing the Nazi extermination of the Jews, the Bergson group believed, would Americans put pressure on their government to act.

At the same time, Jewish organizations compelled various institutions to shut down the pageant. In Gary, Indiana, for instance, the American Jewish Congress and the Zionist Organization of America (both Rabbi Wise organizations) successfully pressured the town to prohibit "We Will Never Die" from opening. A message arrived at the Bergson group's headquarters. With considerable regret, the message disclosed, "The 'We Will Never Die' pageant cannot be presented in the city of Gary." The message continued, "Considerable agitation was started immediately after it was announced in the papers that the pageant would be presented. . . . All the Jewish organizations met. . . . They unanimously agreed to present a demand . . . that it be stopped."[16]

This struggle within the Jewish community proved disturbing. One of Bergson's aides, Alexander Rafaeli, remarked, "I can easily say that my struggle during those years was often harder, more tense and more depressing than the battles I was to know on the beaches of Normandy. . . ."

At a time when the unprecedented massacre in Europe continued "unabated," to use Roosevelt's word, Jewish leaders chose an internal struggle—disparaging the Bergson group—over rescue. "There could have been no reason why we [and the Jewish leaders] shouldn't work together," Bergson said in *A Race Against Death*. "There were a lot of very able people there. But we couldn't get them to budge. . . ."

Despite the obstacles, the Bergson group carried on its agitation. That included a conference attended by fifteen hundred delegates, including former President Herbert Hoover and New York Mayor Fiorello La Guardia, both of whom helped the conference attract national media attention. The Bergson group "focused attention on the problems," the pro-Zionist journal *Furrows* commented, not on "the vacillations and temporizing of official Jewish leadership."[17] At the conference, the Committee for a Jewish Army changed names. "The Emergency Committee to Save the Jewish People of Europe" came into existence.

The Jewish establishment responded to the conference with contempt. What bothered Jewish leaders, specifically, was that the conference shunned the issue of Jewish statehood in Palestine. One month later, the first American Jewish Conference convened in New York City. All Jewish organizations were invited, with the exception of the Bergson group. Peter Bergson did attend, as a member of the audience. "At long last," he thought to himself, "the Jews are going to get together and do something for rescue."

He was wrong. The issue of rescue was added to the agenda at the last minute and didn't play a significant role in the Conference's proceedings. Palestine did. In fact, Palestine was the crucial issue. "I remember being flabbergasted," Bergson said in *A Race Against Death*. A conference to "come up with a unified Jewish position on postwar Palestine. But not on the saving of the Jews. In the middle of the extermination!"

The conference, the advertisements, the media attention, the diverse array of supporters signing the Emergency Committee's petitions: all of this brought the Bergson group significant attention. So much attention, in fact, that Secretary of State Cordell Hull could not refuse Bergson's request for a meeting.

That appointment took place on August 12, 1943. Bergson used the opportunity to plug a governmental rescue organization. In typical fashion, Hull didn't take a position. His assistant, in typical fashion, did. Breckinridge Long dismissed the rescue agency imperative. "He was hostile to the issue," Bergson said in *A Race Against Death*. "You couldn't get it across to Long—I didn't meet him so many times, maybe four or five times in all, I think, and not always alone. Once he sat in the meeting with Hull. . . . I remember the feeling of getting absolutely nowhere in terms of conveying the human urgency to it." From that sense of futility, Bergson began to turn his energies to Congress.

Meanwhile, in another meeting with Breckinridge Long, Stephen Wise and Nahum Goldmann denounced Bergson. They saw him as a threat to their establishment. They saw him as misrepresenting American Jewish opinion. They voiced concerns that his activities might stir up anti-Semitism, fearing that "Bergson would bring pogroms to America."[18] Goldmann advised that the State Department either draft Bergson or deport him.

Halfway around the world, the Nazis declared martial law in Denmark and put into action a plan to deport all the Danish Jews to concentration camps. The plan was leaked. On the eve of the deportation, Danish sea captains and fishermen ferried nearly 6,500 Jews to neutral Sweden. When the Nazis began the deportations, only 500 Jews remained in Demark. All were sent to the concentration camp Theresienstadt.

Seizing upon the Danish rescue operation as an example of what was possible, the Bergson group took out a full-page advertisement in both the *New York Times* and the *Washington Post*. Its "call to action" included a petition, signed by millions of Americans, calling for both a rescue agency and American intervention in Britain in terms of opening Palestine; an appeal to Christian churches to honor Sunday, October 10, 1943, as a "Day of Intercession"; and a pilgrimage for rescue, with Orthodox rabbis marching through the capital.

On October 6, three days before Yom Kippur, some 400 rabbis gathered at Union Station. It was early in the afternoon on a cool Wednesday. The rabbis made for a conspicuous sight: long flowing beards, black coats, many of the men wearing overcoats, nearly all of them donning black fedoras.

The rabbis marched to the Capitol. There, Vice President Henry Wallace and a group of Congressmen gathered. The rabbis, upon arrival, read aloud their petition, calling for a rescue agency and for all nations to open their doors to Europe's Jews. Vice President Wallace, toeing the party line, advocated the rescue-through-victory refrain.

The rabbis then marched to the Lincoln Memorial. In front of the Great Emancipator, they prayed for American soldiers and European Jews. Then the rabbis marched to the White House. While most of the congregation prayed outside the gate, a small delegation met with Marvin McIntyre, the presidential secretary. Afterward, the rabbis marched to the synagogue for more prayer.

The President was nowhere to be seen. Officially, he did not meet with the rabbis because of other business. What did "other business" constitute? That Wednesday, Roosevelt went to Bolling Field to witness a ceremony: the integration of forty Yugoslavs into the United States Air Force. Directly after the ceremony, Roosevelt traveled to Hyde Park for a five-day weekend.

Roosevelt's decision to avoid the march stemmed from the influence of his Jewish advisers. Both Stephen Wise and Samuel Rosenman, Roosevelt's closest consultant on Jewish affairs, counseled the President. Rosenman, in particular, offered the most resistance. His counsel tended to minimize Jewish issues. And Rosenman "had the most influence on Roosevelt of any Jew. On Jewish matters, Roosevelt would turn to him and say, 'What do I do now?' because Roosevelt never had time or energy to understand the factions within the Jewish community."[19]

Another Jew who opposed the rabbis was Congressman Sol Bloom. Bloom, who did not have a particularly strong influence on Roosevelt but nevertheless had an influential position within the government, argued publicly that it would be "undignified for such an un-American-looking group to appear in Washington. . . ."[20]

Meanwhile, in Moscow, the foreign ministers of the Allied powers deliberated for two weeks. A stern war crimes warning was issued, naming many victims of Nazi atrocities. The list included the Czechs, the Greeks, the Serbs, the Russians, French hostages, Polish officers, Cretan peasants, but no mention of the Jews.

Soon after the Moscow Conference adjourned, a reporter asked Roosevelt if the foreign ministers had taken action in favor of Jewish rescue. Roosevelt replied, "That I don't know. I won't be able to tell you that until I see Mr. Hull, because that is, as you know, that whole problem is—the heart's all right—it's a question of ways and means."[21]

A full-page advertisement appeared in the *New York Times* on November 5, 1943. In response to the Moscow Conference and to the President, Ben Hecht wrote a story called, "My Uncle Abraham Reports." The ad began, "I have an Uncle who is a Ghost. But, he is no ordinary Ghost like so many dead uncles. He was elected last April by the Two Million Jews who have been murdered by the Germans to be their World Delegate."

Hecht's story followed the ghost named Uncle Abraham. First Abraham sat on the windowsill at the Kremlin and listened to Foreign Ministers Anthony Eden, Cordell Hull, and V. M. Molotov address everything but the Jews. Then the ghost met with the "Two Million murdered Jews" in a place called the "Jewish Underground" where "only Ghosts belong." Uncle Abraham began, "Dishonored dead, Fellow Corpses and Ghosts from All Over, of the Moscow Conference I have this to report." Uncle Abraham then mentioned the other victims of the Nazis, as the Moscow Conference participants had. "Only the Jew had no name," Uncle Abraham reported. "He had no face. He was like a hole in Europe on which nobody looked." Why was that, another ghost asked? Uncle Abraham did not know. "In the Kremlin in Moscow, in the White House in Washington, in the Downing Street Building in London where I have sat on the window sills, I have never heard our name," Uncle Abraham reported. "The people who live in those buildings—Stalin, Roosevelt, and Churchill—do not speak of us. . . .We were not allowed by the Germans to stay alive. We are not allowed by the Four Freedoms to be dead."

The advertisement ended with Uncle Abraham sitting on the windowsill at the White House, "two feet away from Mr. Roosevelt. But he has left his notebook behind." Clearly, Uncle Abraham was not going to hear anything that needed to be recorded.

A more attention-grabbing advertisement could not have been conceived. "This was a unique ad," Peter Bergson said in *A Race Against Death*, "one of its kind." He concluded, "The whole text is obviously a political drive at Roosevelt."

The political drive hit its mark. According to Sam Rosenman, President Roosevelt both noticed the ad and found it disturbing. According to Eleanor Roosevelt, President Roosevelt remarked that such an advertisement hit below the belt. Mrs. Roosevelt voiced this opinion directly to Peter Bergson, whom she met on a few occasions in her unofficial capacity as the President's eyes, ears, and legs. "I told her that I am very happy to hear that he is reading it and that it affects him," Bergson responded.

In the same month as the Uncle Abraham advertisement appeared, Peter Bergson convinced two of his supporters, Senator Guy Gillette and Representative Will Rogers, Jr., to introduce a non-binding resolution in the Congress. To quote from the resolution, Gillette-Rogers recommended and urged "the creation by the President of a commission of diplomatic, economic, and military experts to formulate and effectuate a plan of immediate action designed to save the surviving Jewish people of Europe. . . ."

At the same time the Bergson group placed an advertisement in the *New York Times*. "HOW WELL ARE YOU SLEEPING?" the ad asked. "Is There Something You Could Have Done to Save Millions of Innocent People—Men, Women, and Children—from Torture and Death?"

The Chairman of the House Foreign Affairs Committee, Congressman Sol Bloom, reacted to the resolution by calling for hearings. The Senate Foreign Relations Committee, on the other hand, did not hold hearings. "I was angry at having the hearings," Bergson said in *A Race Against Death*. "The hearings were a stall. There was no purpose. . . . This was not the type of resolution that required hearings. It wasn't a law. They didn't do it to help us. Bloom did it against us."

Behind the scenes, another force maneuvered. According to Bergson, "Wise arranged the hearings." On the surface, Wise gave the impression that he supported the resolution but that it contained a major flaw: a lack of pressure on the British in response to opening Palestine. When his time came to testify, Wise called the resolution "inadequate."

According to Congressman Will Rogers, Jr., "Rabbi Wise knew that putting Palestine in was just going to kill it. It was a method, a means, which he used to try and kill this resolution. He did not openly oppose it. He really couldn't. There was no way, nobody can openly oppose trying to be a humanitarian. But they just wanted to wiggle around and sabotage and change the wording. . . ."[22] The sponsors had omitted the issue of Palestine because they didn't want to alienate an ally in the middle of a war.

A series of leading figures endorsed the resolution, including Wendell Willkie and the incomparable Fiorello La Guardia. As

New York's mayor from 1934 to 1946, La Guardia represented the city with the largest concentration of Jews in the world. As such, he spent 1943 voicing his concerns. "We cannot tell others to take in the doomed while we keep our own door closed," he criticized American immigration policy. He felt America had a moral responsibility to open its doors, and consequently ask other countries to do the same.[23]

At the resolution hearings, La Guardia called for an agency to "save the Jewish people of Europe from extinction at the hands of Nazi Germany." Aside from speaking for his constituency, La Guardia also had personal reasons. His sister, Gemma, had married a Hungarian Jew employed with the Budapest Central Bank. Some four months after the hearings concluded, the Nazis turned their attentions to the hundreds of thousands of Jews living in Hungary. Gemma La Guardia became a prisoner. At the instruction of Reichsführer Heinrich Himmler she was sent to the concentration camp for women, Ravensbrück, as were her daughter and grandson. Her husband died at the concentration camp Mauthausen.

At Ravensbrück, Gemma La Guardia, at age sixty, was put in line to be gassed. However, the Camp Commander pulled her out. "The camp personnel director told me afterward that I was kept from the gas chamber because they were fearful that some harm would come to the Germans in New York in reprisal," she wrote in her memoirs.[24] As the sister of the Mayor of New York, Gemma La Guardia was spared. Because of her brother, she was classified as a political prisoner and given special status. That allowed her to observe the crematorium. "As I could sleep little, I watched the grim flaming smoke pouring out of the chimneys of the crematory," she wrote. "And oh, the terrible odor. We could force our eyes shut, but we could not keep the stench of death away from our nostrils. When we were awakened at four a.m., the first thing we saw was the flaming smoke, the first thing we were aware of was the smell." Gemma La Guardia survived Ravensbrück. She survived Berlin immediately after liberation. Eventually, through her brother's help, she made her way back to the United States. As a Displaced Person, that process took two years. In 1943, however, when Mayor La Guardia appeared at the resolution hearings, he knew that his sister was under Nazi dominion.

Following Mayor La Guardia and others, Peter Bergson took the stand. Bergson was the only witness required by Sol Bloom to testify under oath. Bloom turned the hearings into a grilling, discrediting Bergson on every conceivable level, from Bergson's Irgun connections; to his alien status in America; to the prohibitive cost of rescue (Bloom claimed the price to save one Jew was two thousand dollars and to save two million, a few billion would be needed); to Bloom's insistence that the Bermuda Conference (to which Bloom was a delegate) had explored all viable ways of implementing rescue; to a telegram the Bergson group sent to supporters "to force passage resolution." "To force passage," Bloom roared. "What the hell's this all about? You're going to *force* us to act?"[25]

"I greatly admired and respected the old man [Sol Bloom]. . . . We were very friendly," Will Rogers, Jr. remembered. "But when I began to go over to the Bergson group, this friendly attitude changed almost immediately. He said, 'What are you doing over there? This is going to wreck your career.' Well, I didn't worry about that very much, but he said, 'This is not the people you should be associated with.' And then he cut off all communication with me."

Bloom's shakedown of Bergson, however, was not the decisive moment of the hearings, nor was Wise's testimony. The decisive moment came when Breckinridge Long testified. Long claimed that the United States alone had accepted approximately 580,000 refugees since the beginning of the Hitler regime. In fact, he had confused, or purposefully muddled, the total number of visas issued and the number of refugees who had actually arrived. In that time period, 476,930 immigrants arrived from all countries, and 296,032 from Europe. As for Jews, an estimated 165,756 came from Europe.[26]

Long's comments set off a controversy. The *New York Post* labeled Long's testimony, "false and distorted." Congressman Celler accused Long of shedding "crocodile tears" and blamed him for the "tragic [visa] bottleneck." According to Congressman

Samuel Dickstein, Long created a false impression of action.

As 1943 ended, the Gillette-Rogers Resolution received unanimous support from the Senate Foreign Relations Committee. A floor vote was scheduled for late January 1944. A poll of both houses of Congress in mid-January revealed "a sufficient margin of votes to insure passage."

The question within the Bergson group became: How would Roosevelt react? The Bergson group wasn't the only organization with that question in mind.

Chapter 19

◄►

"Relief, Like Water to the Thirsty"

Shortly before the vote on the Gillette-Rogers Resolution, Secretary of the Treasury Henry Morgenthau, Jr. visited the White House. Two aides, John Pehle and Randolph Paul, accompanied their boss. The scene was the President's private study, the Oval Room. The date was Sunday, January 16, 1944. Morgenthau felt "very anxious."[1] He was, according to Randolph Paul, "taking his political life in his hands."

Morgenthau carried with him two important documents: the "Report to the Secretary on the Acquiescence of This Government in the Murder of the Jews" and the draft of an executive order by which Roosevelt's signature would implement a rescue agency.

Three days earlier, in a meeting at the Treasury, Morgenthau had received the "Report," an eighteen-page memorandum documenting State Department obstructions and conspiracies. State Department deception included Gerhart Riegner's plan for the Transnistria Jews during the winter of 1943. Seventy thousand lives were at stake. Riegner proposed a scheme for purchasing those lives. He needed a license to transfer funds overseas; licenses of that type had to be signed by both the State and Treasury Departments. Treasury signed it on August 14. Rather than grant the license, the State Department consistently searched for excuses. "Vaguely phrased" became State's official response.

In truth, the State Department feared the possible success of the plan. The question within State Department circles became: What would be done with the Jews once they gained their freedom? One answer was Palestine. Yet only 30,000 openings remained available within the White Paper quota. R. Borden Reams, the man in charge of Jewish Affairs for the State Department, remarked that he "did not know of any other areas to which the remaining Jews could be evacuated."[2]

The State Department consulted with the British over Palestine. The Foreign Office's position was summarized in a cable to the State Department from John Winant, the American Ambassador to Great Britain. The Foreign Office was "concerned with the difficulties of disposing of any considerable number of Jews should they be rescued from enemy-occupied territory. . . . For this reason they are reluctant to agree to any approval being expressed."[3]

When Cable 354, which shut off the flow of information from Riegner to Wise, came under Treasury Department scrutiny, Treasury officials went to the Secretary. Randolph Paul called State's policy, "one of the cleverest conspiracies of silence and suppression."[4] Treasury officials wanted Morgenthau to take the information directly to the President.

Morgenthau reacted cautiously. He knew the President would insist on involving the State Department. He therefore went to Secretary Hull first. That meeting took place on December 20, 1943. To Morgenthau, it could not have been any more enlightening. In the first place, Secretary Hull was so removed from the internal workings of his own Department that he couldn't introduce four of the five officials involved in refugee affairs (who were present at the meeting). In addition, Hull attended the meeting unprepared, despite the complete files at his fingertips. Finally, Hull blamed his Department's obstruction on "the fellows down the line." In echoing his boss, Breckinridge Long mentioned aides Bernard Meltzer and Herbert Feis. Meltzer "was one of the fellows who had been raising technical difficulties. I think you ought to know that," Breckinridge Long cautioned Morgenthau. "I know he had been creating a lot of trouble."[5] Aides Herbert Feis and Bernard Meltzer were the two most prominent Jews in the State Department.

Following the meeting, Breckinridge Long asked Morgenthau for a private audience. The topic of Breckinridge Long's anti-Semitism came up. "Breck, we might be a little frank," Henry Morgenthau said. "The impression is all around that you particularly are anti-Semitic."[6] Long acknowledged that he too had heard the rumors but denied the charge. However, Morgenthau, from this time forward, realized that he had to remove refugee issues from State Department domain.

Still, Morgenthau needed a push to confront the President. A Treasury aide, Josiah DuBois, provided it. DuBois, who wrote the "Report" on Christmas Day (along with John Pehle), threatened to resign from the Treasury and go public with his findings if Morgenthau didn't meet with the President.

What accounted for Morgenthau's reservation? The Secretary, like nearly every other Jew in the nation, venerated President Roosevelt. (In the general elections of 1936 and 1940, 90 percent of American Jews voted for the Roosevelt ticket.) In Morgenthau's case, he'd known the Roosevelts for many years, dating back to their neighborly friendship in Dutchess County, New York. In the early 1920s, Morgenthau joined the Roosevelt team. He quickly demonstrated his fierce loyalty and talents as an administrator. In addition, his wife Elinor became close to Eleanor Roosevelt, and the couples went out socially. The Morgenthaus, in fact, were the only Jews who socialized with the Roosevelts. Henry Morgenthau valued his relationship with FDR above all others; he was hesitant to do anything that might jeopardize the friendship.

At the same time, Henry Morgenthau was a Jew of his era. "He didn't want to stand out as a Jew," John Pehle explained. "He wanted to stand out as a Secretary of the Treasury."[7] Like the other Jews in the Roosevelt Administration, Morgenthau originally avoided Jewish issues. He found the matter of anti-Semitism perplexing and incredible. Once, when Father Charles Coughlin went on an attack, ridiculing Secretary Morgenthau for upholding the gold standard and calling for silver as a replacement, a "Gentile" metal in Coughlin's words, Morgenthau "was nonplussed."[8]

Holocaust news, however, began to have a deep impact on Morgenthau. On one occasion, Rabbi Wise visited the Secretary at the Treasury Department. Wise began to speak of Nazi atrocities. "Please, Stephen," Morgenthau replied, "don't give me the gory details." But Wise persisted; he talked about the Germans making soap out of concentration camp victims. Morgenthau kept "getting paler and paler" and his personal secretary "thought he was going to keel over."[9]

On that Sunday in January, 1944, a dapper Roosevelt greeted Morgenthau, Pehle, and Paul. This surprised Randolph Paul. Roosevelt was suffering from a case of influenza, contracted during the recently completed conference at Teheran. Still, according to Paul, he was "well-dressed."

Roosevelt listened to the Treasury's presentation. He did not read the "Report" but rather received an oral summation. He glanced at the executive order. He heard Morgenthau's attack on State Department duplicity and, in particular, Breckinridge Long's obstruction. Morgenthau asked that Long be stripped of refugee responsibility. At the same time, Morgenthau suggested that Congress had become tired of State Department subterfuge. If Roosevelt chose not to act, Congress would, with the effect of making Roosevelt look indifferent toward the Jews of Europe. The fact that 1944 was an election year perhaps added weight to Morgenthau's argument.

President Roosevelt did not commit himself. Forty minutes into the meeting, Eleanor poked her head into the Oval Room. "Now, come on, Franklin," she said. "Remember, you've not been well." The meeting ended abruptly.

For the rest of the day, Morgenthau felt ill at ease. "I was very serious," he wrote in his diary, "and he [Roosevelt] didn't seem to like it too much." That same evening, to assuage his anxieties, Morgenthau called the President. Roosevelt "joked and kidded with me and seemed to be in a grand humor," Morgenthau wrote in his diary. Roosevelt's jocularity calmed Morgenthau's nerves. Six days later, Roosevelt signed Executive Order 9417, bringing to life the War Refugee Board. The date was January 22, 1944.

In retrospect, Morgenthau wondered how the War Refugee Board came into existence. He gave credit to the Gillette-Rogers

Resolution. "When you get down to the point," Morgenhau mentioned during a staff meeting, "this is a boiling pot on the Hill. You can't hold it; it is going to pop, and you have either got to move very fast, or the Congress of the United States will do it for you."[10]

John Pehle argued otherwise. He praised "the Emergency Committee: Peter Bergson and his group."[11] For Peter Bergson, throughout 1943, had taken his campaign directly to Morgenthau. He repeatedly pressed the Secretary on the issue of a rescue agency. Morgenthau repeatedly echoed the Administration's line: only a military victory would solve the problem. Bergson's appeal, however, tempted the Secretary. And once his aides compiled all of the evidence against the State Department, Morgenthau felt compelled to confront the President.

On the implementation of the War Refugee Board, Peter Bergson reflected, "We had a sense of victory. . . . During the euphoric period after the War Refugee Board was born, we thought that now, you know, not only *we* get up in the morning worrying about the Jews, but there's a government agency worrying about them. The War Refugee Board gave us a relief, like water to the thirsty—and we wanted to believe. . . ."[12]

As for Henry Morgenthau, he continued to question the steps that led to the War Refugee Board. "I think that six months before [the rescue resolution] I couldn't have done it," he said. "Now, what I'm leading up to is this: I am just wondering who the crowd is that got the thing that far."[13]

Six months before Gillette-Rogers came to a floor vote, six months before Treasury Secretary Henry Morgenthau pleaded with the President for a rescue agency, FDR had welcomed a member of the Polish Underground into his office. The man's name was Jan Karski.

Chapter 20

◄ ►

Contact with Karski

The scene was FDR's private study, the Oval Room. The President sat behind his desk. Two men, Jan Ciechanowski, the Polish Ambassador to the United States, and Jan Karski, a courier representing the Polish Underground, entered the room. The date was July 28, 1943.

The President welcomed the visitors with the wave of his trademark cigarette holder. Karski was immediately impressed. "He really projected majesty, power, greatness," Karski later recalled.[1]

"Mr. President," Karski nervously began. "I cannot express my feelings. I cannot find the right words. When I was leaving Poland on my journey to England and to America I could hardly promise the men who sent me abroad that I would be able to reach you. They did not dare to think that it would be possible for an Underground courier to report to you personally at the White House in Washington. And here I am, Mr. President. . . ."[2]

At age thirty-two, Jan Karski appeared before the President as a learned warrior. His journey to the White House had been a long, instructive one. As a young man, Karski dreamed of becoming an ambassador. In his early twenties, he served as an apprentice diplomat, working at the Polish Consulates in Rumania, Switzerland, Germany, and England (and becoming fluent in French, German, and English). His internship in Germany coincided with the Nuremberg Laws of 1935. In fact, Karski attended the Nazis' Parteitag (Party Day) celebration as an invited guest. He listened to Hermann Gœring's nationalistic frenzy and wondered to himself, "Why couldn't I be born German, so I can be superior, too?"[3] Jan Karski was twenty-one years old at the time.

In the summer before the war began, Karski found a position as the administrative assistant to the Foreign Ministry's Director of Personnel. This was a major career step for a twenty-five-year-old. The grooming of Karski for a highly successful career in diplomacy seemed in full swing.

However, like all Polish young men, Karski had to serve in his country's military. An excellent horseman, he had become a Lieutenant in the Cavalry Brigade. On August 23, 1939, he received his mobilization orders. A few hours later Jan Karski boarded a train heading for the southwest corner of Poland, not far from the German border. The nearest town was named Oswiecim. The world would come to know the place as Auschwitz.

Following the German occupation of Poland, Karski joined the Underground as a courier. Eventually, that duty led to a mission to the West. In the winter of 1943, Karski made a harrowing trek across occupied Europe by train, from Warsaw to Berlin to Paris to Spain and finally on to London. In an ordinary house key, he carried microfilm welded into the shaft. The microfilm contained material documenting the many facets of life in Nazi Poland, from reports written by political leaders, to an analysis of the Underground, to a ten-page letter detailing the Holocaust under way in Warsaw. In London, under the direction of the Polish government-in-exile, Karski reported to both the Jewish leadership and the top echelon of the British government, including Lord Selbourne, the Chief of Special Operations, and Anthony Eden, the Foreign Minister. Eden reacted defensively to Karski. "He said that Great Britain had already done enough by accepting 100,000 refugees," Karski reported.[4]

In June, General Sikorski, the leader of the Polish government-in-exile, gave Karski new orders. He would travel to Washington to report on Poland's plight. Karski set sail from Scotland on June 10. He arrived on June 16.

The only ships that crossed the Atlantic in six days at that time were the *Queen Mary* and the *Queen Elizabeth*. The convoy ships, traveling at 8 to 10 knots, simply didn't move fast enough. The only port in Scotland in which the *Queens* entered was Gourock. In June of 1943, I'd just arrived in Gourock. As a Port Officer, it was altogether possible that I might have embarked Jan Karski on his mission to America. It's strange, when I reflect on this possibility, that I might have been so close to a man with first-hand knowledge of the Holocaust, and later on in my life I would pursue as much first-hand knowledge of the Holocaust as possible. It's ironic.

In America, Polish Ambassador Jan Ciechanowski introduced Karski to many top officials, from Assistant Secretary of State Adolf Berle to William Bullitt, the former Ambassador to the Soviet Union and France, to Attorney General Francis Biddle to Secretary of War Henry Stimson. To each member of the government, Karski told of the circumstances in war-torn Poland. "I have never met a man," Ambassador Ciechanowski later wrote, "who could with such simplicity, such telegraphic brevity, and such absolute frankness, describe events and complicated situations."[5]

Supreme Court Justice Felix Frankfurter met with Karski in the midst of these appointments. After a dinner with Karski and two other Jews within the Roosevelt Administration, adviser Ben Cohen and Assistant Solicitor General Oscar Cox, Frankfurter took Karski aside. Polish Ambassador Ciechanowski joined the conversation. "There are so many conflicting reports about what is happening to the Jews in your country," Frankfurter began. "Please tell me exactly what you have seen."

For the next half hour Karski spoke about the eradication of the Jews. When he finished, Frankfurter lifted himself from his chair and paced the room. Then he sat down again. "Mr. Karski," Frankfurter said, "a man like me talking to a man like you must be totally frank. So I must say: I am unable to believe you."

"Felix, you don't mean it!" Ambassador Ciechanowski replied. "How can you call him a liar to his face! The authority of my government is behind him. You know who he is!"

Frankfurter replied softly, "Mr. Ambassador, I did not say this young man is lying. I said I am unable to believe him. There is a difference."[6]

At the White House, Karski continued with his introduction. "Permit me to tell you, Mr. President, that not only we, the Poles, but hundreds of millions of people in Europe look up to you as the only man on earth who can bring us liberation and organize a peace based on justice and human principles. . . ."

The President "was visibly pleased," Jan Ciechanowski wrote in his remembrance of that era, *Defeat in Victory*, "but apparently wanted to get to the point quickly." Roosevelt asked, "Is the situation in Poland as bad as they say?"

In his explanation, Karski described Polish suffering under occupation, from severe food shortages to coal deprivation (and therefore unheated homes) to psychological demoralization. Karski recounted how, during a sugar shortage, the Nazi Governor of Poland mockingly thanked the Poles for making sugar available to the "heroic German army, which fights self-sacrificingly to protect Poles from Communism, British and American imperialism, and international Jewry."

"That's amazing," Roosevelt responded. "Their perfidy is just beyond understanding."

That comment sparked the President. He launched into a series of questions. He asked about the Polish Underground. He asked about German conduct, from the rumors of prisoner sterilization to German property confiscation to abuses. He wondered if the Germans were easy to bribe. He asked if demoralization in the German army and administration had reached any considerable degree.

In his autobiography, Karski wrote of the President's inquiries: "On every topic he demanded precise and accurate information. He wanted to know, to be able to realize, not merely imagine, the very climate and atmosphere of Underground work and the minds of the men engaged in it."[7]

"Tell me about the German methods of terror," Roosevelt said.

"They're different than the Bolsheviks' methods," Karski

responded. A significant part of Karski's mission to the West was to reveal Soviet abuses. Karski, in fact, had been captured by the Soviets in the initial days of the war. The Soviets used the German blitzkrieg as an excuse to attack from the east. Karski spent about a month in a detention center in central Ukraine. (At the time, Karski thought he was in an arctic region of Russia, judging from the frigidity and the five-day journey in a boxcar.) He managed to escape, but some twenty-two thousand of his fellow Polish officers were murdered by Soviet troops, under Stalin's orders, and buried in the Katyn Forest. In addition, the Russians had deported hundreds of thousands of Poles to the Soviet Union and were sending "agents and provocateurs" to infiltrate and expose the Polish Underground.

"That's a very tough situation," Roosevelt responded. "Old Joe is playing a wily game."

"The Germans have other techniques," Karski then interjected. This was a subject that Karski knew intimately. In 1940, he'd been captured by the Gestapo while on a mission to Slovakia, tortured to the edge of his life, given time to recover, and then tortured again. The persecution went on interminably. Knowing that he'd eventually break, knowing that at some point he'd reveal invaluable information, Karski slashed at his wrists with a razor blade hidden in his shoe. The injuries didn't kill him; they did, however, land him in a hospital. Word of his confinement spread. When the Underground learned of his presence, a commando team performed a daring rescue. The commando team had specific orders. The first was to save Karski at any price. The second was to shoot him if the rescue didn't succeed.

To Roosevelt, Karski described German methods of terror in a different way. He chose to focus on the technique of mass arrests. "They find a doctor in some small town who's involved in the Underground movement, and they arrest most of the doctors," he told the President. "They find a printing press, and they arrest everybody living for several blocks around." For instance, in a street roundup in the summer of '42, the Germans arrested thirty-five thousand Poles in a matter of days.

The notion of arrests steered Karski to mention Auschwitz.

"The most horrible concentration camp," he called it. And though he introduced the camp in terms of Poles and Polish suffering, he soon turned to the treatment of the Jews. "There is a difference between the German-orchestrated systems of terror against the Poles and the Jews," Karski told Roosevelt. "The Germans want to ruin the Polish state as a state; they want to rule over a Polish people deprived of its elites. . . . With regard to the Jews, they want to devastate the biological substance of the Jewish nation."

In August 1942, when plans for Karski's mission to the West were in the works, Jewish guides smuggled him into the Warsaw ghetto. "There was hardly a square yard of empty space," Karski recalled. "As we picked our way across the mud and rubble, the shadows of what had once been men or women flitted by us in pursuit of someone or something, their eyes blazing with some insane hunger or greed." Naked dead bodies filled the gutters. Karski asked his guides about their significance. "When a Jew dies," a guide replied, "the family removes his clothing and throws his body in the street. Otherwise they would have to pay a burial tax to the Germans. Besides, this saves clothing." Karski began to feel sick to his stomach. A final sight made him flee the ghetto in haste. From an upstairs window he watched "while two pudgy teen-aged boys in the uniforms of the Hitler Youth hunted Jews for sport, cheering and laughing when one of their rifle shots struck its target and brought screams of agony."[8]

The assault of witnessing the Warsaw ghetto was further compounded, a few weeks later, when Karski was smuggled into a small concentration camp (near the town of Izbica Lubelska). There, the Jews were sorted and transported to the extermination camp at Belzec some forty miles away. Dressed as a Ukrainian militiaman, he saw an expanse completely covered by "a dense, pulsating, throbbing, noisy human mass" of "starved, stinking, gesticulating, insane" Jews. He "thought he smelled burning flesh. Soon he witnessed the arrival of several thousand starving and frightened Jews who had been brought to the camp from Czechoslovakia. He watched as their bags were taken away from them. Then he saw Jews being beaten and stabbed." The experience left Karski physically ill and psychologically torn. Later in life, Karski, like many actual survivors, would refuse to go into the details of what he witnessed. Instead, he would say, "I saw terrible things."

To Roosevelt, Karski warned, "If the Germans don't change their methods of dealing with the Jewish population, if there is no effort at Allied intervention, whether through reprisals or other actions, barring some unforeseen circumstance, within a year and a half of the time I left the Homeland, the Jewish people of Poland, beyond those actively working in the Jewish Underground in cooperation with us, will cease to exist."

Karski's information was not new to Roosevelt. A week earlier, for instance, Rabbi Wise had been in the same office reporting similar stories. Roosevelt chose to return to the Polish Underground. He asked about the levels of cooperation between the Jewish and Polish Undergrounds. He asked about Poland's postwar preparedness. He raised the issue of Poland's western (East Prussia) border, assuring Karski and Ambassador Ciechanowski that the corridor connecting Germany to Danzig (Gdansk) would not exist after liberation. "No more Polish corridor," Roosevelt promised, "no more corridor this time."

Regarding the eastern border, Roosevelt wondered, "What can we do if Stalin calmly announces, for instance, that the question of Lithuania must be left out of the discussions? I presume that he will insist on his demands for some rectification of the eastern boundaries of Poland. . . . I am afraid that Stalin will raise a question which will be very difficult for us; namely, that of compensation for giving East Prussia to Poland."

At this moment in the discussion, the President paused. Ambassador Ciechanowski suggested that an unyielding position on the part of America would stop Soviet territorial demands. "Well, yes," Roosevelt replied, "but we cannot afford a war with Russia."

An hour and fifteen minutes into the meeting, an exorbitant amount of time for the President to spend with an envoy, Roosevelt glanced at his watch. He was, he announced, a half hour late for another appointment. Jan Karski had time for one final question. "I am going back to Poland," he said (although, in fact, he did not; his identity had become known to the Germans). "People will know that I was received by the President of the United States. Everybody will ask me: what did President Roosevelt tell you? What am I to tell them?"

"You will tell them that we shall win this war," Roosevelt responded. "You will tell them that the guilty ones will be punished. Justice and freedom shall prevail. You will tell your nation that they have a friend in this house."[9]

The meeting between Karski and Roosevelt left an indelible impression on both men. Karski, in the immediate aftermath, felt "not an ordinary fatigue." He felt "the satisfied weariness of the workman who has just completed his job with a last blow of his hammer or an artist who signs his name under the completed picture."

Secretary of State Cordell Hull was amazed at the impact Karski had on FDR. In a conversation with Ambassador Ciechanowski a few days later, Hull said, "The President seems so thrilled by his talk with your young man that he can talk of nothing else." Ambassador Ciechanowski confirmed the impact of Karski on Roosevelt when he wrote to his associates in London, "I find that never before have I seen him [Roosevelt] so deeply interested, and even completely absorbed, as upon this occasion. . . . I emphasize the fact that the President, who so enjoys dominating conversations himself, listened to Mr. Karski without interrupting him and held his questions until Mr. Karski had finished with each topic. . . ." According to John Pehle, the War Refugee Board's first Executive Director. "Over night," Karski's meeting "changed U.S. government policy from . . . indifference at best to affirmative action."

Pehle's statement tended toward exaggeration. Six months would pass before the President signed Executive Order 9417.

Chapter 21

◀▶

Counterforces

Executive Order 9417 called for the War Refugee Board (WRB) to "take all measures within its power to rescue the victims of enemy oppression who are in imminent danger of death and otherwise to afford such victims all possible relief and assistance consistent with the successful prosecution of the war."

The WRB immediately met roadblocks. From the beginning there was inertia. President Roosevelt, for instance, appointed the Secretaries of the three most powerful Cabinet agencies to supervisory roles. Secretary Morgenthau, of course, was the European Jew's best hope in Washington. Secretary of State Hull had no time, or inclination, for rescue. As for Secretary of War Henry Stimson, he may have initially supported the WRB but he "could spare almost no time for it because of his other heavy duties."[1] In addition, Stimson's track record exposed his attitude of immigration restriction. During Herbert Hoover's Administration, Stimson, then the Secretary of State, supported the National Origins Act of 1929, which tightly squeezed immigration for Europeans beyond Great Britain.

Due to his heavy duties, Stimson appointed Assistant Secretary John McCloy to be his representative at the WRB. That appointment had far-reaching effects on rescue. McCloy, in the summer of 1944, rejected the WRB's call for bombing Auschwitz and the railway lines leading to it (see chapter 22).

From the beginning there was delay. When Roosevelt signed the Executive Order, he suggested a nationally prominent person to serve as Executive Director. Secretary Morgenthau pushed for pushed for his assistant, John Pehle. The Cabinet Secretaries compromised. Pehle would lead the rescue work while a prestigious public figure would guide the WRB's relations with the Administration, the Congress, and the public. Morgenthau suggested Wendell Willkie, who had previously taken up the rescue cause, personally confronting British leadership on its closed-door policy in Palestine in 1942. However, 1944 was an election year and with Willkie the possible Republican nominee, Roosevelt would not put him in a position where he might attract attention. Morgenthau then suggested Frank Graham, the President of the University of North Carolina and a leading advocate for the passage of the Wagner-Rogers Bill of 1939. The President rejected the nominee outright. Morgenthau then returned to his first suggestion, John Pehle. By the time Roosevelt signed off on the candidate, two weeks had passed. Meanwhile, the trains continued to depart from points throughout Europe for Auschwitz. On February 3, a train carrying 1,214 Jews left Drancy, the despicable transit camp in France. Nine hundred and eighty-five of those people died in the gas of Auschwitz. On February 8, a train carrying one thousand Jews left Westerbork, the despicable transit camp in Holland. Eight hundred of those people, including all the children, died in the gas of Auschwitz.[2]

From the beginning there was limited government funding for so large an undertaking. In its entire existence, the WRB used about $1.6 million of government monies: $547,000 drawn from the President's Emergency Fund and $1,100,000 from the general appropriation for foreign war relief as voted on by Congress. Contrast those numbers to the $16,300,000 provided by private Jewish organizations, including $15 million supplied by the Joint Distribution Committee. The United States government provided 9 percent of the WRB's budget. Is it not unusual for a government agency to operate on privately drawn funds?

From the beginning there was State Department obstruction. The State Department, in fact, adhered to its pre-WRB days of anti-rescue. Three examples speak specifically to State Department subterfuge:

1. The Department insisted on clearing all cables drafted by the WRB. In the first few weeks of the Board's existence, the WRB sent out cables to all Embassies, Consulates, and missions explaining the major shift in American policy. All personnel were now expected to help save refugees. The State Department, however, found those cables disturbing, particularly the phrase, "the Department is determined to do everything in its power to carry out this Government's policy." James Dunn, a State Department official, reacted: "That Jew Morgenthau and his Jewish assistants like Dubois are trying to take over this place."[3] Dubois was a Protestant, as was Pehle. And even after the demotion of Breckinridge Long, the anti-Semitism continued to prevail.

2. In March, officials at the Department squelched six urgent cablegrams, one of which involved warning Nazi satellites to refrain from collaborating in Nazi atrocities.

3. That spring, the Germans captured a group of Polish Jews hidden in France and transported them to Camp Vittel near Paris. The Jews, many of whom were rabbis, held false Latin American passports. These passports gave Jews a better chance of survival. Officially, Nazi policy incarcerated, rather than murdered, Jewish citizens from countries not under Axis control. The Polish Jews, however, were clearly not Latin American nationals and the Nazis began to question the authenticity of their papers. The WRB, upon hearing the news from Camp Vittel, asked the State Department to petition the Swiss government. In the past, the Swiss had achieved a measure of success in appealing directly to the Nazi government. The State Department stalled. Officially, the Department took a position condemning the use of false papers. Two months passed. Eventually, through WRB persuasion, State changed course. That change took place in the early summer. By then, the Polish rabbis were on their way to Auschwitz.

The WRB spent a good portion of its time wondering how to push rescue policy through State, rather than actually pursuing rescue. Had State been more cooperative, could the WRB have been effective earlier? How many more Jews could have been saved? Considering the earlier period of the War Refugee Board, Peter Bergson compared the WRB to a train that "didn't jump, it slowly got off, it didn't turn over."[4]

This then was the situation that Executive Director John Pehle and his colleagues from the Treasury inherited. To be certain, the WRB staff recognized the desperate urgency associated with their work. They were, one observer commented, "young, dynamic, bold, clear and a bit brash."[5] They began by meeting with the many private agencies involved in rescue and relief activities. There was no shortage of suggestions. The American Jewish Committee, for instance, advocated bombing Auschwitz and the railway lines. The Bergson group proposed threatening the Nazis with the use of poisonous gas on the German population if the mass murders continued. "If this would have been tried," Bergson declared, "it might have stopped the massacre right there and then."

The WRB put forth a multi-faceted, ambitious plan for rescue. The strategy hinged upon the cycle of moving Jewish refugees from enemy territories into neutral countries and onto temporary havens and therefore opening up the neutral countries for more refugees. Two elements were needed to facilitate the flow of refugees: field representatives in the neutral countries and havens for resettlement. Considering the latter, a number of sites were suggested and pursued. In Libya, the British stalled. Opening a refugee camp for Jews in North Africa, the British argued, would lead to "involved political problems." In other words, Arab opposition. In Fedala, near Casablanca, the French procrastinated for three months before opening the army barracks to 2,000 refugees, although the space could hold 15,000. In the Soviet Union, the Russians, who had moved 120,000 Polish nationals to refugee camps in Iran, refused to help Jews. In America, President Roosevelt opened a shelter at Fort Ontario in Oswego, New York, in August 1944. Roosevelt permitted nearly one thousand refugees from southern Italy to enter the United States outside the quota system. This caused considerable consternation and criticism within the Congress. Roosevelt reacted by calling his decision, "the humanitarian thing to do." He then stressed that the refugees would remain in an army camp "under appropriate security restrictions" and "upon the termination of the war they will be sent back to their homelands."[6]

At Fort Ontario, resentment immediately surfaced on all sides. The refugees felt shackled by their surroundings. Their living conditions were shabby; they had to adhere to a curfew; their futures were uncertain; they were in a holding tank of sorts—isolated, their lives shattered by the immediate past, with no opportunity to rebuild—and they felt like prisoners of war. Curt Bondy, a psychologist and expert on camp life, reported "the high level of tension in the shelter, despite the almost complete absence of physical violence."

In the town of Oswego, anti-Semitism pervaded. The residents who befriended the refugees were socially ostracized. In the Oswego schools, which allowed the refugee children to enroll, the name-calling—with terms like "Dirty Jew" and "filthy refugee"—became a regular part of the day. The town residents considered the refugees an affliction and called Fort Ontario "a dumping ground for the unwanted."

In the country, the isolationists and anti-Semites flooded the newspapers with vitriol. "None believed that the refugees would go back," David Wyman wrote in *The Abandonment of the Jews*. "Many saw the thousand as the entering wedge for hundreds of thousands more, mostly Jews." A Colorado man, writing to the newspaper, summarized the general impression: "What country would want a Jew back?"

What were President Roosevelt's intentions in opening Fort Ontario? And why did he stop at one thousand refugees? The need was great and there were many vacant military bases throughout the country. Why couldn't more have been opened? The fact that no other havens opened within the United States stifled the rescue of European Jews. The governments of Central and South America viewed the Fort Ontario haven as tokenism; there was no groundswell therefore to open other havens in the Americas. In the neutral countries, those refugees who had reached safety couldn't move on. There was simply no place to go. That meant that new refugees from enemy lands couldn't enter. The roadblock was stifling.

In its hope to facilitate the flow of refugees from enemy-occupied lands into the neutrals, the WRB placed representatives in Portugal, Spain, Sweden, Switzerland, and Turkey. In Switzerland Roswell McClelland, who had worked for the Quakers in France since 1941, financed a series of covert operations. They included protecting thousands of Jewish children in France (mainly through false documents like counterfeit birth certificates, fake work permits, and baptismal certificates); organizing escape routes across the Pyrenees from France into Spain; funding Underground fighters in Slovakia who freed over a thousand Jews from concentration camps; funding prison breaks in Italy, liberating partisan leaders; and bribing guards so that refugees could move into Switzerland. Through McClelland's leadership, some 27,000 Jewish refugees escaped into Switzerland during the WRB era, as did approximately 20,000 non-Jewish refugees.

In Turkey Ira Hirschmann identified hundreds of thousands of Jews in Rumania, Bulgaria, and Hungary. He saw Turkey as a "window into the Balkans." The job, according to Hirschmann, "was to attempt to make out of the window, a door."[7]

Hirschmann had previous experience in dealing with Jews in dire circumstances. In the immediate aftermath of the Evian Conference (1938), Hirschmann visited Vienna. There, he witnessed the long lines of Jews at the U.S. Consulate. Without financial sponsorship, he knew that the refugees had no chance of gaining admittance to America. Hirschmann rented a hotel suite and let it be known that he would serve as a guarantor. In one day he "accepted financial responsibility for more than two hundred prospective immigrants he had never seen before." These refugees all entered America and none of them became public charges.[8]

In Turkey Hirschmann put forth an ambitious plan. He endeavored to set up evacuation routes into Turkey and on to Palestine. He opened a land route for the Jews in Bulgaria and a sea route for those in Rumania. At the same time, he pressured the governments of Turkey, Rumania, and Bulgaria to ease immigration restrictions. Due to Hirschmann's persuasion, the Rumanian government moved the Jews of Transnistria, where some 48,000 of the original 70,000 still remained and were in the direct path of the retreating German army. In total, some 7,000 Jews fled into Turkey and reached Palestine under WRB guidance.

Why were Hirschmann and the WRB effective in Rumania and Bulgaria? German hegemony was crumbling. That made President Roosevelt's March 24th war crimes declaration even more threatening. "In one of the blackest crimes of all history—begun by the Nazis in the day of peace and multiplied by them a hundred times in time of war—the wholesale systematic murder of the Jews of Europe goes on unabated every hour . . . ," Roosevelt roared. "None who participate in these acts of savagery shall go unpunished. . . . That warning applies not only to the leaders but also to their functionaries and subordinates in Germany and in the satellite countries. All who knowingly take part in the deportation of Jews to their death in Poland or Norwegians and French to their death in Germany are equally guilty with the executioner. All who share the guilt shall share the punishment." And so the fear of FDR's declaration coupled with Germany's diminishing ability to wage war forced the Balkan nations into a level of cooperation.

An interesting side story. When John Pehle suggested to Roosevelt that he issue a war crimes warning, Roosevelt responded positively. But in a request similar to the one asked of Rabbi Wise back in December of 1942, Roosevelt wanted the WRB staff to write the warning. That draft wasn't the one issued. Roosevelt's chief speechwriter and counsel on all issues Jewish, Samuel Rosenman, weakened the speech. Rosenman thought the original version placed excessive emphasis on the Jews, which had been in fact the WRB's purpose. Like many American Jews in positions of authority, Rosenman believed that placing an emphasis on the Jews of Europe would fuel American anti-Semitism and lead to a rise of anti-Roosevelt sentiment. Peter Bergson called Rosenman, "the most guilty of the bunch. . . . If he would have had the healthy attitude of saying . . . , 'I cannot be your adviser on Jewish things. I can be your speechwriter. Please don't rely upon me in Jewish matters.' But he didn't. He functioned as a Jew all the time."[9] In the original version of the war crimes warning, the destruction of Europe's Jews dominated the tone of the entire warning. In Rosenman's version, the annihilation of Europe's Jews had a secondary quality.

In March of 1944 rumors began to circulate that the Hungarian government was considering an armistice with the Allies. The Nazis' grasp on Europe appeared perilous. The Red Army approached from the east. The Western Allies controlled North Africa and southern Italy. Although the Hungarians couldn't have known it, the Normandy invasion was only a few months away.

Hitler reacted to the rumors by forcing the Regent of Hungary, Admiral Miklos Horthy, to appoint an anti-Semitic government. Horthy vacillated. He was not a friend of the Jews. He detested foreign Jews, particularly those from Poland. However, his daughter-in-law was Jewish and he found the assimilated Jews of Hungary loyal and therefore less objectionable.

Hungary at that time held some 800,000 Jews. In fact, Hungary had served as sort of an oasis. The incessant massacres throughout Europe hadn't materialized under the Horthy regime. Therefore, thousands of Jews from Poland, Slovakia, and Rumania had sought refuge there.

Adolf Eichmann arrived in Budapest at the end of March. As he did in Vienna during the *Anschluss* and Poland after the invasion, Eichmann quickly put in place the Nazis' Jewish policy: enforcing the wearing of the yellow star, confiscating Jewish property, rounding up the Jews and forcing them into a ghetto. Afterward, as per Nazi policy, he formed a Jewish council which served as the liaison between the Nazis and the general Jewish population. Within two months, the deportations to Auschwitz began. From May 15 to July 7, 437,000 Jews were transported to the death camp. The crematoria simply couldn't handle the volume. To compensate for the massive influx, the Commandant of Auschwitz, Rudolf Höss, ordered pits to be dug. Before the deportations ended, nearly 300,000 Jews from Hungary were either gassed or shot.

The War Refugee Board reacted to the Hungarian crisis in substantive ways. Aside from Roosevelt's war crimes warning of March 24th, the WRB convinced the President to threaten the bombing of Budapest in hopes of ending the deportations. Roosevelt did so on a number of occasions, including the end of June. When the deportations didn't end, the Allies bombed Budapest in early July. The U.S. Fifteenth Air Force hit targets (an oil refinery, the city's rail yards, an airfield) in and near Budapest with twelve hundred tons of bombs. The bombing damaged private homes and governmental buildings. The psychological effects were unmistakable: The Hungarian government realized that the Allies controlled the air and therefore could, at Allied whim, inflict inestimable damage.

In addition, the WRB called on the Pope to personally intervene. Pope Pius XII, in fact, had numerous opportunities to intervene, even to possibly facilitate rescue. In August 1941, for instance, the Vichy government asked the Vatican for its position on its anti-Jewish laws. "I have never been told anything which—from the standpoint of the Holy See—implied criticism and disapproval of the legislative and administrative acts in question," Léon Bérard, Vichy's Ambassador to the Vatican, reported. An authorized spokesman at the Vatican simply responded that Vichy should show "justice and charity."

Subsequently, the Vichy government issued a press release. "Nothing in the legislation designed to protect France from the Jewish influence is opposed to the doctrine of the Church." Pope Pius did not object to the statement.[10]

Another opportunity for the Pope to save Jews occurred in the fall of 1943. On October 16, under the watchful eye of Adolf Eichmann, German troops entered the ghetto of Rome, rounded up one thousand Jews and transported them by trucks to a transit building. The trucks passed the boundary of St. Peter's Square. The imprisoned Jews, according to various reports, called out to the Pope for assistance. Two days later the Jews were sent to Auschwitz. Only fifteen of the one thousand survived the war.

Pope Pius XII was one of the first to hear of the round-up and deportation. According to the German Ambassador to the Holy

See, "pressure from all sides was building, calling for a demonstrative [Papal] censure of the deportation of the Jews of Rome."[11] Much of the pressure came from the Germans in Italy. The German Consul in Rome, for instance, feared that the deportation would instigate a general Italian uprising against the Nazis. But Pope Pius never offered a word of protest. Not during the first deportation of one thousand Jews, nor during subsequent deportations. His one action was to open the sanctuaries of Vatican City to all "non-Aryans" seeking refuge. The Pope's compliance with the deportations stemmed from a fear of Communism. In the absence of Nazism, he anticipated a "Communist takeover." (His fear never abated and to the end of his Papacy in 1958 he threatened to excommunicate Catholics who supported Communism.) Harold Tittman, American representative to the Vatican, summarized the Pope's behavior in a message to the State Department. Tittman wrote, "The Holy Father appears to be occupying himself exclusively with spiritual matters, charitable acts, and rhetoric, while adopting an ostrich-like policy toward these notorious Nazi atrocities. . . ."[12] Within two months of the first deportation from Rome, the Nazis rounded up 7,345 Jews, mainly in northern Italy. A staggering 6,746 of the Jews were gassed upon arrival at Auschwitz.[13]

"I came back from Auschwitz on my own," a Roman Jewish woman said. "I lost my mother, two sisters, a niece, and one brother. Pius XII could have warned us about what was going to happen. We might have escaped from Rome and joined the partisans. He played right into the Germans' hands. It all happened right under his nose. But he was an anti-Semitic Pope, a pro-German Pope. He didn't take a single risk. And when they say the Pope is like Jesus Christ, it is not true. He did not save a single child. Nothing."[14]

As for the Pope's reaction to the WRB and its call for the Holy See to intervene in Hungary, Pius waited a month before sending a plea to Admiral Horthy. His cable to Horthy read, "Use all possible influence in order to stop the suffering and torments which countless people are undergoing simply because of their nationality or their race." By then hundreds of thousands of Hungarian Jews had been murdered.

The WRB, in addition to applying pressure on the Pope and President Roosevelt, pursued ransom opportunities, including Eichmann's trucks-for-Jews scheme. Eichmann's deal—significant amounts of coffee, tea, soap, and 10,000 trucks in exchange for one million Jews—was met with U.S. skepticism. The State Department, in consultation with the WRB, agreed on a delay tactic, stringing out negotiations as long as possible. Morgenthau and Pehle "strongly supported continuing negotiations in the hope that Eichmann's offer might be the forerunner of other proposals." President Roosevelt agreed. The other Allies did not. The British feared that negotiations might "lead to an offer to unload an even greater number of Jews onto our hands." The Soviets denounced "any conversations whatsoever with the German government" on this issue.[15] The deal died, officially, when the British leaked it to the press.

Was the trucks-for-Jews scheme an actual ransom possibility or was it, like other Nazi proposals, an olive branch to the West, a façade, and an effort to cozy up to the Western Allies with the Soviet Union bearing down upon the Germans? As far as ransom possibility goes, a secondary story suggests an answer. After collecting a sizable ransom from Hungary's Jews, Eichmann promised that a train carrying 1,700 Jews would be sent to Spain. Instead, those Jews were sent to the concentration camp Bergen-Belsen in Germany. Would Eichmann have pulled a similar maneuver in this case?

The WRB, in addition to ransom opportunities, placed a field representative in Hungary. His name was Raoul Wallenberg. A thirty-one-year-old Swede, Wallenberg reached Budapest on July 9, 1944. By then, nearly 600,000 Jews had disappeared. The countryside had been cleared. The Jews in Budapest, some 230,000 in number, held a perilous position. Although the deportations had ended two days earlier, another round could commence at any moment.

Wallenberg arrived carrying two knapsacks, a sleeping bag, a windbreaker, and a revolver. "The revolver is just to give me courage," Wallenberg told Per Anger, the Second Secretary at the Swedish Legation in Budapest, who quickly became Wallenberg's colleague in rescue.[16] Wallenberg, a member of a prominent family, a world traveler and linguist, an architect with a degree from the University of Michigan, immediately began the most dramatic life-saving operation of the war. He concocted a protective passports scheme, giving tens of thousands of Jews identification papers. He rented a building and applied Swedish territorial status to it. The building became a safe haven for several hundred Jewish religious leaders. In the course of a few months, he added several additional buildings to his scheme. The total number of Jews under Swedish protection swelled to an estimated 20,000 people.

The stories of Wallenberg's heroics during this period are legendary. Hungary's pro-Nazi Party, the Arrow Cross, wanted to kill him. So did Eichmann, who referred to Wallenberg as the "Jew-dog." Wallenberg did not let the danger deter him. For instance, when an armed patrol entered the Swedish house and began rounding up Jews, Wallenberg intervened. "This is Swedish territory," he declared. "If you want to take them you will have to shoot me first." The patrol released the Jews.

On another occasion, he received word of a deportation. Although the general deportation policy had ceased, the Germans sporadically shipped Jews off to Poland. To try to counter these transports, Wallenberg utilized lookouts at strategic rail points. When his informers passed on information of the deportation, he went to the train station. He brought with him a list filled with those holding protective Swedish passports. He suggested to the Germans that these Jews had been put on board by mistake. "The Germans were taken by surprise," Per Anger wrote, "and right under their noses, Wallenberg pulled out a large number of Jews. Many of them had no passport at all, only various papers in the Hungarian language—driver's licenses, vaccination records, or tax records—that the Germans did not understand. The bluff succeeded."

How many Jews did WRB representative Raoul Wallenberg save? He sheltered and protected some 20,000 Jews in the Swedish houses. Both the Spanish and the Swiss legations joined in his example, saving anywhere from 10,000 to 30,000 Jews. In total, 120,000 Jews in Budapest survived the war. How many of these people owed their survival to Wallenberg? He provided food to the Jews in the ghetto. In addition, when word trickled out that the Arrow Cross planned to destroy the ghetto and its inhabitants in the final days of Nazi occupation, Wallenberg went to see the SS commander. He promised the German that if he didn't prevent the killing, Wallenberg would make certain that he swung from the gallows when the Russians came. The German stopped the operation.

Historians estimate that Wallenberg saved as many as 100,000 lives. One life he couldn't save was his own. When the Russians took control of the country, he traveled to their headquarters in Debrecen. Tragically, he was never directly heard from again.

The Swedish government continually pursued information on Wallenberg. In 1945, Moscow reported that Wallenberg was under the protection of Soviet troops. In 1957, Moscow reported that Wallenberg had died of a heart attack back in 1947. However, in 1979, reports emerged, placing Wallenberg in the Soviet prison system and in relatively good health. He would have been sixty-six years old at that time.

How many refugees did the War Refugee Board save? The exact numbers are not known. There are only approximations, and they vary from historian to historian. A quarter of a million lives seems reasonable. That total, of course, comes nowhere near the need. The history of the WRB is a legacy of possibility. The WRB, which started as a governmental agency endowed with broad-based authority, quickly turned into something else. "An effective, large-scale charitable effort to save some Jews of Europe," Peter Bergson summarized. Such an "effort" wasn't powerful enough. To re-quote Bergson, the "magnitude of the slaughter wasn't anything that a charitable organization would handle. Only a government could handle it."

Peter Bergson attributed the breakdown to, in his words, "various counterforces." The culprits are clear: the State Department, the British who feared a major resettlement, the Soviets who shunned rescue operation, the governments of the neutral countries. The Turks feared Axis saboteurs crossing an open border and flooding the country before dispersing into Allied lands. The Swiss severely limited Jews crossing their frontier. According to official Swiss policy, groups who could cross the border without impediment included: those in danger due to political belief, escaped prisoners of war, and military deserters. Jews who could cross the border included: young children and their parents (if present), pregnant women, the sick and the old, and relatives of Swiss citizens. Outside of those categories (and within these categories, too), most Jews were turned away.

At the same time, the Swiss government acted in partnership with the Nazis. Switzerland accepted looted gold. In his testimony at the Nuremberg Trials, Walther Funk, the President of the Reichsbank, recalled, "The other countries with which we still had business relations introduced gold embargoes. Sweden refused to accept gold at all. Only in Switzerland could we still do business through changing gold into foreign currency."[17]

The Reichsbank dealt predominantly with the Swiss National Bank, Switzerland's central bank. The Swiss National Bank bought the gold at a discount, charged a commission of 0.5 percent to the Nazis and sold the gold to other neutral European banks (mainly in Spain and Portugal) at significantly higher prices. Estimates vary but it is believed that the Swiss National Bank made nearly $400 million (around $4 billion in today's currency) in profits and $20 million (nearly $200 million in today's currency) on the commission alone. The evidence was "incontrovertible," according to Stuart Eizenstat, an Undersecretary of Commerce who conducted a study of Nazi gold in 1997. "The Swiss National Bank . . . knew as the war progressed that the Reichsbank's own coffers had been depleted, and that the Swiss were handling vast sums of looted gold."

In the early 1940s, with Germany on the verge of bankruptcy, the Nazis filled their coffers in two ways. As its armies conquered various nations, the Nazis looted the treasuries of the occupied countries, in violation of international law. The Hague Convention of 1907 stipulated that occupying powers could only secure publicly held property for the administration of the occupation, not for the financing of a war effort. The Nazis, of course, didn't respect international law. In Belgium, for instance, the Nazis looted the entire gold reserve, valued at $223 million (around $2.2 billion today).

Simultaneously, the Nazis filled their coffers by confiscating property belonging to the Jews, including the bullion the Jews brought to the concentration camps. The Nazis sent the bullion (such as jewelry, rings and, of course, gold extracted from teeth) to the mint in Prussia. There, the gold was melted into bars. These were the bars that the Reichsbank sold to the Swiss National Bank.

The Swiss partnership with the Nazis didn't end there. From the Swiss, the Nazis received munitions, machine tools, and electrical equipment throughout the war. The munitions, in particular, worried Secretary of State Cordell Hull. In a letter to Admiral William Leahy he wrote that the Swiss were "materially decreasing the military effectiveness of our air attacks on the Axis." Leahy agreed. He replied that the Swiss were increasing Nazi munitions supplies "at the very time that the British and American combined bomber offensive is beginning to substantially affect German production of munitions." An Allied blockade of Switzerland was discussed, but never put into effect.

And what of the accounts opened in Switzerland by Jews during the 1930s and early 1940s? Many thousands of Jewish families entrusted their fortunes to the Swiss banks, believing the neutrality of Switzerland would bring about a measure of security. The Swiss banks, after the war, denied access to the accounts. The banks, employing the tactic of obstruction, asked for death certificates. While over a quarter of a million Jewish survivors suffered in poverty in Displaced Persons Camps, Swiss banks held an estimated $8.9 million (in today's currency) in accounts that might have been opened by some of those survivors. And to add insult to injury, in more recent years, as Swiss complicity has been fleshed out, the Union Bank of Switzerland ordered the shredding of files from the 1930s and 1940s. A young security guard, Christoph Meili, happened to notice two large bins filled with documents in the bank's shredding room. For fifteen minutes, he perused German contracts from the war era. Included in the material, Meili read about "forced auctions," or confiscation of property in Berlin. Meili absconded with as many documents as he could carry, turning them over to Israeli officials. Some of the materials about to be shredded came from Eigenoessiche Bank, a subsidiary of the

Union Bank. "There were several Swiss banks that cultivated close connections with Germany in the 1930s and Eigenoessiche was one of them," Swiss journalist Gian Trepp, an expert on Swiss banks, responded. "They attached their fate to the fate of Nazi Germany. What that means is that anything about Eigenoessiche has a possible relevance to the Holocaust."[18]

Considering the Swiss-Nazi alliance, it is easy to see why the WRB, in Peter Bergson's words, "got worn out." Some of those "counterforces" were actually Nazi accomplices.

Back in America, there was a counterforce of another kind. Though clearly not a Nazi accomplice and in no way linked to the work of the WRB, the case of Arthur Sulzberger demonstrated the tremendous influence of one man.[19]

Like most successful Jews of the time, Sulzberger was culturally assimilated: American first, Jewish second. Sulzberger, in fact, feared "being continually classified" with other Jews, particularly the less-educated, more recent immigrants. At the same time, Sulzberger suffered the indignities of anti-Semitism, from being called a "sheeny" as a child to being turned away from a Cape Cod resort as a young father. How much these experiences impacted Sulzberger during his run as owner and publisher of the *New York Times* is difficult to say, but he did worry that his Protestant readership might feel alienated by his Jewish status and he did fear that anti-Semitism might rise further, as society saw another Jew in a position of power.

In Sulzberger's worldview, Jews were neither a race nor a people. Judaism was simply a religion. Sulzberger staunchly believed that Jews could become as integrated as their non-Jewish neighbors, with only the place of worship serving to differentiate. This was Reform Judaism, as espoused by Rabbi Isaac Wise. In Wise's version, Jews had a mission: to champion the principles of the Enlightenment, to teach integration, to castigate divisions based on race, religion, or nationality. In Wise's version, the United States was the proving ground for his brand of Reform Judaism. America, with its code of morality, with its laws of justice, with its melting-pot immigration, became "our Zion." Arthur Sulzberger bought into this philosophy whole-heartedly.

As Adolf Hitler came to power in 1933, Sulzberger assumed control of the *Times*. The era for Sulzberger was full of controversial decisions. He opposed the boycott of German goods, believing that the international community should not delve into what he considered an internal German affair. He supported the immigration system of quotas. Only once, according to Laurel Leff in *Buried by the Times*, did the *New York Times* advocate loosening the restrictions: during the Wagner-Rogers debate of 1939. But even then, the *Times'* editorial emphasized that the children would be "of every race and creed." Sulzberger railed against Zionism. He even helped to form an anti-Zionist organization, the American Council for Judaism. And as an anti-Zionist, Arthur Sulzberger supported the White Paper. Finally, Sulzberger was part of a group of Jewish leaders who went to President Roosevelt in an effort to persuade him not to appoint Felix Frankfurter to the Supreme Court in 1939. Sulzberger feared an anti-Semitic reprisal.

Sulzberger's editorial decisions at the *Times* reflected his quietly Jewish approach. "I cannot tell you what difficulty we have in getting the publicity we need in the pages of the *Times*," Stephen Wise said. "The *Times* seems to consider nothing as news which originates from and through Jews." (Peter Bergson might be considered an exception; his group, however, paid for their advertisements.) Jews, Sulzberger announced, should "not be treated as a group in the pages of the *Times* or in public policy." In fact, the word "Jew" was to be used sparingly. Sulzberger wrote to his editors, "Thus, when the American Jewish Congress meets, our headline does not say 'Jews Meet' but emphasizes the fact that it is the Congress. When the Zionists meet it is not Jews, but Zionists." That policy did not change during the Holocaust, as the *Times* referred to Jews as "refugees" or in the case of the Warsaw ghetto uprising, "the unfortunate citizens of Poland."

As Henry Morgenthau did not want to be known as a Jewish Secretary of the Treasury, Arthur Sulzberger did not want the *Times* to be known as a Jewish newspaper. So the editorials "never emphasized the Jewish side of the question." And the stories themselves were buried. On July 2, 1944, for instance, the *Times* reported that 400,000 Hungarian Jews had been deported to their deaths and 350,000 more were to be deported in the coming weeks. The story appeared on page 12. On the front page that day, the *Times* examined the problem of New York holiday crowds on the move.[20]

Did the burying of such stories influence other newspapers in their coverage? According to *Time* Magazine, "What Harvard is to U.S. education, what the House of Morgan has been to U.S. finance, the *New York Times* is to U.S. journalism." And if the *New York Times* didn't elevate Holocaust news to a paramount position, why would a newspaper in Middle America?

"We didn't know" was the cry in the United States regarding the Holocaust. How responsible was the *Times* for the public's lack of knowledge? Had the *Times* prioritized Holocaust stories, placing them on the front pages, what would have been the effect? Might America, with a greater knowledge of the Nazis' atrocities, have pressured the government to take action?

The question, of course, is rhetorical. "If ever there was a case where the *Times* should have risen superior to fear of consequences, it is this," declared the publisher of the *New York Post*. "For never were human beings more entitled to be defended and championed by a great organ of public opinion; certainly, never have men and women anywhere been tortured and slaughtered in such numbers for less reason."[21] His words sound like an obituary for the *Times's* coverage of the Holocaust.

In Europe, a Jewish cry emanated from Amsterdam to Auschwitz to Budapest and into the Balkans: "When are the Americans coming?" A second cry was just as powerful: "Where is Roosevelt?"

Where was Roosevelt? In the spring of 1944 the President, along with his generals and the British, was committed to the planning of the Normandy invasion. That was his top priority. All of his energies went into the war, from keeping abreast of military strategy and operation to nursing the terribly complicated relationship between the Soviet Union, the British, and the United States. Simultaneously, Roosevelt presented to the American people a forceful and determined leadership. His involvement took an enormous amount of time and energy and creativity. Sadly, Roosevelt couldn't bring to rescue the same kind of creativity and tenacity that he brought to his other policies, the New Deal included. Back in 1933, during the first hundred days of his Administration, Roosevelt introduced a bevy of ground-breaking programs known, affectionately, as alphabet soup. The torrent of proposals instilled in the American public hope for the present and future. The Jews within imprisoned Europe hoped for a parallel plan.

Roosevelt did not go public with news of the Final Solution. This was typical Roosevelt policy. He severely limited the flow of information coming from his Administration: no minutes of Cabinet meetings, no presidential tapes, no presidential notes or writings. For instance, Harry Truman, after taking office, had to interview everyone present at Yalta in order to discern Roosevelt's tactics during the Conference. But in all the journals and diaries published later by Roosevelt's colleagues, rescue operation does not hold even a slight presidential priority. Roosevelt, from all the evidence, put his energies into one enormous task: winning the war.

The Holocaust was a Nazi policy, perpetuated by the Germans and their Allies. To hold Roosevelt responsible for the murder of six million Jews is irrational. Roosevelt fought anti-Semitism the best way he knew how. In America, he continually supported the Jewish minority (evidenced by the Jewish minority's adoration of the President). In Europe, he tried to end the war as soon as possible. Ending the war, in fact, served as Roosevelt's answer to rescue. He clarified this position when he implemented the WRB. The Executive Order called for rescue "consistent with the successful prosecution of the war."

This policy would have far-reaching effects as a debate raged over another option to save the Jews of Europe: the bombing of Auschwitz.

Chapter 22

◄►

A Sense of Agony?

In April of 1944 two Auschwitz prisoners, Rudolf Vrba and Alfred Wetzler, hid for three days in a wood pile just outside the main camp. While the SS and their dogs searched the camp and its surroundings, the prisoners waited silently, cautiously, gripping their stolen knives, as if such weaponry might effectively combat machine guns. After the three-day period expired and the SS discontinued its search, as SS procedure dictated, Vrba and Wetzler escaped.

One hundred miles and two weeks later, after a harrowing journey through countryside controlled by the Nazis and their Polish partisans, the men crossed into their homeland, Slovakia. There, Vrba and Wetzler met with leaders of the Jewish community. Their aim was clear; they had escaped the Auschwitz camp, in part, to tell their stories to the world, to broadcast to both the Allies and the remaining European Jews the exact purposes of Auschwitz. The Vrba/Wetzler report—taken on April 25, 1944— went into specific and broad detail concerning the inconceivable slaughter at Auschwitz. Vrba and Wetzler had held administrative positions within the camp; their access to its full operation was extensive. The report, known as the Auschwitz Protocols, included camp history, lay-out, classification scheme of prisoners, security guarding the camp, frequency of trains arriving, selection process, and numbers of dead. The Protocols were descriptively chilling. In depicting the crematoria, for instance, Vrba and Wetzler wrote:

> At present there are four crematoria in operation at Birkenau, two large ones, I and II, and two smaller ones, III and IV. Those of type I and II consist of 3 parts, i.e.: (A) the furnace room; (B) the large halls; and (C) the gas chamber. A huge chimney rises from the furnace room around which are grouped nine furnaces, each having four openings. Each opening can take three normal corpses at once and after an hour and a half the bodies are completely burned. This corresponds to a daily capacity of about 2,000 bodies. . . . The gassing takes place as follows: the unfortunate victims are brought into hall (B), where they are told to undress. To complete the fiction that they are going to bathe, each person receives a towel and a small piece of soap issued by two men clad in white coats. Then they are crowded into the gas chamber (C) in such numbers that there is, of course, only standing room. To compress this crowd into the narrow space, shots are often fired to induce those already at the far end to huddle still closer together. When everybody is inside, the heavy doors are closed. Then there is a short pause, presumably to allow the room temperature to rise to a certain level, after which SS men with gas masks climb on the roof, open the traps, and shake down a preparation in powder form out of tin cans labeled "CYKLON" "For use against vermin. . . ."

The Vrba/Wetzler Protocols were translated into German and Hungarian and sent to Dr. Rudolf Kastner, the leader of the Jewish Agency Rescue Committee in Hungary. Dr. Kastner chose not to reveal the information to the Hungarian Jews. Instead, using the report as a bargaining chip, he entered into negotiations with Adolf Eichmann. Those negotiations proved fruitless for Hungarian Jews, as the deportations soon began. According to Rudolf Vrba, the negotiations "were only for the purposes of distracting the Jews from the knowledge of their extermination." Years later, Kastner admitted as much. "I also felt the same thing in my heart," he confessed.[1] Kastner saved 1,684 lives. But that total paled in comparison to the number possible. Years later, Kastner recounted Eichmann's fear of "another Warsaw." Eichmann did not want, in Rudolf Vrba's words, "a repetition of that twenty-seven-day battle during which 33,000 men, women and children held at bay thousands of Wehrmacht and SS troops, armed with tanks and cannon."[2]

What would have happened had Kastner revealed the Vrba/Wetzler Protocols to Budapest's Jews? Would that knowledge have caused a revolt? How would the Nazis, lacking the manpower to deal with a large-scale uprising, have changed their tactics? Would the deportations have begun? Would 400,000 Jews have gone to their deaths?

In his book, *I Escaped from Auschwitz*, Rudolf Vrba wrote, "Why did Doctor Kastner betray his people when he could have saved many of them by warning them, by giving them a chance to fight, a chance to stage the second 'Warsaw' which Eichmann feared?" That question might be asked of many Jewish council leaders, including Adam Czerniakow in Warsaw and Chaim Rumkowski in Lodz and Leo Baeck in Berlin, all of whom negotiated with the Nazis while their people were slaughtered. In the case of Kastner, he survived the war and made his way to Israel. He became the editor of Israel's most popular Hungarian language newspaper and the spokesman for the Ministry of Trade and Industry. In 1957, he was murdered outside his house in Tel Aviv. Not by a Hungarian avenger, as might seem poetic justice, but by Zeev Eckstein, a self-proclaimed agent of the Israeli Secret Service. The motive for the murder, to this day, remains a mystery.

Eventually, the Vrba/Wetzler Protocols made their way through a Czechoslovakian Minister to Gerhart Riegner in Switzerland. "Now, what did I do?" Riegner asked rhetorically. "I went to the American Legation and to the British Legation in Berne . . . and I asked them to relay the reports to the competent authorities."[3]

Roswell McClelland, the War Refugee Board's representative in Switzerland, received a summary of the report in June. He reacted by sending a cable to John Pehle in Washington, calling for bombing. "It is urged by all sources of this information in

Slovakia and Hungary that vital sections of these lines especially bridges . . . be bombed as the only possible means of slowing down or stopping future deportations," McClelland's cable read. "There is little doubt that many of these Hungarian Jews are being sent to the extermination camps of Auschwitz and Birkenau in western Upper Silesia where, according to recent reports, since early summer 1942, at least 1,500,000 Jews have been killed."

In late June John Pehle sent the cable to John McCloy at the War Department. McCloy responded on July 4 (three days before the halting of deportations), "The War Department is of the opinion that the suggested air operation is impracticable. It could be executed only by the diversion of considerable air support essential to the success of our forces now engaged in decisive operations and would in any case be of such very doubtful efficacy that it would not amount to a practical project."

The proposal to bomb Auschwitz and the railway lines leading to the camp turned into a hotly contested debate, both in 1944 and currently, as historians continue the disputation. The historians' debate began with a David Wyman article, published in 1978, entitled "Why Auschwitz Was Never Bombed." His second book, *The Abandonment of the Jews*, furthered his contention that Auschwitz should have been bombed and had it been, tens of thousands of lives would have been saved. Since Wyman's publications, many historians have joined his side of the argument, including two of the foremost Holocaust scholars, Martin Gilbert and Richard Breitman. In 1985, only one year after the publication of Wyman's *Abandonment*, Lucy Dawidowicz responded in her article, "Could the United States Have Rescued the European Jews From Hitler?" Dawidowicz wrote, "The lack of evidence has not inhibited Wyman from indulging his historical imagination."[4] James Kitchens, a scholar once based at the Air Force Historical Research Agency, furthered Dawidowicz's refutation of Wyman's scholarship. He was soon joined by a series of scholars, Richard Levy among them. In 1997 William Rubinstein wrote a book called *The Myth of Rescue* in which he asserted that Wyman's scholarship was "not merely wrong, but egregiously and ahistorically inaccurate." Rubinstein then claimed that not one additional Jew could have been rescued. Wyman responded, in brief, in a letter to the *New York Times.* "The real myths in Rubinstein's book are the new ones he has created," Wyman wrote, calling Rubinstein's work, in general, "nonsense." Historian Richard Breitman, a cautious proponent of bombing Auschwitz, wrote in *Official Secrets* that "Rubinstein's argument is fundamentally misleading and methodologically flawed."

In 1944, the dispute was just as divided. Within the Jewish community of that era, for instance, leaders advanced both sides of the issue. Chaim Weizmann, the head of the Jewish Agency, lobbied Foreign Minister Anthony Eden and the British to bomb the railway lines connecting Budapest to Auschwitz and the death installations at Birkenau. Nahum Goldmann, the President of the World Jewish Congress, proposed knocking out the crematoria with, in his view, a few dozen bombs. Jacob Rosenheim, the President of Agudas Israel World Organization, wrote a letter to Henry Morgenthau pleading for a bombing raid on the railway lines. "This slackening of the process of annihilation could be achieved by paralyzing the railroad traffic from Hungary to Poland, especially by an aireal [sic] bombardment of the most important railway junctions . . . through which the deportations-trains pass. By such a procedure, precious time would be won and thousands of human lives preserved. On the other hand, every day of delay means a very heavy responsibility for the human lives at stake."[5] Peter Bergson called the bombing scheme, "the one suggestion that came out of the Jewish leadership that had merit."[6]

On the other side of the issue David Ben-Gurion, the Chairman of the Jewish Agency Executive in Jerusalem (and future Prime Minister of Israel), argued, "We should not ask the Allies to bomb places where there are Jews."[7] Leon Kubowitzki, the head of the Rescue Department of the World Jewish Congress, agreed with Ben-Gurion's viewpoint. Destruction of the "death installations cannot be done from the air," Kubowitzki wrote the WRB, "as the first victims would be the Jews who are gathered in these camps." In addition, Kubowitzki believed that "such a bombing would be a welcome pretext for the Germans to assert that their

Jewish victims have been massacred not by their killers, but by the Allied bombing."[8] Kubowitzki did suggest an alternative. "Why don't we send a commando [unit] with arms and ammunition and explosives and parachute them in by plane and tell them to blow up the ovens from inside?"[9]

Kubowitzki's assertions pointed toward the deep split among Jews. Within the same organization—the World Jewish Congress—its President (Goldmann) called for bombing; its lead Rescue Department official (Kubowitzki) deplored the idea.

Outside Jewish organizations, the debate was just as divisive. In the United States government, WRB agent Benjamin Akzin, a Jew originally from Latvia, wrote an interoffice memo claiming that destroying the "physical installations" at the Auschwitz camp "might appreciably slow down the systematic slaughter at least temporarily."[10] On the other hand, Azkin's superior, John Pehle, expressed a series of doubts: "(1) whether it would be appropriate to use military planes and personnel for this purpose; (2) whether it would be difficult to put the railroad line out of commission for a long enough period to do any good; and (3) even assuming that these railroad lines were put out of commission for some period of time, whether it would help the Jews in Hungary."[11] Pehle did, however, suppress his doubts and send the bombing request to McCloy. And later, in November, when he received the Vrba/Wetzler report in full, Pehle jumped on the bombing bandwagon.

The most forceful and vehement voice against the bombing scheme within the United States government belonged to John McCloy. As an Assistant Secretary in the War Department and liaison to the WRB, McCloy held a pivotal position. Though he was a civilian, he championed the interests and needs of the military and he clung to official Roosevelt policy. "We must constantly bear in mind," he wrote in an internal War Department memorandum, "that the most effective relief which can be given victims of enemy persecution is to insure the speedy defeat of the Axis."[12]

For years, McCloy maintained that the orders not to bomb the Auschwitz camp were made by himself and the War Department's operations staff. However, in an interview conducted in 1986 by Henry Morgenthau III, the son of the Secretary of the

Treasury, McCloy reported that President Roosevelt made the decision. "I remember talking one time with Mr. Roosevelt about it
and he was irate," McCloy recalled. " 'Why, the idea!' " McCloy
quoted Roosevelt. " 'They'll say we bombed these people, and
they'll only move it down the road a little way and bomb them
all the more. . . . We'll be accused of participating in this horrible
business.' "13

McCloy blamed the proposal for the bombing of Auschwitz
on "a bunch of fanatic Jews who seemed to think that if you did-
n't bomb it was an indication of lack of venom against Hitler."
Roosevelt, McCloy believed, reacted in a prudent manner. McCloy
reported, "The President had the idea that that [bombing] would
be more provocative and ineffective and he took a very strong
stand, took it right out of our hands." The President's words,
according to McCloy, were very succinct. " 'I won't have anything
to do with it.' "

McCloy's statement to Henry Morgenthau III stands alone.
No other members of the Roosevelt government corroborated it.
Why? Why was McCloy, if indeed his memory is accurate, the
only member of the government who took the bombing proposal
to the President? Where were the other voices of influence? John
Pehle, who had ample opportunity to discuss it with Roosevelt,
followed the bureaucratic chain of command and took his appeal
to McCloy. Benjamin Akzin urged Pehle to go directly to Roosevelt.
"I am certain," Akzin proposed, "that the President, once
acquainted with the facts, would realize the values involved and,
cutting through the inertia-motivated objections of the War
Department, would order the immediate bombing of the objectives suggested."14 Pehle declined to do so. Secretary Morgenthau,
who had felt compelled to risk his political life in proposing the
War Refugee Board to Roosevelt, did not approach Roosevelt on
this issue. Winston Churchill, the most enthusiastic advocate of
the bombing proposal, did not press the President. On July 7, after
reading Riegner's summary of the Vrba/Wetzler report, Churchill
ordered Anthony Eden to confer with the Royal Air Force (RAF)
regarding bombing possibilities. Churchill, not only the Prime
Minister but the Minister of Defense as well, told Eden to "get

anything out of the Air Force you can and invoke me if necessary."
On July 15, Sir Archibald Sinclair, the Secretary of State for Air,
spurned an RAF bombing run. "The distance of Silesia from our
bases entirely rules out anything of the kind," Sinclair explained.
He did, however, suggest that the Americans might be in position.

While the British did press the Americans on a Foreign Minister
level (Anthony Eden, not exactly the Jews' greatest friend, supported the proposal), and Churchill strongly advocated it to his
own people, they did not address Roosevelt. And so Roosevelt,
who clearly did not sense an overwhelming necessity or a political expediency to act, never voiced his opinion publicly on the
bombing proposal.

The statistics simply stagger the mind. During the Hungarian
deportations, 10,000 to 12,000 Jews were gassed at Auschwitz
per day. On September 30, some 2,000 Jews who had survived
Theresienstadt arrived at Auschwitz and were gassed. Three days
later, another 1,200 Theresienstadt Jews were gassed. On October
17, 2,000 Auschwitz prisoners were designated as "unfit for work"
and gassed. One day later, 3,000 Jews from Slovakia and 300 Jews
from Hungary were gassed. During that third week of October,
some 17,392 Jews died in the gas chambers. The total number of
Jews gassed at the Auschwitz camp for the month of October was
33,000. On November 26, Heinrich Himmler stopped the car-
nage. He turned his attention to destroying the evidence.[15]

What effect would bombing the Auschwitz camp have had on
these incomprehensible statistics? There is no definitive answer.
Rather, there are many questions. To begin with, could the
Fifteenth Air Force reach Auschwitz from its headquarters in southern Italy? The answer is an unequivocal yes. Starting in early July,
the Air Force began to pound the Axis oil industry in Eastern
Europe, including the oil plants of Upper Silesia, Blechhammer
and Odertal. From July 7 to November 20, Blechhammer, within
thirty-five miles of the Auschwitz camp, was hit by heavy bombers
on ten different occasions. The factory areas of Auschwitz became
a target late that summer. For instance, on August 20, the Air
Force dropped over one thousand high explosive bombs on the

Auschwitz factories. August 20 was a Sunday. According to survivor Ernest Michel, "some people got killed. Not many. Because on Sundays the workers didn't work."[16] Michel was among those who transported the bodies back to the camp. The distance between the factories and the crematoria was less than five miles.

Did the Fifteenth Air Force have the aerial reconnaissance to recognize gas chambers? According to David Wyman, the crematoria stuck out like sore thumbs. "The four huge gassing-cremation installations stood in two pairs, spaced along the westernmost edge of the Auschwitz complex . . . ," Wyman wrote. "Two of the extermination buildings were 340 feet long, the others two-thirds that length. Chimneys towered over them." Clearly, in Wyman's perspective, identification was not at issue.

Dino Brugioni, a member of the Air Force during World War II and, later, an expert in aerial photographic interpretation (he in fact won a citation from President Kennedy for his excellent work during the Cuban missile crisis), believed there was another force at work: disbelief. He explained, "Photo interpreters depend heavily on precedence or existing knowledge about a subject or installation. I did not find a single reference in which interpreters were told to look for gas chambers or crematoria that were killing thousands each day. There was simply no historical or intelligence precedence for genocide on such a scale. Most World War II photo interpreters I have spoken to found this concept unbelievable, unimaginable and completely incongruous."[17]

Did the technology of the day permit precision bombing? If the Air Force had used its medium bombers, the B-25s, which flew at lower altitudes, would Nazi anti-aircraft have knocked the planes out of the sky? Historian Stuart Erdheim, a bombing advocate, pointed to a B-25 attack on the Toulon harbor as a parallel to a proposed Auschwitz camp raid. The B-25s destroyed their targets (a battleship, a cruiser, and a submarine) despite "extremely intense" flak. Could something similar have been accomplished by bombing Auschwitz?

The same question could be raised concerning the Allies' most accurate planes, the P-38 Lightning dive-bombers. According to Wyman, such planes "could have knocked out the murder buildings without danger to the inmates." Wyman then wrote about a Lightning mission, dive-bombing the oil refineries at Ploesti in Rumania. But according to Richard Levy, in that raid at Ploesti, twenty-three of seventy-five planes did not return.[18]

The only American planes that flew high enough to avoid Nazi flak were the heavy bombers, the B-17s and B-24s. From an altitude of 20,000 to 25,000 feet, though, how accurate were they? Historian James Kitchens used another raid as a possible comparison. He called the hit at an armament factory next to the concentration camp Buchenwald "as analogous to Auschwitz as history permits." B-17s dropped 303 tons of bombs, according to Kitchens, destroying the objectives. "Despite good knowledge of the targets and much-above-average accuracy, however," Kitchens wrote, "315 prisoners were killed, 525 seriously wounded, and 900 lightly wounded."[19]

At the Auschwitz camp, where the gas chambers were located just a few hundred yards from rows and rows of barracks populated with prisoners, what would the effects of a missed target have been? Doesn't it seem likely that a stray bomb or two might have killed thousands of prisoners?

On September 13, 1944, a stray bomb, intended for the I.G. Farben chemical plant, struck one of the Auschwitz barracks. Fifteen SS men died in the bombing. Over forty prisoners perished. And a spontaneous celebration ensued. Prisoners throughout the camp looked to the sky and cheered. "The American are coming," the refrain reverberated. "We are not alone."

"We were no longer afraid of death," Elie Wiesel wrote in *Night*, concerning Allied bombs dropping on the Auschwitz camp, "at any rate, not of that death." Ernest Michel echoed the sentiment. "We did not expect to live, although I never gave up hope. But I would have welcomed to be bombed by the American Allies in destroying the gas chambers of Auschwitz. Yes, I would have welcomed that."[20]

In *The Abandonment of the Jews*, David Wyman wrote that successful bombing raids begun in July 1944 and knocking out the crematoria might have saved upwards of 150,000 lives. That number is derived from the total murdered in the chambers from

July through November. That number represents a best-case estimate. For instance, in the event of a successful bombing raid, doesn't it follow that the Nazis would have found other ways to kill Jews, perhaps returning to the days of machine-gun slaughter? There can be no doubt that as the Nazis saw their conquest of Europe eroding, they stepped up their war against the Jews. Crematoria or not, the Nazis would not have been deterred.

Due to that determination, wasn't there a moral imperative to knock out the crematoria? "It would have been a sign of Allied horror at Nazi genocide and Allied determination to do something about it, even at the risk of military and Jewish casualties," Richard Breitman argued. "It would have forced high Nazi authorities to turn to less efficient means of murder, and it might have made some subordinates think twice about continuing their own role in the Final Solution of the Jewish question. It would have been humanitarian, and it should have been done, but it was no panacea."[21]

The crematoria, of course, were never purposefully bombed by the Allies. One of them however was destroyed. On October 7, 1944, the *Sonderkommando* (prisoners who dragged the bodies from the gas chambers to the crematoria) blew up Crematorium IV with explosives smuggled in from the nearby Union explosives factory. About six hundred prisoners broke out of the camp. None of them escaped. All of them died from machine-gun fire.

Meanwhile, at the White House, President Roosevelt continued to wage a world war. He focused on the big picture, the entire world map, as Axis power at one point reached from the Pacific to Europe to North Africa. FDR did not micro-manage the war. Yes, he liked to discuss covert military operations. For instance, he spent hours with OSS head Bill Donovan, considering various projects, including a bat drop over Japan. (In theory, the bats, armed with incendiaries tied to their bodies, and dropped from B-17s, would fly onto wooded roofs and explode, burning the structures to the ground. In reality, bats dropped from 20,000 feet invariably froze to death.) FDR made or approved major policy decisions, such as invading North Africa, invading Normandy, and the Atlantic First policy, emphasizing the war in Europe over the war in the Pacific. FDR, though, did not make day-to-day military decisions. Unlike Churchill, he placed his trust in his generals. And his actions, his policies, his transition from American isolation to neutrality to Cash-and-Carry to Lend-Lease to all-out warfare, hastened the end of the Nazi empire.

Countless proposals on many war fronts must have crossed Roosevelt's mind, if not his desk. Was one of them the bombing of the Auschwitz death camp? Did Roosevelt, secretly, look into its efficacy, its possibility? Did he consult, in private, with his generals? In the strictest confidence, did he ever talk with Marshall or Eisenhower?

While these are purely hypothetical questions, it should be noted that his office did receive numerous telegrams from Jewish organizations calling for the bombing. One appeal, dated July 24, from J.J. Smertenko, the Vice-Chairman of the Committee to Save the Jewish People of Europe, pleaded for bombing retaliation, from "Railways and bridges leading from Nazi-occupied territory to extermination centers in Poland" to "the extermination camps themselves . . . where thousands of people are assassinated daily" to "a specific statement . . . that the extermination of Hebrew men, women, and children by continued use of poison gas will be considered a provocation for retaliation in kind."[22]

If Roosevelt read this telegram, or others, there is no record of it. What remains then are questions, estimates. On the bombing of Auschwitz, the fact that the President did not publicly address the issue has sparked a debate as to its potential efficacy. That debate will never be satisfactorily resolved.

Chapter 23

◄►

Why I Call Myself a Rooseveltian

My journey with Roosevelt began over the radio. The year was 1933. I was a month away from my fifteenth birthday. The country teetered on the verge of collapse when President Franklin D. Roosevelt, during his first inaugural, put priorities in perspective. "Happiness lies not in the mere possession of money; it lies in the joy of achievement, in the thrill of creative effort," he announced. "The joy and moral stimulation of work no longer must be forgotten in the mad chase of evanescent profit. These dark days will be worth all they cost us if they teach us that our true destiny is not to be ministered unto but to minister to ourselves and to our fellow men." Roosevelt became my hero from that day forward. His humanitarian efforts during the New Deal phase and his dynamic leadership throughout the war era inspired me to be a Rooseveltian.

My journey with Roosevelt changed sometime in the 1980s—forty years after the President's death. A student's question took me by surprise. "What about the *St. Louis*?" the girl asked in class. I was frightfully embarrassed. I didn't know the first thing about the *St. Louis*. I've gone back and searched through the archives of the *New York Times* and I've found extensive articles and multiple headlines. For instance, in the second week of June 1939, the *Times* ran articles on the *St. Louis* every day, and from June 5 to June 8, it featured the ship as front-page headline news. I don't remember reading this. Neither do my peers, I've found through my inquiries. Why? Were we so into our lives that we didn't pay attention? Did we block out the suffering? Did we forget? These are confounding questions.

My journey with Roosevelt, following the student's question, took me down a different path. You see, I couldn't let it go. I couldn't tell the student to answer her own question and report her findings to the class at the next session. I saw a different side to my hero. I needed to do the research for myself. That led to further research. Suddenly, I was hooked. And with each event researched, the question in my head grew louder and louder. "Where was Roosevelt?" the Jews of the Holocaust asked. That question hounded me.

Where was Roosevelt during the sailing of the *St. Louis*? The passengers on board the ship sent a telegram to the White House, asking for assistance. If the President read that telegram, there is no record of it. Why? How could the President, my hero, not respond to the crisis? This wasn't during the war. His attentions were not single-mindedly focused on destroying Nazi Germany. How could he ignore the pleas of refugees without responding in any way?

I didn't want to write this history. I want to write something in keeping with my heroic image of Franklin Roosevelt. I want to write a fantasy: President Roosevelt made a phone call. With the *St. Louis* harbored in Havana and the passengers staring at the city and their many relatives awaiting their landing at the port, Roosevelt called his Cuban counterpart, President Laredo Brú. In that conversation, Roosevelt pressed for the passengers' disembarkation, even going as far as declaring that "the full force of the U.S. government is behind my request." I want to write that, in response to this plea, Cuban President Brú opened the port to the passengers.

Why didn't Roosevelt sign an Executive Order when the *St. Louis* paralleled America's coastline? Why didn't he grant temporary visitor's visas? Why didn't he, at the very least, cable the ship and explain his situation? Why did he turn away? Where was the Great Humanitarian?

His silence gave a form of permission for others to do the same. There is plenty of blame to go around. Nobody doubts the State Department's nonchalance during the crisis. Nobody doubts Congress's lack of action. But the President's lack of leadership had a strangling effect and the other institutions joined in his acquiescence. The *St. Louis*, as we all know, sailed back to Europe.

If only it had ended there. If only I could report that in the next crisis, Roosevelt changed course. He didn't. During the Wagner-Rogers legislative deliberations, he again took a position of silence. This pains me. In the margin of a letter urging him to act he wrote "File. No Action." Today I am at a loss to explain these words. And here again, the war hadn't started. Nazi Germany was not his sole focal point. Couldn't he have used the bully pulpit to influence the debate in Congress? It's puzzling to me why a debate occurred. This was not a question of finance. This was not a question of immigration. These were children in dire circumstances. My God, they were about to be thrown into concentration camps.

Again, I want to write a different history. I want to write that the President took a stand on behalf of the children. I want to write that in a press conference or in a speech or in a surprise visit to Congress, Roosevelt admonished the legislators with the words, "How can 20,000 children, all under fourteen years of age, cause so much debate? What are we afraid of? What possible harm could they bring to our country?" Various politicians and public figures tried to pressure the President regarding Wagner-Rogers, his wife included. Roosevelt remained silent. Shamefully, the legislation died.

If only it had ended there. In September of 1939 Germany invaded Poland, prompting a brutal war. Western Europe fell to the Nazis in a series of lightning strikes. By the summer of 1940 the Nazis controlled Europe from the eastern edge of Poland to Dunkirk and as secretly as possible began their insidious war on the Jews. In September of 1939, President Roosevelt appointed his trusted ally to a powerful position. Breckinridge Long became Special Assistant to the State Department. Four months later, he was elevated to Assistant Secretary. His "postpone, postpone, postpone" visa policy cut off immigration at the precise moment when it was most needed. His obsession with Fifth Columnists consigned Europe's Jews to an inescapable prison. And Roosevelt had been briefed, in a sense. In 1940, four years before Henry Morgenthau brought up Long's visa obstruction in the meeting that led to the War Refugee Board, Eleanor Roosevelt mentioned the subject of Breckinridge Long to her husband. "Franklin," she said, "you *know* he's a fascist."

"I've told you, Eleanor," the President responded, "you must not say that."

"Well, maybe I shouldn't say it," Eleanor replied, "but he is!"[1]

Roosevelt chose to concentrate on security, and for that task he chose to put his trust in Breckinridge Long. I know that Long was not responsible for the concentration camps; his five-year tenure, however, ensured that few Jews would be allowed to flee the prison of Europe. The President remained above it all, ensconced in the White House and firmly believing, to quote Jan Karski, that Europeans suffering under the Nazi regime had "a friend in this house."

Regarding Jan Karski, in his meeting with Roosevelt in 1943, he warned that the Polish Jews would "cease to exist" if the Germans continued with their program. Roosevelt heard these words. Again, he took no action. This is difficult for me to accept. I want to write that Karski's words pushed Roosevelt into an urgent response. I want to write something, anything. I want to write that he formed the War Refugee Board at the end of 1942. He certainly had the intelligence. He knew about the Nazi death machine. In December of that year he welcomed Rabbi Stephen Wise and other members of the American Jewish leadership into his office. They asked him to issue a war crimes warning. He complied. Why didn't they ask him to go further? Why didn't he go further on his own? Why didn't he attempt some kind of rescue operation?

Would a rescue operation in the year 1942 have been effective? Germany still controlled most of Europe. The battle for air supremacy continued. Militarily, the Allies could not reach Eastern Europe. Certainly, bombing Auschwitz and the railway lines then was not an option. So the efficacy of rescue becomes hypothetical. All we can go on are other rescue operations: Varian Fry (in the early part of the war, while a sense of instability encompassed Vichy, France), Japanese Consul-General Chiune Sugihara in Lithuania, the Danes ferrying 6,500 Danish Jews to Sweden. Still, I want to write that in his year-end press conference of 1942 President Roosevelt said, "Rescue operation is now an American responsibility. A new agency, the War Refugee Board, will do everything in its power to free the enemies of Hitler." I want to write that Roosevelt followed that statement with the immortal words, "This is my Emancipation Proclamation." And when questioned as to why he implemented the War Refugee Board, Roosevelt responded "Our flourish of humanitarianism depends on doing all we can. The world watched through the 1930s as Hitler constructed the foundation for what would become a death trap for the enemies of Nazi Germany. The world will not make the same mistakes in the 1940s. Nobody in the future will accuse this government, and this country, of abandoning the Jews."

As you know, none of this took place. Roosevelt did not take a pro-rescue position. Not in 1942 following the Riegner Report. Not in the summer of 1943 following his meeting with Jan Karski. And not in the autumn of 1943, as the Gillette-Rogers Rescue Resolution gained support. Only in 1944, only when Morgenthau went to him, only when Congress was on the verge of passing Gillette-Rogers, did Roosevelt implement the War Refugee Board.

The WRB pursued rescue as if handicapped. Its powers weren't broad enough. It lacked financial backing. It received little assistance. For instance, few havens opened in the WRB's attempt to funnel refugees out of the neutral countries. One or two opened in North Africa. The United States opened a camp at Fort Ontario in Oswego. No other empty army barracks in America were used. "The real hurdle," Arthur Morse wrote in *While Six Million Died*, "was the White House. . . . The President said that it would not be necessary to establish havens in the United States because there were many countries to which the refugees could go."

To be accurate, Roosevelt did address refugee issues. Following the Nuremberg Laws of 1935, he ordered his Consulates to offer the "most generous" and "favorable" treatment to German Jews seeking immigration (his orders were not heeded). After the

Anschluss of Austria, he convened the Evian Refugee Conference. He removed his Ambassador to Germany following *Kristallnacht.* In 1939, he began to anticipate the pending refugee crisis. In typical Roosevelt creativity, he entertained numerous hypotheses for dealing with some 10 to 20 million postwar refugees, according to his calculations. That led to his talk of "self-sustaining civilization[s]." Roosevelt envisioned one or two large settlements able to support millions of people. Secretly, he created the "M" project (M for Migration), which compiled demographic studies on possible settlement areas in the postwar period. Some of Roosevelt's favorite areas included the grasslands of Venezuela, the North African desert (after desalinization), and Palestine.

In 1942, Roosevelt even went so far as to privately consult with Treasury Secretary Morgenthau. Could the Arabs in Palestine be moved to other parts of the Middle East in order to make room for Jewish refugees? he wondered. To Morgenthau, Roosevelt proposed putting a "barbed wire around Palestine, and I would begin to move the Arabs out of Palestine. . . . I would provide land for the Arabs in some other part of the Middle East. . . . Each time we move out an Arab we would bring in another Jewish family. . . . It would be an independent nation just like any other nation. . . . Naturally, if there are 90 per cent Jews, the Jews would dominate the government."[2]

In 1943, Roosevelt conducted his own unscientific study. "The President consulted his neighbors in Marietta County, Georgia [the site of his home in Warm Springs] and at Hyde Park," Vice President Henry Wallace recorded in his diary, "asking whether they would agree to have four or five Jewish families resettle in their respective regions. He claimed that the local population would have no objection if there were no more than that."[3]

In March of 1944, he called the murder of the Jews "the blackest crime in history" and promised retaliation against Germany and its satellites. He warned Hungary regarding the deportation of Jews to Poland. Initially, he threatened to bomb Budapest. At the end of June 1944 he ordered the bombing. However, he took no stance on the bombing of other sites. He offered no opinion.

What would Roosevelt have thought had he lived to see

Auschwitz and the other camps liberated? Would he have had the same reaction as General Dwight D. Eisenhower when the General toured a concentration camp? On the day before President Roosevelt died, General Eisenhower toured Ohrdruf-Nord, near Gotha. The sight was appalling. In their effort to stop eyewitness testimony, SS guards had murdered everyone before fleeing. Piles of bodies filled the expanse. The smell of death hovered. Eisenhower said that the sight was "beyond the American mind to comprehend." If he had reviewed General Eisenhower's report, would Roosevelt have been just as confounded?

What do we make of Roosevelt's actions? He recognized, without a doubt, the deep and troubling aggression of Nazi Germany. He offered a variety of alternative solutions. The record suggests that, at best, Roosevelt was sympathetic to the Jews and, at worst, Roosevelt resorted to political expediency. David Wyman wrote, "America's response to the Holocaust was the result of action and inaction on the part of many people. In the forefront was Franklin D. Roosevelt, whose steps to aid Europe's Jews were very limited. If he had wanted to, he could have aroused substantial public backing for a vital rescue effort by speaking out on the issue. . . . But he had little to say about the problem and gave no priority at all to rescue."

What comes across in reviewing this period is Roosevelt's sincere belief that it was essential to put all of America's resources and his own influence into winning the war. That became his preoccupation. Germany's best hope for winning the war was to divide the Allies, to cut the Soviet Union off from the West. Roosevelt pacified the Allies. Throughout the war, and including the conferences at Teheran and Yalta, he kept the disparate parts intact. His methods were evident following the Yalta Conference. On his way back to America, Roosevelt met with three of the leaders in the region at Great Bitter Lake in the Suez Canal (a case could be made that Roosevelt met with four leaders of the region as Winston Churchill, the leader of the dwindling British empire, visited President Roosevelt after the other three). After FDR had visited with Emperor Haile Selassie of Ethiopia and King Farouk of Egypt, King Saud of Saudi Arabia came on board the *USS Quincy*. Their conversation, after discussing the progress of the war, turned toward the Jews and Palestine. FDR, in his congenial manner, asked King Saud for advice regarding the problem of Jewish refugees driven from their homes in Europe. The King replied, "Give them and their descendants the choicest lands and homes" in the Axis countries, Germany included.[4] Roosevelt remarked that Poland might be considered a possibility, saying, "The Germans appear to have killed three million Polish Jews, by which count there should be space in Poland for the resettlement of many homeless Jews."[5] King Saud responded by discussing the Arab claims to Middle East lands. He stated that the Arabs and the Jews could never cooperate, neither in Palestine nor in any other country.

An analysis of the conversation shows Roosevelt in his political comfort zone. He knew that he needed to hold the alliance together. At the same time, he realized the tricky nature of discussing Palestine and the Jews with the King of Saudi Arabia. So he "suggested" a resettlement in Poland. Did he really believe his own words or was he brokering a friendship with the King while laying the groundwork for a Jewish resettlement in Palestine? His history indicates the latter. Roosevelt, throughout the war, continually sought refugee settlements in Palestine. In addition to his conversation with Henry Morgenthau, Roosevelt floated to other colleagues the idea of moving thousands of Arabs out of Palestine. According to Felix Frankfurter, for instance, FDR realized the need for keeping Palestine "whole and of making it Jewish." He was "tremendously interested—and wholly surprised—on learning of the great increase in Arab population since the war; and of learning of the plentitude of land for Arabs in Arab countries, about which he made specific inquiries."[6] Roosevelt then wanted to transfer 200,000 Arabs across the Jordan River.

Still, Roosevelt focused on postwar resettlement. Did he miss opportunities to save lives during the war? The follow-up question, for a Rooseveltian, would be: What exactly could he have done? Perhaps the simplest yet most profound answer came from Congressman Emanuel Celler, who blamed Roosevelt for not providing "some spark of courageous leadership." Grudgingly, I agree.

Why then am I still a Rooseveltian? I see the man's prescience.

In 1937, he took a stab at warning the world. In his Quarantine Speech he condemned the "10 percent who are threatening a breakdown of all international order and law." He reasoned that the other 90 percent "must find some way to make their will prevail." To an isolationist nation, his speech was a major risk. He gave it anyway. For that action, I admire his insight, judgment, and courage. I admire that he was willing to go against the grain of American isolationism.

Why am I still a Rooseveltian? I admire the man's creativity. In 1940–1941, Great Britain was broke and the Nazi Air Force was pummeling London nightly. Churchill cabled Roosevelt regularly, desperate for assistance. Roosevelt, in the face of American neutrality and isolation, wondered how to keep Britain afloat. The idea hit him during a fishing voyage: Lend-Lease. He explained the program during a press conference. "Let me give you an illustration," he told a room full of reporters.

Suppose my neighbor's home catches on fire, and I have a length of garden hose four or five hundred feet away. If he can take my garden hose and connect it up with his hydrant, I may help him to put out the fire. Now what do I do? I don't say to him before that operation, "Neighbor, my garden hose cost me $15; you have to pay me $15 for it." What is the transaction that goes on? I don't want $15—I want my garden hose back after the fire is over. All right. If it goes through the fire all right, intact, without any damage to it, he gives it back to me and thanks me very much for the use of it. If his neighbor smashed it up he could simply replace it.

This was Roosevelt at his creative best. Lend-Lease saved both Great Britain and Russia and, in return, made America much stronger. Could he have used some of his creativity for rescue? The question is hypothetical.

Why am I still a Rooseveltian? I regret his lack of leadership regarding the Holocaust but I greatly admire his war leadership. At the end of 1940, at a time when Nazi Germany controlled all of Western Europe, threatening Britain while America maintained its neutrality and isolation, President Roosevelt gave one of his fiercest Fireside Chats. "If Great Britain goes down," Roosevelt said, "the Axis powers will control the continents of Europe, Asia, Africa, Australasia, and the high seas and they will be in a position to bring enormous military and naval resources against this hemisphere. It is no exaggeration to say that all of us, in all of the Americas, would be living at the point of a gun." Roosevelt then offered his vision of the future. "We must have more ships, more guns, more planes, more of everything. We must be the great arsenal of democracy."

One year later, immediately following Pearl Harbor, Roosevelt turned the arsenal of democracy into war production challenges. In his State of the Union message, delivered on January 6, 1942, Roosevelt promised the increase of airplanes, from "60,000 planes, 10,000 more than the goal we set a year and a half ago" to "125,000 airplanes, including 100,000 combat planes" by 1943. He promised the increase of tanks, from 25,000 to 75,000 by 1943. He promised the increase of anti-aircraft guns, from 20,000 in 1942 to 35,000 in 1943. He promised the increase of merchant ships, raising the tonnage of material from 1,100,000 in 1941 to 6,000,000 in 1942 to 10,000,000 tons in 1943. "These figures," Roosevelt said, "and similar figures for a multitude of other implements of war will give the Japanese and the Nazis a little idea of just what they accomplished in the attack at Pearl Harbor."

Roosevelt's leadership galvanized the war effort. Sacrifice to the great cause became a way of life. There was a draft beginning in 1940. After Pearl Harbor there was a rush to join the military. The recruits included some of the most famous men of the day. Clark Gable, considerably over draft age, enlisted as a private in the Army Air Force. He flew operational missions over Europe in B-17s. Jimmy Stewart entered the Army Air Force as a private, too. He flew more than twenty missions over Germany. Ted Williams, who received a deferment because his mother depended upon her son for financial support, enlisted in the Naval reserves. Fiorello La Guardia campaigned relentlessly for a military appointment.

Within the United States, there was a migration to the war production factories of the North. Americans took unfamiliar jobs in unfamiliar cities. All automobile factories were converted into war material plants, building munitions, planes, ships. American factories would increase Liberty Ship production to one per day, a staggering statistic.

These were the days of rationing. There were shortages of butter and sugar, tires, and gasoline. These were the days of the seven-day work week. These were the days of housing scarcity, of workers sharing "hot beds," with shifts of workers crowding into rooming houses. These were also the days of the dreaded telegrams: "We regret to inform you" those War Department telegrams began, and then they named the individual soldier who died in defense of this country. These were the days that the telegram trickle turned into a telegram deluge and the grieving could be felt from cities to villages to farms. These were the days of a great and inestimable national sacrifice. And all of us looked to the White House and President Roosevelt for stability, for hope, for guidance. And Roosevelt responded. He was the greatest wartime leader in the history of this nation.

Why am I still a Rooseveltian? After Pearl Harbor, Roosevelt made one of his most difficult decisions: he recognized that Germany had to be defeated first. This again showed his leadership ability; the nation and Roosevelt's admirals, aroused by the Japanese, wanted to fight in the Pacific. Still, Roosevelt pushed for the Atlantic First strategy. Had Roosevelt gone along with popular opinion, how much longer would the war in Europe have lasted?

Why am I still a Rooseveltian? To return to an earlier theme, in my mind there was a direct link between Roosevelt and my father, an intertwined moment. My father and I sat in the dining room of our apartment. It was sometime in the mid-1930s. It was seven in the evening. The Depression continued but there was a feeling of hope in the air, something that wasn't there before Franklin Roosevelt. From the radio, the sonorous tones of President Roosevelt's voice filled the room. "My friends," Roosevelt began, as he always began his Fireside Chats, "I want to talk to you tonight about. . . ." And then he launched into whatever particular theme he had in mind. In his voice, there was assurance and power and optimism. I looked over at my father. He was nodding his head. He was agreeing with the President. I was a teenager, young, eager, impressionable. And in my teenage eyes, these two men, my heroes at the time, not only agreed but connected, at least by radio.

Why am I still a Rooseveltian? Because in the photographs I see the President now and I'm reminded of my father. And I see my father now and I'm reminded of the President. And I realize that because of one man, my father, I became involved in the other.

The Holocaust tears me to shreds. Researching and writing about it has taken a tremendous toll. I've envisioned myself as a European Jew. I've envisioned myself in the Auschwitz camp. I've wondered if I would have survived. I know that I would have prayed for American bombs to obliterate the crematoria. I feel guilty as a Jew that more wasn't done.

Revisionists view Franklin D. Roosevelt in light of every Holocaust-related event. This is a narrow vision. To study America's response to the Holocaust is to study a series of mistakes, inactions, and inexplicable responses by nearly everyone involved. The State Department was egregiously anti-Semitic and anti-immigrant. Were it not for State Department "bureaucratic bungling and callousness," Rabbi Wise wrote, "thousands of lives might have been saved and the Jewish catastrophe partially averted."[7] Speaking of Rabbi Wise, he seemed to hold onto his own power, and his own connection to Roosevelt, at the expense of pushing for action to aid European Jews. He seemed seduced by the President. His heart was in the right place, I believe, but I wonder if his relationship to Roosevelt served his European brethren.

Pope Pius XII chose to acquiesce to Nazi demands. And when he did break out from that mode, he took an oblique and seemingly detached tone. "One is inclined to conclude that the Pope and his advisers—influenced by the long tradition of moderate anti-Semitism so widely accepted in Vatican circles—did not view the plight of the Jews with a real sense of urgency and moral out-rage," the learned and prolific historian Guenter Lewy wrote.[8] On the question of anti-Semitism, the Pope never offered "a single liturgical act for the deported Jews of the Eternal City." When Hitler died, however, the Cardinal Archbishop of Berlin ordered all the parish priests "to hold a solemn Requiem in memory of the Führer and all those members of the Wehrmacht who have fallen in the struggle for our German Fatherland, along with the sincer-est prayers for Volk and Fatherland and for the future of the Catholic Church in Germany."[9] If Pius objected to any of this liturgy, he never publicly voiced it.

Whether Pope Pius was anti-Semitic or not, he clearly found it difficult to comprehend and respond to the enormity of the Final Solution. And in that reaction, Pius was like nearly all the leaders of the day.

The British, who could have greatly enhanced rescue by open-ing their protectorate, Palestine, chose a harsh restriction, the White Paper. Churchill, who disliked the White Paper, did not change course. Nor did he pressure his government to implement a WRB-type agency. A British government committed to rescue in 1944, or earlier, might have saved thousands of refugees.

The Jewish organizations in America were involved in internecine warfare, each going in a different direction. The Yiddish newspaper *Yiddisher Kemfer* found it unfathomable that "the chief organizations of American Jewry . . . could not in this dire hour, unequalled even in history, unite for the purpose of seeking ways to forestall the misfortune or at least to reduce its scope. . . ."[10]

Other than Henry Morgenthau, the Jewish advisers around Roosevelt did not press for rescue. This makes for a bitter legacy. President Roosevelt appointed more Jews to his Administration than any other President, prior or subsequent, and yet those men did not use their faith to agitate for the Jews in Europe. It's ironic and devastating.

The media kept Holocaust stories off the front pages. The *New York Times*, for instance, from the years 1939 through 1945, printed 1,186 Holocaust stories, or an average of 17 stories per month.[11] And yet only 26 stories mentioning the "discrimination, deportation, and destruction" of the Jews made the front pages. And of those stories, only six identified Jews as the primary victims. Six stories in six years. Six stories while six million died. The *New York Times* was owned by the quietly Jewish Arthur Sulzberger

But, as this is primarily a Roosevelt story, let us end with the protagonist. He was not an anti-Semite. He was not responsible for the Holocaust. He believed, as we have read over and over again, that the best way to save Jewish lives was to defeat Nazi Germany. His commitment to that belief never wavered.

That same commitment, it should be noted, allowed Roosevelt to gain a place within the pantheon of great U.S. Presidents. Because of his drive, because of his prescience, because of his confidence and creativity, and because of his commitment to defeating Hitler, Roosevelt joins Abraham Lincoln and George Washington at the top of the pyramid of great Presidents. Like those other two giants, he had his faults. I started this project as a Rooseveltian, and I will end it as one, but along the way I've learned a simple though profound truth: Great people are not great all the time.

Bob Beir gives his best Roosevelt imitation during the opening of the Robert L. Beir Education Center at the Franklin D. Roosevelt Library and Museum. October 28, 1996.

Chapter 24

◀ ▶

This Is What's Happening

"The Jew I am belongs to a traumatized generation," Elie Wiesel, a survivor of Auschwitz and a subsequent Holocaust chronicler and Nobel Peace laureate, said. "We have antennas— better yet, we are antennas. And if we tell you that the signals we receive are disturbing, indeed alarming, people better listen."[1]

I have an antenna, too. No, it's not the antenna of the Auschwitz survivor, or the antenna of a European Jew who somehow survived the Nazi Reich. It's a different kind of antenna, the kind molded here in America, during an era of demeaning prejudice. My antenna developed during the 1930s and 1940s. It was built by personal experiences: the "dirty Jew" comment in school, classmates raiding my room late at night and dumping me out of bed, a roommate in graduate school declaring that he couldn't room with a Jew. These experiences formed a sixth sense, a gauge, an antenna. And the world I see today, a world of fundamentalism and prejudice and scapegoating, gives me great pause. I am filled with fear.

In Europe, the indicators are frightening. The number of anti-Semitic incidents in 2004 jumped by 20 percent over the previous year. Polls conducted by the Anti-Defamation League speak to the increase: 40 percent of Europeans believe that Jews have "too much power" in the business world; 29 percent of Europeans believe that Jews "don't care what happens to anyone but their own kind"; and 63 percent of Europeans believe that Jews "stick together" more than other people.[2]

In Russia and the Ukraine, there were 482 anti-Semitic attacks in 2004, according to the Stephen Roth Institute at Tel Aviv University, a scholarly think-tank that studies contemporary anti-Semitism and racism. Most of the incidents involved vandalism of cemeteries and property. Nineteen incidents, however, were considered "major attacks" (identified as intent to kill). The year 2005 began with the assault on two rabbis on a Moscow street. "Moreover," the Stephen Roth Institute reported, "Russia is perhaps the only country where officials openly express anti-Semitic opinions and slurs at meetings of state institutions, such as the Duma [lower house of Parliament], and where anti-incitement laws exist but are not enforced."[3]

Take General Albert Makashov as a case study. In the late 1990s he became infamous worldwide for his anti-Semitic rants. In a Russian newspaper he stated that a "Yid is a bloodsucker feeding on the misfortunes of other people. They drink the blood of the indigenous peoples in the state; they are destroying industry and agriculture." At a rally commemorating the Bolshevik Revolution, Makashov shouted, "I will round up all the Yids and send them to the next world."[4]

General Makashov was not some separatist spewing his vitriol to a small counterculture enclave in central Russia; instead, Makashov was a member of the Duma and a rising star within the Communist Party. The Duma, upon hearing his tirades, failed to censure the General. In addition, Gennady Zyuganov, the Communist Party leader, supported Makashov with his own harsh anti-Semitic references. Today, Albert Makashov continues to serve in the Duma and Gennady Zyuganov continues to lead the Communist Party of the Russian Federation.

This is what's happening.

In Poland, where fewer than 10,000 Jews now live (from a pre-World War II population of 3.2 million), a recent poll found that 25 percent of the population holds anti-Semitic opinions.[5] The rise of anti-Semitism is unmistakable. In September 2003, the windows of a Jewish school in Wroclaw were smashed, and the perpetrators scrawled anti-Semitic slogans on the walls. The incident was followed by an anonymous phone call to the principal, describing this as "the first stage in a war [against the Jews]." In October, in a restaurant in Krakow, a group of high school students from Israel were thrown out after one of the employees discovered their religious roots. In December, the Jewish cemetery of Oswiecim (Auschwitz) was desecrated, with ten tombstones overturned.

In January of 2005, the world gathered at Auschwitz to commemorate the 60th anniversary of the camp's liberation. Forty-four world leaders, U.S. Vice President Richard Cheney included, joined 1,000 survivors in sub-zero temperatures with snow falling softly. The event began with the whistle of a train, symbolizing the arrival of a cattle car once used across Europe to transport Jews to the extermination camp. Polish President Aleksander Kwasniewski then called for "future generations never to forget." And yet Kwasniewski's government, in a proposed compensation package to survivors, offers a fraction of the value of their Holocaust-era possessions.

This is what's happening.

In France, the home of 600,000 Jews (the country with the world's third largest Jewish population), anti-Jewish violence has reached epidemic proportions. There have been attacks on 147 Jewish institutions (schools, synagogues, businesses) since September 2000, according to Vérité-Sécurité, an anti-Semitic watchdog organization. That includes the burning of the main synagogue in Marseilles in 2002. That includes an arson attack on a Jewish school in Paris in November 2003. That includes the reported assaults on rabbis, and schoolteachers canceling classes on the Holocaust, and in January 2004, a group of North African youth heckling a Jewish singer named Shirel, shouting, "Filthy Jew! Death to the Jews!"

This is what's happening.

In February 2004, a comedian named Dieudonne (full name, Dieudonne M'Bala M'Bala), appeared on French television. Dressed as an orthodox rabbi, he delivered a Nazi salute. Jewish organizations immediately accused Dieudonne of anti-Semitism or, at the very least, racial insensitivity. A theater, which was to

stage the comedian's act, canceled his run of shows, claiming that
it couldn't guarantee the safety of the audience. Dieudonne reacted
by denying any anti-Semitism. His sketch, he said, was intended
to criticize the policies of Prime Minister Ariel Sharon toward the
Palestinians. "The Jewish communities of Europe are seen by the
public as extensions of and advocates for a regime in Israel that
is rapidly losing its legitimacy in the eyes of the intelligentsia, the
media, the left, and the anti-globalization crowd," according to
David Harris, head of the American Jewish Committee. "So the question really becomes, how do you fight anti-Semitism in France or
Belgium if the image of their Jewish citizens is inextricably linked to
Israel?"[6] Israel, with the only freely elected government in the Middle
East, with the only free press, with a citizenry still decidedly in favor
of a two-state solution with Palestine, has become a pariah. Such a
sentiment was voiced by Daniel Bernard, the French Ambassador to
England, in December 2001. Speaking off the record, Bernard
remarked that the world's troubles were because of "that shitty lit-
tle country Israel." He continued, "Why should we be in danger of
World War III because of these people?"[7]

This is what's happening.

In America, the indicators are nearly as frightening. At Duke
University in North Carolina, a student named Philip Kurian wrote
an editorial for the university newspaper, *The Chronicle*. Under
the title, "The Jews," Kurian mentioned all the old anti-Semitic
diatribes, from "shocking overrepresentation" at universities to
"exorbitant Jewish privilege" and an "overwhelming sense of entitlement" to usurping civil rights from other, more needy segments
of society. The Jewish agenda, according to Kurian, "uses its influence to stifle, not enhance, the Israeli-Palestinian debate, simultaneously belittling the real struggles for socioeconomic and political
equality faced, most notably by black Americans."

Kurian's article was not shocking in its substance; such rhetoric can be found in numerous places, now and in the past. The
same tone and temper flowed during the era of the Wagner-Rogers
legislation debate, from the mouth of Congressman Jacob
Thorkleson, who called the Jews an "obnoxious tribe;" from the
mouth of Congressman John Rankin, who referred to news colum-

nist Walter Winchell as "that little kike;" from the Nazi-like rhetoric of the Daughters of the American Revolution. Kurian's article, however, produced a shocking reaction.[8] *The Chronicle* listed 539 responses, some from Duke and the state of North Carolina but many more from around the country. Kurian's article struck a nerve. And yes, most of the responses were critical of, if not deploring, Kurian's position. For instance, an attorney in New York wrote, "Am I reading *The Chronicle* or *Der Stürmer?*" But there were other respondents, those who not only congratulated Kurian but thanked him for his "courage" and his resolve.

A computer technician in New York wrote, "I can see form [sic] the letters received that the Jewish lobby is getting into high gear to try and silence you. . . . The Jewish power must be stopped. . . ."

An engineer in California wrote, "I enjoyed your article, however you did not dwell on recent Jewish problems such as 9/11 and the war in Iraq." The 9/11 reference referred to the theory (for lack of better word) that Jews who worked in lower Manhattan were warned in advance to stay away from the World Trade Center. According to that absurd claim, four thousand Jews heeded the warning.

A student in Michigan wrote, "I am glad you have the courage to stand up to the Jews. I agree with everything in your article, except you pointed out that the holocaust is a fact, when in reality what happened is still open for debate."

And then there was a reply from a man named Michael who addressed those respondents who had condemned Kurian's column: "Seriously, did any of you actually read the article? . . . Yes, he made his argument in a sensationalist manner, but there's no need to get all huffy about it. The more you complain about the article, the more you validate the point he's trying to make, that the Jewish [sic] seem to have developed a (false) sense of entitlement to immunity from any kind of speech that is slightly derogatory or not in their interests."

This is what's happening.

In New York, the statistics are startling. The city saw 57 anti-Semitic crimes in the fourth quarter of 2003. There were 21 incidents alone in November. In 2004, just in the borough of

Manhattan, there were 105 anti-Semitic incidents.[9]

At Columbia University, professors in the Middle East Studies Department were accused of intimidating their pro-Israeli students, choosing selectively to silence and humiliate those with a different political opinion.

At a basketball game in 2004 between two private, prestigious high schools in New York City, an ugly scene occurred. The students of one high school directed a series of mocking references at a player with the surname Goldberg. "Gefilte fish," the students yelled. When the player committed a turnover, the students yelled, "passover." When the player missed a shot, the students yelled, "not kosher." When the player scored a basket, the students yelled derisively, "light the menorah."

A parent in the crowd became inflamed. Yes, he felt burned by the students yelling the insults (some of whom, as it turns out, may have been Jewish and may have actually known the player and therefore may have been "kidding around"). But beyond that, he couldn't believe that other parents could permit the taunts and jibes. He called the parents' reaction "a kind of betrayal." In a letter to the school's head administrator, he wrote, the "parents [were] sitting idly by in tacit approval. . . . But as it has for generations, the anti-Semitism started to spread. Like a cancer, it grew—as people all around started to laugh and encourage this small, vocal group."[10]

This is what's happening.

At a restaurant on the New Jersey shore, a young couple received quite a shock. On their bill, alongside various sushi items, were the words, "Jew Couple." The manager of the restaurant explained: "We use it as a form of identity." She added that the words were not intended to be offensive. "My grandfather went through all that in old-school Europe," the male member of the couple said. "But that happened more than fifty years ago. You don't expect it to happen in 2005. . . ."[11]

But this is what's happening.

At the intersection of Amsterdam Avenue and 96th Street on Manhattan's Upper West Side (a neighborhood which has become heavily Jewish) a sight took the breath away of Sunday strollers passing by. On the windows of a dry cleaning store three swastikas glowed in anger and ridicule. "It's that one symbol that symbolizes hatred, bigotry, and persecution, even to death," Abraham Foxman, the Director of the Anti-Defamation League said. "It's a very selective graffiti. You can make circles and squares and triangles. But all you have to do is the swastika, and it communicates 80 years of hatred."[12]

According to the Anti-Defamation League, there has been "a tremendous increase in the number of swastikas painted in apartment buildings, in lobbies and elevators, as well as on synagogues, on shops and other buildings." There is, in fact, a pandemic. The swastika can be seen all over New York: on a building in Brighton Beach, on a Jewish school in Woodhaven, on the walls of a subway station in Greenwich Village, on the hood of a car at Sheepshead Bay, on the windows of a dry cleaning establishment on the Upper West Side.

This is what's happening.

The American Ambassador to the European Union, Rockwell Schnabel, reported that anti-Semitism "is getting to a point where it is as bad as it was in the 1930s."[13] If that's the case, then a recent conference might be considered the Evian Conference of the 21st century, with perhaps a different result. Back in 1938, in response to the imperialism of Nazi Germany and the *Anschluss* and reports of Nazi atrocities committed against Jews, President Roosevelt called for the Evian Conference to try to address the Jewish refugee crisis. On April 28–29, 2004, the Organization for Security and Cooperation in Europe (OSCE) sponsored a conference to condemn and fight modern anti-Semitism. The differences between Evian and the OSCE Conference were striking. To start with, the OSCE picked Berlin, the former capital of the Third Reich, as the site for the Conference. The date too was emblematic. Fifty-nine years earlier, on April 29, 1945, Adolf Hitler married his girlfriend of many years, Eva Braun, in his Berlin bunker. The next day, with the Soviet army controlling large swaths of Berlin and frantically searching to take the leader of Germany alive, Adolf Hitler bit into a cyanide capsule, then shot himself in the right temple. His body, alongside his wife's, was cremated the same day.

At Evian in 1938, thirty-two nations gathered for the nine-day conference. The American delegation was led by Myron C. Taylor, who had no experience in refugee or Jewish issues. At the Berlin Conference in 2004, representatives of fifty-five nations gathered, with more than five hundred participants. The American delegation, led by former Mayor of New York Ed Koch, included former Secretary of State Colin Powell and two of the most fervent fighters of anti-Semitism the world over: Elie Wiesel and Abraham Foxman.

During the Evian Conference, the Nazi Foreign Minister, Joachim von Ribbentrop, threatened to retaliate against German Jewry if Evian encouraged anti-German propaganda. At the Berlin Conference, Germany's Foreign Minister, Joschka Fischer, took a far different position. In his opening remarks, Fischer said, "I would like us to condemn all forms of anti-Semitism as actions demeaning our human dignity; to create instruments that would help detect any acts of anti-Semitism . . . ; and to take appropriate measures. I would like us to assume a common political responsibility to fight all forms of anti-Semitism openly and decisively."[14]

Fischer's remarks built upon the words of Germany's President Johannes Rau, who opened the Berlin Conference with, "It's sad to see that in 2004, there is still need for a Convention to devote itself to battling anti-Semitism." Rau's statement, clearly, was in direct opposition to his predecessor of the 1930s and 1940s, Adolf Hitler. After the Evian Conference Hitler gloated, "It is a shameful spectacle to see how the whole democratic world is oozing sympathy for the poor tormented Jewish people, but remains hard hearted and obdurate when it comes to helping them."

During the Evian Conference, the U.S. State Department did not put forth a policy position. Roosevelt's Secretary of State at that time, Cordell Hull, neither attended the Evian Conference nor addressed the refugee crisis. Contrast that to Secretary Colin Powell in Berlin. "Today, we confront the ugly reality that anti-Semitism is not just a fact of history, but a current event," he said. "Indeed we're appalled that in recent years the incidence of anti-Semitic hate crimes has been on the increase within our community of democratic nations. All of us recognize that we must take decisive measures to reverse this disturbing trend."

At the Berlin Conference, the President of Israel, Moshe Katsav, said, "We very much appreciate this gathering in Berlin. This step to fight anti-Semitism sends a very important message that this issue has a significant place in the European agenda, in the relations between Israel and Europe and between Europe and world Jewry. It is a sign that the security of Jews touched directly basic human values." At Evian, of course, the state of Israel did not exist.

The Evian Conference quickly revealed world opinion. Country after country came forward with reasons for not accepting Jewish immigration. The Australian delegation declared, "As we have no real racial problem, we are not desirous of importing one."

The Berlin Conference showed the opinion of the participating nations, too. By recognizing the growing tide of anti-Semitism, the European nations seemed to end their days of denial, realizing that anti-Semitism threatens "democracy, civilization, and security." The Evian Conference, of course, did not have a keynote speaker like Elie Wiesel (who was ten years old at that time). At Berlin, he implored the delegates to "Stop! Stop a disease that has lasted so long. Stop the poison from spreading." Later, Wiesel called for a "manifesto to be composed, distributed in all schools where, one day every year, it be read and studied as a sacred document." And while the delegates did not go that far, they did adopt a "Berlin Declaration." The measures included:

1. Collecting data on anti-Semitic crimes and reporting such information to the OSCE.
2. Strengthening—and in some cases, creating—national laws against anti-Semitism and hate crimes in general.
3. Advancing educational programs to combat anti-Semitism.
4. Opposing hate crimes fueled by racist propaganda in the media and on the Internet.
5. Asserting that the Israeli-Palestinian conflict should not be allowed to serve as a cover for the expressions of anti-Semitic positions and opinions.

The Berlin Declaration resonated with Congressman Robert

Wexler of Florida, an American delegate to Berlin, who saw "a dramatic shift in the international community's response to anti-Semitism in Europe." Wexler wrote in the aftermath of the Berlin Conference, "Possibly for the first time in history, there is genuine reason to hope."[15]

Contrast the Florida Congressman's words with those of a predecessor. The Evian Conference, according to Congressman Emanuel Celler of New York, "did not even have the dignity of announcing its failure; it merely fizzled out."

This is the good news. Unlike the Evian Conference, when the nations of the world turned away from the crisis, nations today seem to recognize what's at stake. There is, of course, the flip side. In Palestine, the reaction to the Berlin Conference was outrage. The author and Palestinian activist Mahmud Nammura called the Conference a "red herring" and a "sly distraction." The real purpose of the Conference, according to Nammura, was to cover up "the shameful Israeli crimes in Rafah, Jenin and Nablus." Nammura added: "I want to ask the leaders of Europe: Which crime is more serious? The desecration of a Jewish grave in some French town, or destroying an entire neighborhood in Rafah? Scrawling a swastika on the wall of a Jewish synagogue in Italy or turning Palestinian towns and villages into virtual concentration camps?"[16]

This is, unfortunately, the state of the world. We compare atrocities. We attempt to make political points. We attempt to convince others that we're right and they're wrong. The Israeli-Palestinian conflict is a horrible, seemingly endless and complex quagmire. Many regard it as an occupation. To others, it's a means of self-preservation. But comparing Israeli practice, no matter how severe, to the Nazis' Final Solution is a demonization. At the Berlin Conference, Colin Powell declared, "It is not anti-Semitism to criticize Israel, but the line is crossed when the leaders of Israel are demonized and vilified by the use of Nazi symbols." The same can be said of using Nazi symbols to speak of Arab leaders. We must be very careful. We live in a precarious time: an age of crusades. Hatred is the prevailing emotion.

In *Conversations with Elie Wiesel*, Wiesel said, "After the war

[WWII], the Germans were afraid. They weren't afraid of the Americans. Nor were they afraid of the French. Of the Russians, yes. But above all, they were afraid of the Jews. Somehow they felt that the Jews would come back and avenge the blood that was shed. And it didn't happen. There were no acts of vengeance."[17]

Should this be our motto today? We live in a vengeful world. We're an eye-for-an-eye culture, an eye-for-an-eye civilization. Take, as an example, Prime Minister Mahathir Mohamad of Malaysia. In 1997, he sounded an age-old anti-Semitic rant and blamed an economic crisis on the Jews, who purportedly control the world financial systems. "We are Muslims," he said, "and the Jews are not happy to see Muslims progress. . . . If viewed from Palestine, the Jews have robbed Palestinians of everything, but they cannot do this in Malaysia, so they do this [cause a financial panic]."[18] The Prime Minister followed up those comments in 2003, at the Tenth Islamic Summit. The Jews, he said, "rule the world by proxy" and "get others to fight and die for them." Mohamad called for a "final victory" by the world's 1.3 billion Muslims who "cannot be defeated by a few million Jews."[19]

Mahathir Mohamad's speech found support among the Muslim nations and disdain elsewhere. The German Foreign Ministry called the anti-Jewish remarks "totally unacceptable." President George W. Bush, in a face-to-face meeting with Prime Minister Mohamad, called the remarks "reprehensible . . . divisive and unnecessary."

On the other side, former Iranian President Mohammad Khatami said, "It was a brilliant speech. Very logical." Somalia's former President Abdiqasim Salad Hassan said, "The prime minister was not inciting war. He was just saying that we should be united to face threats from many quarters, including Israel." Or, in other words, he was inciting war. Yemen Foreign Minister Abubakar al-Qirbi said, "I don't think they were anti-Semitic at all. I think he was basically stating the fact to the Muslim world." Or, in other words, his words were blatantly anti-Semitic.

At the Islamic Summit, those in attendance—fifty-seven nations altogether, including supposed moderates like Jordan and Egypt— reacted to Mahathir Mohamad's speech with a standing ovation.

Such a reaction brings to mind the United Nations. Consider some of the UN's blatant anti-Semitic gestures. In 1975, the General Assembly declared that "Zionism is a form of racism" by a vote of 89 to 67. That's pure anti-Semitism. According to Anne Bayefsky, Professor of Political Science at York University in Toronto and an Adjunct Professor at the Columbia Law School, six of the ten emergency sessions ever called by the General Assembly condemned Israeli policy. The UN did not call for emergency sessions during the Rwandan massacre of one million, or the Kosovo slaughter, or the genocide in the Sudan. Why not? Of course Israeli policy should be criticized, but so should the policies of other governments. When that doesn't happen the conclusion is inevitable: The United Nations acts as an anti-Semitic body. In 1991, the "Zionism is racism" resolution was revoked by a vote of 87 to 25. So twenty-five nations still adhered to the insidious clause. That's pure anti-Semitism. In 2001, at the UN-sponsored World Conference Against Racism in Durban, South Africa, the entire Conference degenerated into a forum on Jewish "racism" and "Israeli apartheid." That's pure anti-Semitism. On January 24, 2005, the United Nations marked the anniversary of the liberation of Auschwitz. But previously, the UN had never commemorated the event. Is there any doubt that, in Professor Anne Bayefsky's words, the UN has become "the leading purveyor of anti-Semitism, intolerance and inequity against the Jewish people and its state"?[20]

This is our world today: divided, contemptuous, hateful, and polarized. More and more, it's becoming a world of Muslims versus non-Muslims. That is not to say that all Muslims are anti-Semitic, or that anti-Semitism only flourishes in Muslim countries. But from the perspective of this New Yorker, the moderate voices within the Muslim world seem to be shrinking and the radical voices seem to be growing. What happens when the radical voices within the Muslim world reach out and influence those outside the Muslim world? Is this our future? Will alliances form? Will anti-Semites like Jen-Marie Le Pen of the National Front, who placed second to Jacques Chirac in the French presidential campaign of 2002 (with 18 percent of the vote), or Hans-Günther

Eisenecker, a member of the right-wing National Democratic Party (NPD) in Germany, link with Islamic fundamentalists in a move against Israel and its allies? The ramifications are frightening.

Fortunately, there are those fighting anti-Semitism. There are those who spend their days working tirelessly for justice. The vigilant, I would call them. Abraham Foxman, who was born in Poland in 1940 and survived the Holocaust under the care of a Catholic nursemaid, is one of the vigilant. Wherever there's anti-Semitism, there's Abraham Foxman speaking out. "We can't afford to wait for the next crisis and the explosion of hatred and violence it may provoke," he wrote in his book, *Never Again? The Threat of the New Anti-Semitism*. Foxman suggested a number of steps people might take to combat anti-Semitism and other forms of bigotry, from calling "attacks on Jews and Jewish institutions what they are—acts of anti-Semitism"; to urging both local and national authorities to use the full resources of the law to combat hate crimes; to protesting in the face of anti-Semitism. "When you encounter bigoted attitudes in private life—in the workplace or in your community—have the courage to speak out for tolerance," Foxman wrote. This is Foxman's creed and he lives by it.

Elie Wiesel is one of the vigilant. Like Foxman, he spends his days working to diminish bigotry and intolerance. His is the voice of deep commitment and, because of his history as an Auschwitz survivor, alarm. Regarding the Jews in Europe he said, "I have seen in the last year communities that contain people who came to me and whispered in my ear, saying simply, not, 'Should we leave?' but 'When should we leave?' My god, what a question."

Edgar Bronfman of the World Jewish Congress is one of the vigilant. So is David Harris of the American Jewish Committee. So is Natan Sharansky. As Anatoly Shcharansky in the former Soviet Union, he demanded the right as a Jew to emigrate to Israel. The Soviet authorities reacted with prison sentences. After gaining his freedom in 1986, Sharansky began his crusade for human rights. Now, as Israel's Minister of Diaspora Affairs, he talks about the line between legitimate criticism of Israel and anti-Semitism. This is his "3D test." The first D is the test of demonization. "That was the main instrument of anti-Semitism against Jews," he said in his speech at the Berlin Conference. "The Jews were accused of drinking the blood of children, spoiling the wells, controlling the banks and governments." He called this dynamic "very danger-ous—but at least very easy to identify."

The second D is the test of a double standard. In his speech at the Berlin Conference, Sharansky said, "For thousands of years, a clear sign of anti-Semitism was treating Jews differently than other people, from the discriminatory laws that many nations enacted against them to the tendency to judge their behavior by a different yardstick. Similarly, today we must ask whether criticism of Israel is being applied selectively. If Israel . . . is being condemned by the Human Rights Commission for the violation of human rights more than all the many dictatorial regimes over the past 50 years together, it means that a different yardstick is used toward Israel than toward other countries. And a different yardstick means a double standard and a double standard means anti-Semitism."

The third D is the test of delegitimization. In his speech at the Berlin Conference, Sharansky said, "In the past, anti-Semites tried to deny the legitimacy of the Jewish religion, the Jewish people or both. Today, they are trying to deny the legitimacy of the Jewish state. While criticism of an Israeli policy may not be anti-Semitic, the denial of Israel's rights to exist is always anti-Semitic."[21]

There are other members of the vigilant, of course. Are there enough? Can anti-Semitism be defeated? I am reminded of Peter Bergson's words, spoken in an interview with the historian David Wyman. Regarding the rescue of Holocaust Jews, he said it could-n't be handled by a charitable organization. "Only a government could handle it. You had a government using all its power to do the murder. Only another government could oppose it."

With that in mind, and knowing that circumstantial evidence points to state-supported anti-Semitism, are we not in need of a committed and continual involvement on governmental levels? One such program, from all appearances, has been implemented by President Jacques Chirac of France. After a firebomb gutted a Jewish school in a Parisian suburb in 2003, President Chirac promised to be "uncompromising" and began a crackdown on anti-Semitic activity. "When a Jew is attacked in France," he declared, "the whole of France is attacked." He formed a high level task force—led by the Prime Minister and the Ministers of Justice, Interior, Education and Foreign Affairs—to meet monthly and report on the state of anti-Semitism. The task force introduced various initiatives, including tighter security around Jewish sites, quicker investigations and prosecutions of hate crimes, a movement to teach about the Holocaust in the school system and a crackdown on television channels like Al Manar, which beams its anti-American, anti-Israeli, anti-Semitic messages into France by satellite. At the same time, the government proposed a $7 billion urban regeneration program, aimed particularly at the marginalized Muslim communities (where unemployment among Muslim youth is three times the French national average). And yet, according to the Associated Press, attacks against Jews have reached a ten-year high. The result has been a flow of French Jews to Israel. In 2002, for instance, 2,556 French Jews emigrated, double the previous year's total.

This is what's happening. The doubt continues to resonate. Can all the efforts in the world, by some of the most vigilant people in the world, counteract the rise of anti-Semitism?

As I complete this book, I am eighty-seven years old. I was born at the end of the First World War. That war, we believed, would be the end of violence. The butchery was so incredible; we simply could not foresee future forms of butchery. Today, we see various forms of butchery regularly. Three bombs explode in the London subway, and one explodes on a bus. Another suicide bomber in Tel Aviv. A diplomat in Iraq is tortured on film, then beheaded. Also in Iraq, a suicide car bomber steers his sports utility vehicle toward a group of children congregating around American troops. He detonates the bomb. Over twenty children die in the explosion.

This is what's happening.

The Israeli-Palestinian conflict has heated up anti-Semitism. The inverse is true, too. "Everybody knows that massive anti-

Semitism has been behind some of the criticism of Israeli government policies in the past decades," German President Rau stated at the Berlin Conference.[22] Elie Wiesel might say that the anti-Semite uses the conflict as an excuse. "The anti-Semite doesn't know me, but he hates me," Wiesel said. "Actually, he hated me before I was born."

If a two-state solution for Israel and Palestine comes to pass in the near future, does the anti-Semitism diminish? In our recent past, had Yitzhak Rabin lived to implement the Oslo Accords would the world be in such disarray? Had Yasser Arafat signed the Camp David–Taba peace talks with Ehud Barak, and succeeded in building a peace between the two nations, what would be the state of anti-Semitism now?

I don't know the answers to these questions. I know, now, that we live in an age of vengeance. "Where do you stop?" Elie Wiesel asked, regarding vengeance in the immediate aftermath of the Holocaust. "You know where to begin—the SS first, right? But then there were support groups who helped the SS. And then the bystanders. And then you go back to Hungary—there were quite a few Hungarian fascists who helped the SS in my own town. They hurt and beat up more Jews than the Germans did. The same is true of Rumania and Poland and the Ukraine. Where do you stop? It would be a bloodbath."[23]

We live now in a bloodbath. Will it ever end? In my lifetime, will I see a solution to Israel-Palestine? Will I see a retreating of anti-Semitism? Or, will a greater anti-Semitism commence? My great fear is that a war involving Israel breaks out in the Middle East. A small conflagration, perhaps a border skirmish, becomes enormous. As in both world wars, allies join the fight. The United States, of course, sides with Israel. Britain feels compelled to join its American ally. France and Germany grudgingly do the same. The Muslim world lines up on the other side. It's a vision of World War III. It's a vision of many fronts, and many casualties, and always the threat of nuclear weaponry. It's a vision of increased detainment centers by the Western nations. The Japanese internment of Roosevelt's day would look tiny in comparison to the rounding up of all the Arab-speaking Muslims. This is my fear. And in such an event, what happens to my grandchildren, both of whom are teenagers? Might they be drafted? Might they be forced to serve on some front line? What happens to all of our grandchildren? When does this end?

◄ ►

A Final Note

On September 14, 2004, when I was eighty-six years old, I was diagnosed with bladder cancer. This after living cancer-free for fifty years. I subsequently had surgery. Now I have routine examinations and recurring surgeries. What will happen next, I don't know. But the unknown isn't to be feared. The unknown becomes the next chapter.

Endnotes

Timeline of World and Holocaust Events
   1 James MacGregor Burns, *Roosevelt: The Soldier of Freedom*, p. 250.
   2 David Kennedy, *Freedom From Fear*, p. 438.
   3 *Ibid.*, p. 440.
   4 Burns, pp. 11–12.
   5 Kennedy, p. 467.
   6 Burns, p. 73.
   7 *Ibid.*, p. 103.
   8 Kennedy, p. 524.
   9 Jon Meacham, *Franklin and Winston: An Intimate Portrait of an Epic Friendship*, p. 197.
   10 Burns, p. 537.
   11 Kennedy, p. 802.
   12 For Truman's quote about Churchill, see Kennedy, p. 838. For Truman's quote about his own resolve, see Kennedy, p. 842.
   13 Ernest Michel, *Promises to Keep*, pp. 115–116.

Chapter 2
   1 James MacGregor Burns and Susan Dunn, *The Three Roosevelts*, p. 254.

2 These statistics, as well as the admission policies of Harvard, Yale, and Princeton can be found in Jerome Karabel, *The Chosen.*

3 For an illuminating view of Harvard University and its leniencies toward the Nazi government, see Stephen Norwood, "Harvard's Nazi Ties," *Jewish Standard,* Nov. 19, 2004.

4 John Gunther, *Roosevelt in Retrospect,* p. 324.

5 James MacGregor Burns, *Roosevelt: the Soldier of Freedom,* p. 214.

6 For Roosevelt's hypothetical solution to the internment, see Greg Robinson, "Le Projet M de Franklin Roosevelt: construire un monde meilleur grâce à la science . . . des races," *Critique Internationale No. 27,* Mai 2005, pp. 65–82.

7 Burns, p. 216.

8 For a full story of the Japanese internment, including the efforts of Eleanor Roosevelt, see Greg Robinson, *By Order of the President.*

9 Burns, p. 216.

Chapter 3

1 William L. Shirer, *20th Century Journal: The Nightmare Years, 1930–1940,* p. 594.

2 Martin Gilbert, *The Holocaust,* pp. 601, 611, 616.

3 David McCullough, *Truman,* p. 359.

4 *Ibid.,* p. 424.

5 *Ibid.*

6 "Hiroshima," *The Wall Street Journal,* August 5, 2005.

7 For an analysis of why Truman made his decision to bomb Japan, see Richard B. Frank, "Why Truman Dropped the Bomb," *The Weekly Standard,* August 8, 2005.

Chapter 4

1 For a study of President Roosevelt's psychology, see Richard Thayer Goldberg, *The Making of Franklin D. Roosevelt: Triumph over Disability.*

2 Emanuel Celler, *You Never Leave Brooklyn: The Autobiography of Emanuel Celler,* p. 12.

3 "During the 30s" quote: John Gunther, *Roosevelt in*

Retrospect, p. 239. The quote to Winant: Gunther, p. 237. The quote to Perkins: Gunther, p. 237.

⁴ For the story of the Vice-Presidential nominating process and the 1944 Convention, see David McCullough, *Truman*, pp. 292-324.

⁵ For a second story of the Vice-Presidential nominating process and 1944 Convention, see Frank Freidel, *Franklin D. Roosevelt: A Rendezvous with Destiny*, pp. 529–538.

⁶ Freidel, p. 531.

Chapter 7

¹ Neil A. Lewis, "Nazis and Jews: Insights from Old Diary," *New York Times* (April 22, 2004). The article focuses on the McDonald diaries, which were recently found and donated to the United States Holocaust Memorial Museum. McDonald wrote more than 10,000 pages, including his interviews with Roosevelt, Hitler, Mussolini, and Cardinal Eugenio Pacelli, who would become Pope Pius XII. McDonald, who would become America's first Ambassador to Israel, continually voiced his concerns regarding the Jews of Germany and after the war began, the Jew of Europe. He did not, however, have the ear of the policy makers.

² For Churchill's account of his meeting with Hanfstängl, see Winston Churchill, *The Gathering Storm*, pp. 83–84. For an alternate viewpoint, see Jon Meacham, *Franklin and Winston: An Intimate Portrait of an Epic Friendship*, pp. 189–190.

³ Meacham, p. 190.

⁴ Deborah Lipstadt, *Beyond Belief: the American Press and the Coming of the Holocaust, 1933–1945*, p. 102.

⁵ William L. Shirer, *The Rise and Fall of the Third Reich*, pp. 80–81.

⁶ Frank Freidel, *Franklin D. Roosevelt: A Rendezvous with Destiny*, p. 113.

⁷ For an extensive account of the Reichstag fire, see Shirer, *The Rise and Fall of the Third Reich*, pp. 191–195.

⁸ *Ibid.*, p. 198.

⁹ John Cornwell, *Hitler's Pope: The Secret History of Pius XII*, p. 7.

¹⁰ For the full account of America's response to Nazi Germany in the early years, see Lipstadt, pp. 15–20 and 40–48.

¹¹ For the full account of "The Night of the Long Knives," see Shirer, *The Rise and Fall of the Third Reich*, pp. 213–226.

¹² Albert Speer, *Inside the Third Reich, a Memoir*, p. 51.

¹³ Eric Johnson, *Nazi Terror: the Gestapo, Jews, and Ordinary Germans*, p. 171.

¹⁴ As quoted in Lipstadt, p. 59.

¹⁵ David Kennedy, *Freedom From Fear*, pp. 412–413.

¹⁶ David Wyman, *The Abandonment of the Jews*, p. 8.

¹⁷ Alan Brinkley, *Voices of Protest: Huey Long, Father Coughlin and the Great Depression*, p. X.

¹⁸ A. Scott Berg, *Lindbergh*, p. 362.

¹⁹ *Ibid.*, p. 357.

²⁰ Seymour Hersh, *The Dark Side of Camelot* (Boston: Little, Brown and Company, 1997), p. 63.

²¹ Laurel Leff, *Buried by the Times: The Holocaust and America's Most Important Newspaper*. p. 36.

²² Varian Fry, *Surrender on Demand*, p. XIII.

²³ For a thorough examination of Thomas Watson, IBM, and the alliance with Nazi Germany, see Edwin Black, *IBM and the Holocaust*.

Chapter 8

¹ David Kennedy, *Freedom from Fear*, p. 411.

² Arthur Morse, *While Six Million Died*, p. 174.

³ For the life and times of Avery Brundage, including his reaction to the Berlin Olympics, see Allen Guttman, *The Games Must Go On: Avery Brundage and the Olympic Movement*.

⁴ Patrick Myler, *Ring of Hate*, p. 71.

⁵ *Ibid.*, p. 94.

⁶ Robert Payne, *The Life and Death of Adolf Hitler*, p. 299.

⁷ For the story of Marty Glickman, including the events of the Berlin Olympics, see Peter Levine, *Ellis Island to Ebbets Field: Sport and the American Jewish Experience*, pp. 216–234.

Chapter 9
1 William L. Shirer, *The Rise and Fall of the Third Reich*, p. 233.
2 Charles Peters, *Five Days in Philadelphia*, p. 90.
3 David Kennedy, *Freedom from Fear*, p. 396.
4 As quoted in John Gunther, *Roosevelt in Retrospect*, pp. 136–37.

Chapter 10
1 William L. Shirer, *The Rise and Fall of the Third Reich*, p. 351.
2 Arthur Morse, *While Six Million Died*, pp. 204–205.
3 For the story of Ernest Michel and his father at the American Consulate, see Ernest Michel, *Promises to Keep*, pp. 25–27.
4 Morse, p. 202.
5 For the history of the Joe Louis/Max Schmeling fights, see Patrick Myler, *Ring of Hate*.
6 Conrad Black, *Franklin Delano Roosevelt: Champion of Freedom*, p. 489.
7 David Kennedy, *Freedom from Fear*, p. 415.
8 Morse, p. 212.
9 David Wyman, *Paper Walls*, p. 50.
10 Richard McKinzie, "An Oral History with George L. Warren," *Harry S. Truman Library*, November 10, 1972.
11 Emanuel Celler, *You Never Leave Brooklyn*, p. 88.
12 As quoted in Morse, p. 215.

Chapter 11
1 Arthur Morse, *While Six Million Died*, p. 242.
2 As quoted in David Wyman, *Paper Walls*, p. 54.
3 For the history of the Sosua settlement camp, see Wyman, *Paper Walls*, pp. 61–62.
4 For the history of the Mindanao settlement, see Frank Ephraim, *Escape to Manila: From Nazi Tyranny to Japanese Terror*, pp. 43–50.
5 For the history of the King-Havenner legislation and the Alaska resettlement plan, see Wyman, *Paper Walls*, pp. 99–111.
6 Wyman, *Paper Walls*, p. 114.

Chapter 12

1 William L. Shirer, *The Rise and Fall of the Third Reich*, p. 419.

2 *Ibid.*, p. 423.

3 Martin Gilbert, *The Holocaust*, p. 68.

4 Arthur Morse, *While Six Million Died*, p. 222.

5 Gilbert, *The Holocaust*, p. 117

6 For an account of *Kristallnacht* events, see Gilbert, *The Holocaust*, pp 69–74.

7 Gordon Thomas and Max Morgan Witts, *Voyage of the Damned*, p. 28.

8 Ernest Michel, *Promises to Keep*, p. 6.

9 Deborah Lipstadt, *Beyond Belief*, p. 99.

10 Peter Godman, *Hitler and the Vatican: Inside the Secret Archives that Reveal the New Story of the Nazis and the Church*, p. 163.

Chapter 13

1 The research for this chapter comes from a variety of sources, most of them listed below. Two sources were used extensively: Gordon Thomas and Max Morgan Witts, *Voyage of the Damned* and the official records of the voyage as collected in John Mendelsohn, ed., *The Holocaust volume 7: The SS St. Louis Affair and Other Cases*, 1982.

2 Stephen Wise, *Challenging Years: The Autobiography of Stephen Wise*, p. 299.

3 Interview with Vera Hess-Mahler, New York, April 2004.

4 Steve Lipman, "On Shore, A Silent Protest," *The Jewish Week*, May 7, 2004.

5 Interview with Vera Hess-Mahler, New York, April 2004.

6 Interview with Vera Hess-Mahler, New York, April 2004.

7 David Wyman and Rafael Medoff, *A Race Against Death*, p. 106.

8 "The Tragedy of the *St. Louis*," *The American Jewish Historical Society*, 1997.

9 According to her son James, as quoted in Doris Kearns Goodwin, *No Ordinary Time*, p. 176.

10 Fred Israel, ed., *The War Diary of Breckinridge Long*, p. 130.

11 Arthur Morse, *While Six Million Died*, p. 280.

Chapter 14

1 David Wyman and Rafael Medoff, *A Race Against Death*, p. 2.

2 David Wyman, *The Abandonment of the Jews*, p. 15.

3 The opinion polls in this chapter, unless otherwise notated, come from Hadley Cantril, *Public Opinion, 1935–46*.

4 Arthur Morse, *While Six Million Died*, p. 263.

5 For the story of the Wagner-Rogers legislation, including those individuals and organizations for and against, see Arthur Morse, *While Six Million Died*, pp. 252–269.

6 For another version of the legislative story, see David Wyman, *Paper Walls*, pp. 79–98.

7 James MacGregor Burns and Susan Dunn, *The Three Roosevelts*, p. 415.

8 As quoted in Blanche Wiesen Cook, *Eleanor Roosevelt: The Defining Years, 1933–1938, volume 2* (New York: Penguin, 2000), p. 180.

9 Doris Kearns Goodwin, *No Ordinary Time*, p. 163.

Chapter 15

1 Richard Breitman and Alan Kraut, *American Refugee Policy and European Jewry, 1933–1945*, p. 237.

2 Fred Israel, ed., *The War Diary of Breckinridge Long*, p. XIX.

3 *Ibid.*, p. XXIII.

4 Peter Wyden, *Stella*, p. 48.

5 David Wyman, *Paper Walls*, p. 221.

6 Henry Morgenthau III, *Mostly Morgenthau, a Family History*, p. 325.

7 For a study on Varian Fry and his efforts in Marseilles, including the events at the Commodore Hotel, see Andy Marino, *A Quiet American: The Secret War of Varian Fry*.

8 For the life and times of Varian Fry, from Varian Fry's perspective, see his autobiography, *Surrender on Demand*.

[9] Marek Halter, *Stories of Deliverance*, p. 154.

[10] For another study on Varian Fry, see Sheila Isenberg, *A Hero of Our Own.*

[11] For a loving wife's account of the story of Chiune Sugihara, see Yukiko Sugihara, *Visas For Life.*

[12] Pamela Rotner Sakamoto, *Japanese Diplomats and Jewish Refugees: A World War II Dilemma*, p. 109.

[13] Sugihara, p. 12.

[14] The Chiune Sugihara quote to start the paragraph can be found in Sakamoto, p. 164. His son's quote can be found in Halter, p. 119. Yukiko Sugihara's quote can be found in *Visas for Life*, pp. 18–19.

[15] Hillel Levine, *In Search of Sugihara*, p. 277.

Chapter 16

[1] Otto Friedrich, *The Kingdom of Auschwitz*, p. 20.

[2] An illuminating and introspective interview of Gerhart Riegner can be found in Martin Gilbert, *Auschwitz and the Allies.*

[3] Gilbert, p. 63.

[4] Arthur Morse, *While Six Million Died*, p. 6.

[5] For a record of British intelligence and reaction, see Richard Breitman, *Official Secrets: What the Nazis Planned, What the British and Americans Knew*, p. 63.

[6] Glare Nullis, "Gerhart Riegner, Warned of Holocaust," *The Miami Herald*, December 5, 2001.

[7] Morse, p. 8.

[8] Conrad Black, *Franklin Delano Roosevelt: Champion of Freedom*, p. 815.

[9] Stephen Wise, *Challenging Years*, p. 275.

[10] David Wyman, *The Abandonment of the Jews*, p. 45.

[11] Emanuel Celler, *You Never Leave Brooklyn*, pp. 89–90.

[12] *Ibid.*, p. 90.

[13] Wyman, p. 336.

[14] For the Woodruff, Knutson, and *Chicago Tribune* quotes, see Wyman, p. 57.

¹⁵ As quoted in Wyman, p. 57. See also Breckinridge Long Diary, p. 270.

¹⁶ For Wise's account of the meeting with Welles, see Wise, *Challenging Years*, pp. 275–276.

¹⁷ Deborah Lipstadt, *Beyond Belief*, p. 183.

¹⁸ For a report of the meeting between Roosevelt and the Jewish leaders, including Wise's reaction, see David Wyman, *The Abandonment of the Jews*, pp. 72–73.

¹⁹ Bernard Wasserstein, "Britain and the Jews of Europe, 1939–1945," *Institute of Jewish Affairs*, 1979, p. 173.

²⁰ For a critical analysis of Pope Pius XII and the Vatican, see John Cornwell, *Hitler's Pope: The Secret History of Pius XII.*

²¹ Wise, pp. 276–277.

²² *Ibid.*, p. 278.

²³ Fred Israel, ed., *The War Diary of Breckinridge Long*, pp. 1–2.

²⁴ Irwin Gellman, *Secret Affairs: Franklin Roosevelt, Cordell Hull and Sumner Welles*, p. 330.

²⁵ Morse, pp. 47–48.

²⁶ For British reaction to the Allied Declaration of December 17, see Gilbert, pp. 125–127.

Chapter 17

¹ David Wyman, *The Abandonment of the Jews*, p. 108.

² Jerome Karabel, *The Chosen*, p. 246.

³ David Wyman and Rafael Medoff, *A Race Against Death*, pp. 144–145.

⁴ Marek Edelman, "The Ghetto Fights," *The Warsaw Ghetto: The 45th Anniversary of the Uprising.*

⁵ Excerpts from the Dodd and Law speeches can be found in Arthur Morse, *While Six Million Died*, p. 53.

⁶ Martin Gilbert, *The Holocaust*, p. 559.

⁷ Wyman, *The Abandonment of the Jews*, p. 119.

⁸ *Ibid.*, p. 121.

⁹ For the Kingdon quote, see David Wyman, *The Abandonment of the Jews*, p. 121. For the Celler quote, see Emanuel Celler, *You*

Never Leave Brooklyn, p. 88. For the Dickstein quote, see Wyman, *The Abandonment of the Jews*, p. 121. For the Rabbi Goldstein quote, see Wyman, *The Abandonment of the Jews*, p. 122. For the Richard Law quote, see Morse, p. 63.

[10] Morse, pp. 63–64.

Chapter 18

[1] The statistics in this paragraph come from Martin Gilbert, *The Holocaust*, pp. 534, 540.

[2] Louis Rapoport, *Shake Heaven and Earth: Peter Bergson and the Struggle to Rescue the Jews of Europe*, p. 21.

[3] *Ibid.*, p. 27.

[4] For a study on the life of Jabotinsky, see Shmuel Katz, *Lone Wolf: A Biography of Vladimir (Ze'ev) Jabotinsky.*

[5] Rapoport, p. 32.

[6] As quoted in Katz, p. 1445.

[7] For Peter Bergson's positions and history, see David Wyman and Rafael Medoff, *A Race Against Death.*

[8] *Ibid.*, p. 134.

[9] *Ibid.*, p. 130.

[10] Jon Meacham, *Franklin and Winston: An Intimate Portrait of an Epic Friendship*, p. 190.

[11] David Wyman, *The Abandonment of the Jews*, p. 69.

[12] Rapoport, p. 11.

[13] Wyman and Medoff, *A Race Against Death*, p. 108.

[14] *Ibid.*, p. 31.

[15] Wyman, *The Abandonment of the Jews*, p. 91.

[16] Wyman and Medoff, *A Race Against Death*, p. 207.

[17] As quoted in Wyman and Medoff, p. 39.

[18] Rapoport, p. 11.

[19] Wyman and Medoff, pp. 136-137.

[20] Wyman, *The Abandonment of the Jews*, p. 153.

[21] *Ibid.*, p. 154.

[22] Wyman and Medoff, *A Race Against Death*, p. 142.

[23] For the life and times of Mayor Fiorello La Guardia, see Thomas Kessner, *Fiorello H. La Guardia and the Making of Modern New York.*

[24] For the story of Gemma La Guardia, see Rochelle Saidel, *The Jewish Women of Ravensbrück Concentration Camp* (Madison: The University of Wisconsin Press, 2004), pp. 113–120.

[25] Wyman and Medoff, p. 147.

[26] For immigration statistics during this time, see Richard Breitman and Alan Kraut, *American Refugee Policy and European Jewry, 1933-1945*, p. 144.

Chapter 19

[1] For Morgenthau's reaction to events in 1944, including the January meeting with Roosevelt, see Michael Beschloss, *The Conquerors*, pp. 56–59.

[2] David Wyman, *The Abandonment of the Jews*, p. 180.

[3] Breitman and Kraut, *American Refugee Policy and European Jewry, 1933–1945*, p. 187.

[4] *Ibid.*, p. 189.

[5] Henry Morgenthau III, *Mostly Morgenthau*, pp. 325–326.

[6] *Ibid.*, p. 326.

[7] *Ibid.*, p. 323.

[8] Verne Newton, *FDR and the Holocaust*, p. 67.

[9] Morgenthau, p. 323.

[10] As quoted in David Wyman, *The Abandonment of the Jews*, p. 203

[11] Louis Rapoport, *Shake Heaven and Earth: Peter Bergson and the Struggle to Rescue the Jews of Europe*, p. 153

[12] David Wyman and Rafael Medoff, *A Race Against Death*, p. 165.

[13] Rapoport, p. 153.

Chapter 20

[1] For a version of the meeting between Karski and Roosevelt, as told by Karski's biographers, see E. Thomas Wood and Stanislaw M. Jankowski, *Karski: How One Man Tried to Stop the Holocaust*, pp. 196–202.

[2] For a different version of the meeting, this one told from the perspective of Ambassador Jan Ciechanowski, see Jan Ciechanowski, *Defeat in Victory*, pp. 180–191.

³ Wood and Jankowski, p. 12.

⁴ Michael Kaufman, "How One Man Tried to Stop the Holocaust," *The New York Times*, July 14, 2000.

⁵ As quoted in Wood and Jankowski, p. 191.

⁶ Wood and Jankowski, p. 188.

⁷ For a version of the meeting between Karski and Roosevelt, as told by Karski himself, see Jan Karski, *Story of a Secret State*, pp. 387–389.

⁸ Kaufman, *The New York Times*, July 14, 2000.

⁹ Jan Karski, "Words from the Ghetto," *Newsweek* Magazine, March 8, 1999.

Chapter 21

¹ David Wyman, *The Abandonment of the Jews*, p. 210.

² The statistics in this paragraph come from Martin Gilbert, *The Holocaust*, p. 656.

³ Richard Breitman and Alan Kraut, *American Refugee Policy and European Jewry, 1933–1945*, p. 192.

⁴ David Wyman and Rafael Medoff, *A Race Against Death*, p. 161.

⁵ Wyman, *The Abandonment of the Jews*, p. 210.

⁶ For the story of the refugee camp at Fort Ontario, including the reaction by the country, see Wyman, *The Abandonment of the Jews*, pp. 263–276.

⁷ *Ibid.*, p. 215.

⁸ Arthur Morse, *While Six Million Died*, p. 315.

⁹ Wyman and Medoff, *A Race Against Death*, pp. 136, 166.

¹⁰ Daniel Jonah Goldhagen, *A Moral Reckoning*, p. 149.

¹¹ John Cornwell, *Hitler's Pope*, p. 304.

¹² Morse, p. 14.

¹³ These statistics come from Gilbert, p. 623.

¹⁴ Cornwell, pp. 317–318.

¹⁵ Wyman, *The Abandonment of the Jews*, pp. 244–245.

¹⁶ For the story of Wallenberg in Hungary, including his own letters, see Per Anger, *With Raoul Wallenberg in Budapest: Memories of the War Years in Hungary*.

17 For the secret alliance between Switzerland and Nazi Germany, see Isabel Vincent, *Hitler's Silent Partners: Swiss Banks, Nazi Gold, and the Pursuit of Justice.*

18 *Ibid.*, p. 271.

19 For a study of Arthur Sulzberger, the *New York Times*, and the Holocaust, see Laurel Leff, *Buried by the Times.*

20 Wyman, *The Abandonment of the Jews*, p. 321.

21 Eric Fettman, "Hidden Holocaust," *New York Post*, May 8, 2005.

Chapter 22

1 Rudolf Vrba, *I Escaped from Auschwitz*, p. 280.

2 *Ibid.*

3 Michael Neufeld and Michael Berenbaum, eds, *The Bombing of Auschwitz*, p. 77.

4 Lucy Dawidowicz, "Could the United States Have Rescued the European Jews From Hitler," *This World*, Fall 1985, p. 19.

5 A letter from Rosenheim to Morgenthau, as quoted in Neufeld and Berenbaum, p. 254.

6 David Wyman and Rafael Medoff, *A Race Against Death*, p. 160.

7 Neufeld and Berenbaum, p. 106.

8 Richard Levy, "The Bombing of Auschwitz Revisited: A Critical Analysis," *Holocaust and Genocide Studies*, Winter 1996, p. 271.

9 Neufeld and Berenbaum, p. 78.

10 *Ibid.*, p. 67.

11 Pehle memorandum, as quoted in Levy, p. 270.

12 Neufeld and Berenbaum, p. 48.

13 Henry Morgenthau III interview with John McCloy, New York, October 8, 1986. Small Collections: Oral Histories, *Franklin D. Roosevelt Library*. See also Michael Beschloss, *The Conquerors.*

14 Martin Gilbert, *Auschwitz and the Allies*, p. 312.

15 The statistics in this paragraph come from Gilbert, pp. 325–326.

16 Interview with Ernest Michel, New York, April 2004.

[17] Neufeld and Berenbaum, p. 56.

[18] Levy, p. 284.

[19] Neufeld and Berenbaum, p. 93.

[20] Interview with Ernest Michel, New York, April 2004.

[21] Breitman and Kraut, *American Refugee Policy and European Jewry, 1933–1945*, p. 221.

[22] Neufeld and Berenbaum, p. 272.

Chapter 23

[1] Doris Kearns Goodwin, *No Ordinary Time*, pp. 175–176.

[2] John Blum, *Roosevelt and Morgenthau: A Revision and Condensation from the Morgenthau Diaries*, pp. 519–520.

[3] Greg Robinson, "Le Projet M de Franklin Roosevelt: construire un monde meilleur grâce à la science. . . des races," *Critique Internationale No. 27*, Mai 2005.

[4] For an eyewitness account on the meeting between FDR and King Saud, see "The Conference" in William Eddy, *FDR Meets Ibn Saud* (New York: American Friends of the Middle East, Inc., 1953).

[5] For another account of the meeting between FDR and King Saud, see Memorandum of Conversation between His Majesty Abdul Aziz al Saud, King of Saudi Arabia and President Roosevelt, February 14, 1945.

[6] Leo Kanawada, *Franklin D. Roosevelt's Diplomacy and American Catholics, Italians, and Jews*, p. 116.

[7] Stephen Wise, *Challenging Years*, p. 279.

[8] From Guenter Lewy, *Commentary*, February 1964. As quoted in Cornwell, p. 295.

[9] As quoted in Cornwell, p. 317.

[10] As quoted in David Wyman and Rafael Medoff, *A Race Against Death*, p. 32.

[11] These statistics come from Laurel Leff, *Buried by the Times*.

Chapter 24

[1] Jeffrey Donovan, "OSCE: Berlin Conference Pledges to Fight Anti-Semitism," *Radiofree Europe*, April 29, 2004. Website address: www.rferl.org

2 Abraham Foxman, *Never Again? The Threat of the New Anti-Semitism*, p. 16.

3 "Israeli Report Says Russia, Belarus, Ukraine Condone Anti-Semitism," *The Moscow News*, May 5, 2005. Website: www.mosnews .com/news/2005/antisemitism.

4 "The Reemergence of Political Anti-Semitism in Russia," Anti-Defamation League website: www.adl.org/russia.

5 Andrew Baker, "Poland's Progress?" *New York Post*, January 26, 2005.

6 "The Return of Anti-Semitism," *New York* Magazine, December 15, 2003.

7 *Ibid.*

8 For the article and the various reactions, see Philip Kurian, "The Jews," *The Chronicle* Online: www.chronicle.duke.edu.

9 Stefan Friedman, "Anti-Jewish Crimes Soaring in the City," *New York Post*, March 5, 2004.

10 Lauren Elkies and Patricia Greco, "Furor at Private Schools Rages over Fans' Taunts Construed as Anti-Semitic," *Our Town*, February 12, 2004.

11 Leela de Kretser, "Table for 'Jew'," *New York Post*, August 17, 2005.

12 Dan Barry, "A Dark Stain That Returns All Too Often," *New York Times*, October 6, 2004.

13 Charlemagne, "Europe's Jewish Question," *The Economist*, February 21, 2004.

14 For the proceedings of the Berlin Conference, see the following websites: www.adl.org/anti-semitism (for Abraham Foxman's report), www.adl.org/osce, www.ncsj.org/Berlin2004, www.mfa.gov (for President Katsav's speech), www.state.gov (for Powell's speech), www.dw-world.de (Deutsche Welle), www.rferl .org (Radiofree Europe). See also "Wiesel call for 'Manifesto' on Anti-Semitism," *The Jewish Week*, April 30, 2004.

15 Robert Wexler, "Europe Finally Facing Anti-Semitism Wave," *Palm Beach Post*, May 22, 2004.

16 Khalid Amayreh, "Palestinians Blast Anti-Semitism Meeting," Aljazzera.net, April 29, 2004. Website: www.english.aljazeera.net.

[17] Elie Wiesel and Richard Heffner, *Conversation with Elie Wiesel*, p. 110.

[18] Foxman, p. 33.

[19] For both Prime Minister Mohamad's quotes and the reaction to his speech, see Anti-Defamation League website: www .adl.org/anti_semitism/Malaysian.

[20] Anne Bayefsky, "One Small Step: Is the U.N. Finally Ready to Get Serious About Anti-Semitism?" Ms. Bayefsky delivered this speech at a UN Conference on Anti-Semitism, June 21, 2004.

[21] For Minister Natan Sharansky's speech to the Berlin Conference on Anti-Semitism, see www.mfa.gov (Israel Ministry of Foreign Affairs).

[22] "Wiesel call for 'Manifesto' on Anti-Semitism," *The Jewish Week*, April 30, 2004.

[23] Wiesel and Heffner, p. 110.

◄►

Selected Bibliography

BOOKS

Anger, Per. *With Raoul Wallenberg in Budapest: Memories of the War Years in Hungary*. New York: Holocaust Library, 1981.

Berg, A. Scott. *Lindbergh*. New York: G. P. Putnam's Sons, 1998.

Beschloss, Michael. *The Conquerors: Roosevelt, Truman and the Destruction of Hitler's Germany, 1941–1945*. New York: Simon and Schuster, 2002.

Biss, André. *A Million Jews to Save*. Cranbury, New Jersey: A.S. Barnes and Company, 1975.

Black, Conrad. *Franklin Delano Roosevelt: Champion of Freedom*. New York: Perseus Books, 2003.

Black, Edwin. *IBM and the Holocaust: The Strategic Alliance Between Nazi Germany and America's Most Powerful Corporation*. New York: Crown Publishers, 2001.

Bloom, Sol. *The Autobiography of Sol Bloom*. New York: G.P. Putnam's Sons, 1948.

Blum, John Morton. *Roosevelt and Morgenthau: A Revision and Condensation from the Morgenthau Diaries*. Boston: Houghton Mifflin Company, 1970.

Breitman, Richard. *Official Secrets: What the Nazis Planned, What the British and the Americans Knew*. New York: Hill and Wang, 1998.

Breitman, Richard and Alan Kraut. *American Refugee Policy and European Jewry, 1933–1945*. Bloomington and Indianapolis: Indiana University Press, 1987.

Brinkley, Alan. *Voices of Protest: Huey Long, Father Coughlin and the Great Depression*. New York: Vintage Books, 1983.

Bronfman, Edgar. *The Making of a Jew.* New York: G.P. Putnam's Sons, 1996.

Burns, James MacGregor. *Roosevelt: the Lion and the Fox.* New York: Harcourt, Brace and Company, 1956.

———. *Roosevelt: the Soldier of Freedom.* New York: Harcourt Brace Jovanovich, 1970.

Burns, James MacGregor and Susan Dunn. *The Three Roosevelts: Patrician Leaders Who Transformed America.* New York: Atlantic Monthly Press, 2001.

Cantril, Hadley, ed. *Public Opinion, 1935–1946.* Princeton: Princeton University Press, 1951.

Celler, Emanuel. *You Never Leave Brooklyn: The Autobiography of Emanuel Celler.* New York: The John Day Company, 1953.

Churchill, Winston. *The Gathering Storm: The Second World War.* Boston: Houghton Mifflin Company, 1948.

———. *Closing the Ring: The Second World War.* Boston: Houghton Mifflin Company, 1951.

Ciechanowski, Jan. *Defeat in Victory.* Garden City, New York: Doubleday and Company, 1947.

Cornwell, John. *Hitler's Pope: The Secret History of Pius XII.* New York: Viking, 1999.

Davis, Kenneth. *FDR: The War President, 1940–1943.* New York: Random House, 2000.

Dawidowicz, Lucy. *The War Against the Jews, 1933–1945.* New York: Holt, Rinehart and Winston, 1975.

Eddy, William. "The Conference" in *F.D.R. Meets Ibn Saud.* New York: American Friends of the Middle East, Inc., 1953, pp. 33–37.

Ephraim, Frank. *Escape to Manila: From Nazi Tyranny to Japanese Terror.* Urbana: University of Illinois Press, 2003.

Feingold, Henry. *The Politics of Rescue: The Roosevelt Administration and the Holocaust, 1938–1945.* New Brunswick, N. J.: Rutgers University Press, 1970.

Foxman, Abraham. *Never Again? The Threat of the New Anti-Semitism.* San Francisco: HarperSanFrancisco, 2003.

Freidel, Frank. *Franklin D. Roosevelt: A Rendezvous with Destiny.* Boston: Little, Brown and Company, 1990.

Friedrich, Otto. *The Kingdom of Auschwitz.* New York: HarperPerennial, 1982.

Fry, Varian. *Surrender on Demand.* Boulder, Colorado: Johnson Books, 1977. Published in conjunction with the United States Holocaust Memorial Museum.

Gellman, Irwin. *Secret Affairs: Franklin Roosevelt, Cordell Hull and Sumner Welles.* Baltimore: Johns Hopkins University Press, 1995.

Gilbert, Martin. *Auschwitz and the Allies: A Devastating Account of How the Allies Responded to the News of Hitler's Mass Murder.* New York: Holt, Rinehart and Winston, 1981.

———. *The Holocaust: A History of the Jews of Europe during the Second World War.* New York: Holt, Rinehart and Winston, 1985.

Godman, Peter. *Hitler and the Vatican: Inside the Secret Archives that Reveal the New Story of the Nazis and the Church.* New York: Free Press, 2004.

Goldberg, Richard Thayer. *The Making of Franklin D. Roosevelt: Triumph Over Disability.* Cambridge, Massachusetts: Abt Books, 1981.

Goldhagen, Daniel Jonah. *Hitler's Willing Executioners: Ordinary Germans and the Holocaust.* New York: Alfred A. Knopf, 1996.

———. *A Moral Reckoning: The Role of the Catholic Church in the Holocaust and Its Unfulfilled Duty of Repair.* New York: Viking Books, 2002.

Goodwin, Doris Kearns. *No Ordinary Time.* New York: Simon and Schuster, 1994.

Gunther, John. *Roosevelt in Retrospect: A Profile in History.* New York: Harper and Brothers, Publishers, 1950.

Gutman, Yisrael and Michael Berenbaum, eds. *Anatomy of the Auschwitz Death Camp.* Bloomington and Indianapolis: Indiana University Press, 1994. Published in association with the United States Holocaust Memorial Museum.

Guttman, Allen. *The Games Must Go On: Avery Brundage and the Olympic Movement.* New York: Columbia University Press, 1984.

Halter, Marek. *Stories of Deliverance: Speaking with Men and Women Who Rescued Jews from the Holocaust.* Chicago and La Salle, Illinois: Carus Publishing Company, 1998.

Hamby, Alonzo. *For the Survival of Democracy: Franklin Roosevelt and the World Crisis of the 1930s.* New York: The Free Press, 2004.

Hanfstaengl, Ernst. *Hitler: The Missing Years.* New York: Arcade Publishing, 1957.

Isenberg, Sheila. *A Hero of Our Own: The Story of Varian Fry.* New York: Random House, 2001.

Janeway, Michael. *The Fall of the House of Roosevelt: Brokers of Ideas and Power from FDR to LBJ.* New York: Columbia University Press, 2004.

Johnson, Eric. *Nazi Terror: The Gestapo, Jews, and Ordinary Germans.* New York: Basic Books, 1999.

Kanawada, Leo. *Franklin D. Roosevelt's Diplomacy and American Catholics, Italians, and Jews.* Ann Arbor, Michigan: UMI Research Press, 1982.

Karabel, Jerome. *The Chosen: The Hidden History of Admission and Exclusion at Harvard, Yale, and Princeton.* Boston: Houghton Mifflin Company, 2005.

Karski, Jan. *Story of a Secret State*. Boston: Houghton Mifflin Company, 1944.

Katz, Shmuel. *Lone Wolf: A Biography of Vladimir (Ze'ev) Jabotinsky*. Fort Lee, N.J.: Barricade Books, 1996.

Kennedy, David. *Freedom From Fear: The American People in Depression and War, 1929–1945*. New York: Oxford University Press, 1999.

Kessner, Thomas. *Fiorello H. La Guardia and the Making of Modern New York*. New York: McGraw-Hill Publishing Company, 1989.

Leff, Laurel. *Buried by the Times: The Holocaust and America's Most Important Newspaper*. New York: Cambridge University Press, 2005.

Levine, Hillel. *In Search of Sugihara: The Elusive Japanese Diplomat Who Risked His Life to Rescue 10,000 Jews from the Holocaust*. New York: The Free Press, 1996.

Levine, Peter. *Ellis Island to Ebbets Field: Sport and the American Jewish Experience*. New York: Oxford University Press, 1992.

Lipstadt, Deborah. *Beyond Belief: The American Press and the Coming of the Holocaust, 1933–1945*. New York: The Free Press, 1986.

Long, Breckinridge, ed. by Fred Israel. *The War Diary of Breckinridge Long*. Lincoln, Nebraska: The University of Nebraska Press, 1966.

Marino, Andy. *A Quiet American: The Secret War of Varian Fry*. New York: St. Martin's Griffin, 1999.

Marrus, Michael. *The Holocaust in History*. Hanover: University Press of New England, 1987.

McCullough, David. *Truman*. New York: Simon and Schuster, 1992.

Meacham, Jon. *Franklin and Winston: An Intimate Portrait of an Epic Friendship*. New York: Random House, 2003.

Mendelsohn, John, ed. *The Holocaust volume 7: The SS St. Louis Affair and Other Cases*. New York: Garland Publishing, 1982.

Michel, Ernest. *Promises to Keep*. Fort Lee, N.J.: Barricade Books, 1993.

Morgenthau, Henry III. *Mostly Morgenthau: A Family History*. New York: Ticknor and Fields, 1991.

Morse, Arthur. *While Six Million Died: A Chronicle of American Apathy*. New York: Hart Publishing Company, 1967.

Myler, Patrick. *Ring of Hate, Joe Louis vs. Max Schmeling: The Fight of the Century*. New York: Arcade Publishing, 2005.

Neufeld, Michael and Michael Berenbaum, eds. *The Bombing of Auschwitz: Should the Allies Have Attempted It?* New York: St. Martin's Press, 2000. Published in association with the United States Holocaust Memorial Museum.

Newton, Verne. *FDR and the Holocaust*. New York: St. Martin's Press, 1996.

Novick, Peter. *The Holocaust in American Life*. Boston: Houghton Mifflin, 1999.

Payne, Robert. *The Life and Death of Adolf Hitler*. New York: Barnes and Noble Books, 1995.

Peters, Charles. *Five Days in Philadelphia: The Amazing "We Want Willkie!" Convention of 1940 and How It Freed FDR to Save the Western World*. New York: PublicAffairs, 2005.

Rapoport, Louis. *Shake Heaven and Earth: Peter Bergson and the Struggle to Rescue the Jews of Europe*. Jerusalem: Gefen Publishing House, 1999.

Robinson, Greg. *By Order of the President: FDR and the Internment of Japanese Americans*. Cambridge, Mass. and London, England: Harvard University Press, 2001.

Rubinstein, William. *The Myth of Rescue: Why the Democracies Could Not Have Saved More Jews from the Nazis*. London and New York: Routledge, 1997.

Sakamoto, Pamela Rotner. *Japanese Diplomats and Jewish Refugees: A World War II Dilemma*. Westport, Conn.: Praeger Publishers, 1998.

Shirer, William L. *20th Century Journal: The Nightmare Years, 1930–1940*. Boston: Little, Brown and Company, 1984.

———. *The Rise and Fall of the Third Reich: A History of Nazi Germany*. New York: Simon and Schuster, 1960.

Speer, Albert. *Inside the Third Reich, a Memoir*. New York: Macmillan, 1970.

Sugihara, Yukiko. *Visas for Life*. Translated by Hiroki Sugihara. South San Francisco: Edu-Comm Plus Publishing, 1995.

Thomas, Gordon and Max Morgan Witts. *Voyage of the Damned*. Greenwich, Connecticut: Fawcett Publishing, 1974.

Vincent, Isabel. *Hitler's Silent Partners: Swiss Banks, Nazi Gold, and the Pursuit of Justice*. New York: William Morrow and Company, 1997.

Vrba, Rudolf. *I Escaped From Auschwitz*. Fort Lee, N.J.: Barricade Books, 2002.

Wiesel, Elie. *Night*. New York: Avon Books, 1958.

Wiesel, Elie and Richard Heffner. *Conversation with Elie Wiesel*. New York: Schocken Books, 2001.

Wise, Stephen. *Challenging Years: The Autobiography of Stephen Wise*. New York: G.P. Putnam's Sons, 1949.

Wood, E. Thomas and Stanislaw Jankowski. *Karski: How One Man Tried to Stop the Holocaust*. New York: John Wiley and Sons, 1994.

Wyden, Peter. *Stella*. New York: Simon and Schuster, 1992.

Wyman, David. *The Abandonment of the Jews: America and the Holocaust, 1941–1945*. New York: Pantheon Books, 1984.

———. *Paper Walls: America and the Refugee Crisis, 1938–1941*. New York: Pantheon Books, 1968.

Wyman, David and Rafael Medoff. *A Race Against Death: Peter Bergson, America, and the Holocaust*. New York: The New Press, 2002.

ARTICLES

Barry, Dan. "A Dark Stain That Returns All Too Often." *New York Times*, October 6, 2004.

Charlemagne. "Europe's Jewish Question." *The Economist*, February 21, 2004.

Dawidowicz, Lucy. "Could the United States Have Rescued the European Jews From Hitler?" *This World*, Autumn, 1985.

Eberstadt, Fernanda. "A Frenchman or a Jew?" *New York Times* Magazine, February 29, 2004.

Edelman, Marek. "The Ghetto Fights." *The Warsaw Ghetto: The 45th Anniversary of the Uprising.* Interpress Publishers.

Frank, Richard B. "Why Truman Dropped the Bomb." *The Weekly Standard*, August 8, 2005.

"Hiroshima." *Wall Street Journal*, August 5, 2005.

Kalb, Marvin. "The Journalism of the Holocaust." Lecture, *United States Holocaust Memorial Museum*, February 27, 1996.

Kaufman, Michael. "How One Man Tried to Stop the Holocaust." Obituary, *New York Times*, July 14, 2000.

Kurian, Philip. "The Jews." *The Chronicle: The Independent Daily at Duke University*, October 18, 2004.

Leff, Laurel and Rafael Medoff. "New Documents Shed More Light On FDR's Holocaust Failure." *The David S. Wyman Institute for Holocaust Studies*, October 15, 2004.

Levy, Richard. "The Bombing of Auschwitz Revisited: A Critical Analysis." *Holocaust and Genocide Studies*, Winter 1996.

Lewis, Neil. "Nazis and Jews: Insights From Old Diary." *New York Times*, April 22, 2004.

Lipman, Steve. "On Shore, A Silent Protest." *The Jewish Week*, May 7, 2004.

McKinzie, Richard. "An Oral History with George L. Warren." Harry S. Truman Library, November 10, 1972.

Memorandum of Conversation between Abdul Aziz al Saud, King of Saudi Arabia and President Franklin Roosevelt, on board the *USS Quincy*, February 14, 1945. Map Room, Franklin D. Roosevelt Library.

Morgenthau, Henry III interview with John McCloy, New York, October 8, 1986. Small Collections: Oral Histories, Franklin D. Roosevelt Library.

Moss, Mary. "President Roosevelt and the European Jews of WWII: Did He Protect or Neglect Them?" *The Banyan Quarterly*, Winter 2000.

Norwood, Stephen. "Harvard's Nazi Ties." *Jewish Standard*, November 19, 2004.

Nullis, Glare. "Gerhart Riegner, warned of Holocaust." Obituary, *Miami Herald*, December 5, 2001.

"The Return of Anti-Semitism." *New York* Magazine, December 15, 2003.

Robinson, Greg. "Le Projet M de Franklin Roosevelt: construire un monde meilleur grâce à la science . . . des races." *Critique Internationale No. 27*, Mai 2005.

Vanden Heuvel, William. "America and the Holocaust." *American Heritage Magazine*, July/August 1999.

Wasserstein, Bernard. "Britain and the Jews of Europe, 1939–1945," *Institute of Jewish Affairs*, 1979.

"Wiesel Call for 'Manifesto' on Anti-Semitism." *The Jewish Week*, April 30, 2004.

INTERVIEWS

Interview with Ernest Michel (German Jew, survivor of Auschwitz). New York, April 2004.

Interview with Judy Haber (Hungarian Jew). New York, May 2004.

Interview with Vera Hess-Mahler (German Jew, *St. Louis* passenger). New York, April 2004.

Index